# Halakha and the Challenge of Israeli Sovereignty

# Halakha and the Challenge of Israeli Sovereignty

Asaf Yedidya

LEXINGTON BOOKS
Lanham • Boulder • New York • London

Published by Lexington Books
An imprint of The Rowman & Littlefield Publishing Group, Inc.
4501 Forbes Boulevard, Suite 200, Lanham, Maryland 20706
www.rowman.com

6 Tinworth Street, London SE11 5AL



British Library Cataloguing in Publication Information Available

**Library of Congress Cataloging-in-Publication Data**

Names: Yedidia, Assaf, author.
Title: Halakha and the challenge of Israeli sovereignty / Asaf Yedidya.
Description: Lanham ; Boulder ; New York ; London : Lexington Books, [2019] | Includes bibliographical references and index.
Identifiers: LCCN 2019015987 (print) | LCCN 2019016655 (ebook) | ISBN 9781498534987 (electronic) | ISBN 9781498534970 (cloth)
Subjects: LCSH: Judaism and state—Israel. | Religion and state—Israel. | Jewish law. | Law—Israel—Jewish influences. | Israel—Politics and government.
Classification: LCC BM538.S7 (ebook) | LCC BM538.S7 Y43 2019 (print) | DDC 296.1/8095694—dc23
LC record available at https://lccn.loc.gov/2019015987

# Contents

# Introduction

In December 1976, the 17th government of the State of Israel fell when the ministers belonging to Mafdal—the national religious party—left the coalition. Their reason for so doing was the fact that the ceremony celebrating the arrival of the first F15 aircraft in Israel was held on a Saturday, a clear desecration of the Sabbath. The ceremony was actually slated for Friday afternoon, close to the Sabbath eve, forcing the ministers to travel on the Sabbath in order to return home. The elections held in May 1977 after the government had resigned resulted in the first political upheaval in the State of Israel.

More than a century earlier, the Hebrew poet Judah Leib Gordon (1830–1892) had claimed, in a critical essay directed against the rabbis, that if Go-d will grant them government over the land of Israel, "and you re-establish the four types of capital punishment[1] and other punishments on small secondary acts of the 39 activities prohibited on Sabbath [. . .] all the nations around us will attack and annihilate us, since the world cannot exist this way."[2] Actually, Gordon clarified, the quest for sovereignty challenged Jewish leaders to reinterpret the *halakha* according to political and moral reality.

Gordon's words were calculated to goad the rabbis of his time in the context of the culture war being waged between the two camps. They were not intended as a call to immediate action, and yet, many decades later his condemnation had become extremely relevant. The Zionist movement's political objective to establish a nation-state in the Land of Israel obligated those who were committed to the halakha and its heritage to answer the following question: How could halakha be upheld in the entirely new reality of a modern sovereign Jewish state?[3] The halakha was required to overcome the challenge of sovereignty, a new and complex challenge far greater than any that halakha had hitherto faced in modern times. And this at a time when commitment to halakha was becoming ever weaker among leading groups within Jewish communities throughout the world, and especially in the Zionist movement.

The questions of halakha and the challenge of sovereignty have been discussed from several aspects: philosophical, political, legal, sociological, and historical. Prominent among the general terms used are "'Halakhic state" and "torah state," indicative of a demand to adhere to religious laws to one degree or another, or at least not to go against them.

The slogan "Halakhic state" has been heard from time to time in Israel's religious circles. During the sixty-nine years of the State of Israel, several conflicts on issues of religion and state (Sabbath, autopsy, conversion, etc.) have brought the term to the forefront of public debate. While many religious Jews in Israel do not have a clear position on the actual meaning of this slogan, many secular Jews in Israel are afraid of it.[4] They identify it with medieval, underdeveloped, and irrational states. In his article "Is a Halakhic State Possible? The Paradox of Jewish Theocracy," Aviezer Ravitzki claims that it is only natural that the Jewish religio-political tradition cannot remain indifferent to the state it regards as the state of the Jewish people, and it will strive mightily to influence that state's laws and values and to impose its imprint on its culture and symbols. Therefore, he asks, "if Torah observers gained control over Israeli society, would their faith require them (or permit them) to impose the Torah's laws on one and all, even against the will of the community and its elected representatives?"[5] His answer is negative. He argues that the vision of a halakhic theocracy is vulnerable to challenge on two levels—on the basis of the age-old inner logic of the Jewish tradition and on account of the actual condition of contemporary Jews. He examines the actual meaning of this slogan and concludes that the concern in halakha for the social stability of the Jewish polity takes precedence over its concern for that polity's religious character and halakhic fitness, and that "theocracy" itself proclaims that it depends substantially on the existence of a secular, human and political realm.

Asher Cohen wrote of the religious Zionism's vision of the "Torah state" during the early years of the State of Israel. According to him, beyond the historical claims that no significant preparations had been made to realize this vision, and that realistically it was impossible to implement because most citizens of the state did not accept halakha as their main source of authority, the vision itself was fundamentally problematic due to factors and conditions in the external environment. "Realizing the vision would require a different Torah, a significant change in the existing Orthodox religious tradition, or a different state that is neither democratic nor modern in the accepted sense."[6] Realization of the vision contradicted one of two basic assumptions held by most religious Zionists. Either the Torah state would not be a modern democratic state as we know it because of the halakhic limitations on the principle of equality, or else the Torah state would not be faithful to the accepted halakha of recent generations because of the requirements of liberal democratic principles. Actually, Cohen examined the political aspects of the issue rather than its halakhic aspects. From the point of view of political scientists, for whom the principles of liberal democracy and halakhic tradition are familiar and stable, this was the correct conclusion. But this may not have been the case from the point of view of halakhic research, according to which religious Zionism was unprepared to make the significant changes required considering the challenge of sovereignty.

Alexander Kaye divided the religious-Zionist approaches to the connection between halakha and state into three groups. (1) A revolutionary attitude to law. The leaders of the religious kibbutz movement advocated a revolutionary, almost anarchic, approach to law. They (in theory, at least,) only accepted rules that emerged spontaneously from the spirit of their religious and national life, even if that meant departing from traditional halakha. (2) A pluralistic attitude to law. A group of rabbis, who covered a spectrum from, at one extreme, the call for a complete separation between religion and state to, on the other, the call for a rabbinic oversight of all legislation, who were legal pluralists. They all maintain the idea that Jewish sovereignty may have within it a plurality of legal regimes and a plurality of legitimate sources of legal authority. This position had the advantage that it was able to preserve a distinction between current halakha and the state, thereby avoiding the imposition of current halakha on people who did not recognize its authority and preventing the imposition of radical modifications on halakha in order to engineer its accommodation with the requirements of modern law. (3) A totalitarian attitude to law. Isaac Herzog, the first Ashkenazic chief rabbi of Israel, represented the legal philosophy of legal centralism, which maintained that all legal authority in the state must derive from a single source of authority—the current halakha.[7]

This division is only one aspect of the legal religious Zionist attitude to the subject, along with the question of whether the solution should come through evolution or revolution, and whether the general public also has a role to play, or only the recognized arbitrators of halakha.

Itzchak Geiger wrote about the problems pointed out by contemporary Zionist rabbis, who tackled the halakhic questions that arose in the wake of modern sovereignty. They indicated two central problems: disconnection—the vast period of time that had elapsed since the earlier period of Jewish sovereignty and insufficiency—the scarcity of sources dealing with these issues. These problems required creativity in halakhic rulings, because the halakhic precedents did not allow for routine halakhic discussion.[8] These problems and the awareness of them also hold true for the period of this study, which does not extend to the last decades about which Geiger wrote.

Scholars have dealt with various aspects of the confrontation between halakha and the challenge of sovereignty, beginning with the question of the Shmitta year, the seventh year when agricultural work is suspended. This subject appeared on the national agenda as early as 1888, by way of ordinances of the Chief Rabbinate dealing with personal status, halakha's attitude toward women and minorities, the management of state institutions on the Sabbath, and the regulations governing the army and battle. These studies demonstrated the wide range of halakhic questions that arose in the face of the challenge of sovereignty and the halakhic ways of dealing with them. Some even drew general conclusions. For example, after analyzing halakhic rulings by Rabbi Kook on the question of Heter Mechira during a Shmitta year, Arye Edrei drew conclusions about the general nature of religious Zionist halakha.[9]

In this book, I examine the issue of halakha and the challenge of sovereignty from the point of view of halakha itself and its evolution, by examining the conduct of the sector that adhered to halakhic interpretation—the rabbinical authorities—as well as other groups who endeavored to help or to change it: the Jewish jurists in Eretz Israel who sought to integrate sections of halakha into the Jewish collective; and the religious academics who wanted more meaningful recognition of halakha in non-halakhic values. I will not deal with anarchistic religious attitudes, or the liberal calls for full separation of religion and state heard over the years, or the Haredi concept of Da'at Torah, which has no foundation or discourse on halakhic sources. My assessment extends from the beginning of the Jewish national movement in the last two decades of the nineteenth century to the first two decades of the State of Israel, when weighty problems arose that required a halakhic response to the challenge of sovereignty.

I will examine when the halakhic authorities began to confront the challenge of sovereignty and whether this enterprise was continuously maintained from that time until the establishment of the state; who were the people involved; what halakhic issues were dealt with; how did those who engaged in the work seek to ensure that their suggestions would be made concrete; what obstacles did they encounter; to what extent did the public respond to this topic and the conclusions drawn; and what were the reasons for their actual response.

The selected points of view shed light on methods of halakhic ruling as they were formulated in past centuries and on the social and political aspects of their practical usage in the face of the religious-ideological struggles that divided the Jewish people.

This study also illuminates the very concept of halakha, a concept that at first glance seems to be acceptable to all Orthodox Jews, containing a defined literary corpus (compiled from Talmudic sources, their medieval commentaries, responses from throughout the ages, customs and regulations, both community based and non-community based, and sundry Kabbalistic traditions),[10] certain methods of learning and reasoning, and the limited authority of its believers on its teachings. Yet apparently there is no consensus on the definition of the halakhic literary corpus, certain methods of ruling, and the limits of authority of those who adjudicate. Involvement with the halakhic issues connected to the challenge of sovereignty have stretched the boundaries of the concept of halakha.

I would like to thank my colleagues Professor Guy Miron, Dr. Benjamin Porat, Professor Yosef Salmon, Dr. Shoval Shafat, and Professor

Chaim I. Waxman for reading chapters of this book and providing insightful comments and suggestions.

Efrata College has been my academic home in recent years. I am grateful to the Research Committee for supporting my work.

I would like to thank Shulamit Berman, Professor David Citron and my brother-in-law Hillel Van-Leeuwen, who assisted me in translating the manuscript into English.

I would like to thank editors Sarah Craig and Michael Gibson, and assistant editor Mikayla Mislak for their professional work.

Last, but not least, I would like to thank my parents Hanan and Tova Yedidya, my wife Tsipi, and my children Yifah, Yochai, Ya'ara, Yagel, and Ma'ayan, who always stand by me.

## NOTES

1. The four types of capital punishment in ancient Judaism: Sekila (stoning), serefah (burning) , hereg (beheading), and chenek (strangulation).
2. J. L. Gordon, "Hashmatah," *HaSchachar* 2 (1871): 156.
3. On modern sovereignty, see: J. Bartelson, *A Genealogy of Sovereignty* (Cambridge: Cambridge University Press, 1995); Robert Jackson, *Sovereignty: The Evolution of an Idea* (Cambridge: Polity Press, 2007).
4. On religion and secularism in the context of Zionism, see: Ehud Luz, *Parallels Meet: Religion and Nationalism in the Early Zionist Movement 1882-1904* (Philadelphia: Jewish Publication Society, 1988); Yosef Salmon, *Religion and Zionism: First Encounters* (Jerusalem: Magnes Press, 2002); Shmuel Almog, Jehuda Reinharz, and Anita Shapira, eds., *Zionism and Religion* (Hanover, NH: University Press of New England, 1998); Gideon Shimoni, *The Zionist Ideology* (Hanover, NH: University Press of New England, 1995), chapter 7; Shmuel Feiner, "'Humani nil a me alienum puto': Theodor Herzl's Vision of the Secular Jewish Society and Culture," in *Memoria—Wege jüdischen Erinners*, eds. Brigit E. Klein and Christiane E. Mueller (Berlin: Metropol, 2005), 709–31.
5. Aviezer Ravitzki, *Is a Halakhic State Possible? The Paradox of Jewish Theocracy* (Jerusalem: Israel Democracy Institute, 2004), 49.
6. Asher Cohen, *The Talit and the Flag—Religion Zionism and the Concept of a Torah State, 1947-1953* (Jerusalem: Yad Ben-Zvi, 1998), 164.
7. Alexander Kaye, "The Legal Philosophies of Religious Zionism 1937–1967" (PhD diss., Columbia University, New York, 2013).
8. Itzchak Geiger, *Leaving the Shtetl: Religious Zionists Rabbis and the Challenge of Jewish Sovereignty* (Alon Shvut: Herzog College Press, 2016), 54–68.
9. Arye Edrei, "The Foundations of Religious-Zionist Halakhah: Rabbi Kook and the Polemic over the Sabbatical Year," in *Religion and Politics in Jewish Thought: Essays in Honor of Aviezer Ravitzky*, vol. II, eds. B. Brown, M. Lorberbaum, A. Rosenak, Y. Z. Stern (Jerusalem: Shazar Centre, 2012), 833–96.
10. Maoz Kahana, *From the Noda BeYehuda to the Chatam Sofer: Halakha and Thought in their Historical Moment* (Jerusalem: Shazar Centre, 2015), 15–16.

# ONE

# The Halakha in the Face of Modernity and Zionism

In the modern era, Judaism faced far-reaching changes that influenced it in many ways. The centralized state, which sought to expand its powers, constantly nibbled away at the community's autonomy. The abolition of communal autonomy led to radical changes in the relationship between *halakha* and the community. The communal court, which follows the Talmudic law, lost much of its authority, and Jews began to litigate at state courts. Moreover, as a result of the decreasing authority of the community, people felt less committed, and this was one of the causes of the secularization process of European Jews in the nineteenth century. In 1844, the *kahal*—the autonomic institution of the Jewish community—was abolished in Tsarist Russia.[1] In Western and Central Europe, communal autonomy came to an end as a result of the process of emancipation that began at the end of the eighteenth century, a process that equated the rights of Jews with those of the other citizens of the country while eliminating their former privileges.[2] In Islamic countries, communal autonomy was affected by the European policy of colonial rule throughout the nineteenth century.

In addition, the ideas of the Enlightenment that swept through Western and Central Europe in the eighteenth century, calling for the adoption of religious tolerance and universal human values, even affected the Jewish side of the ghetto walls: a new Jewish elite emerged in Germany during the second half of the eighteenth century, calling for changes in Jewish education and the attitude of Jews toward non-Jews, lowering the barriers between the two societies and the attainment of Jewish emancipation.[3] In the latter part of the nineteenth century, the struggle for emancipation was well advanced among German Jews. Cultural integration and the acceptance of Christian European concepts and values led many Jews to reassess the meaning of being Jewish and to identify more with the state and the nation among whom they lived. Along with the struggle to achieve emancipation, an internal struggle had begun to change the face of the Jewish religion and adapt it to the modern age. As a result, Judaism split into different streams.

## REFORM, ORTHODOXY, MODERNITY

In many German communities the Reform movement grew in strength during the nineteenth century. One of the early changes to the Jewish doctrine initiated by the Reform movement was the replacement of the traditional belief in the coming of the Messiah and the gathering of the exiles with a universal messianic vision. An additional reform introduced at this time was the decision to update the traditional prayer book by excising prayers that mention the construction of the Holy Temple or the reinstatement of the temple sacrifices.[4]

In addition, the reformers instituted changes in the synagogue and the order of prayer: the *bima* was moved from the center to the front of the synagogue, almost the entire service took place in German, and some parts were accompanied by an organ. In some communities *Yom tov sheni shel galuyot* was dropped and radical suggestions for halakhic changes were proposed.

In the 1840s, three liberal rabbinical assemblies were held in Germany: Brunswick (1844), Frankfurt am Main (1845), and Breslau (1846). The most controversial decision of the Brunswick conference was, that the marriage of a Jew with a Christian is not prohibited, provided that the laws of the state permit parents to raise the children of such a union in the Jewish religion. One hundred and sixteen Orthodox rabbis, mostly from Germany and Hungary, signed a protest against the conference. They blamed them as usurpers of authority and destroyers of Judaism and charged them with being "shepherds who err and make others likewise to go astray," with being base men whose only goal was "to purchase temporal and political contentment." The second conference abrogated the importance of Hebrew as the language of the prayer, the prayers for the return to Zion and restoration of the sacrificial cult. In addition, the conference decided that it is permissible for the organ to be played during Sabbath services even by a Jew. The third conference permitted some work on the Sabbath, but rejected the more radical suggestion that the Sabbath be moved to Sunday.[5]

Rabbi Zacharias Frankel (1801–1875), the founder of the positive-historical movement, attended the second rabbinical conference at Frankfurt am Main, but left in the middle, following a dispute with other participants about the preferred language of prayer. He said that he could not cooperate with a body of rabbis who had passed a resolution declaring the Hebrew language unnecessary for public worship. Frankel held that the core of the Jewish religion was "positive"—that is, revealed, and therefore not subject to rational criticism or change. However, the oral law developed within history, and its authority lay in the collective will of average religious Jews: "There is a revelation too, in the common consciousness of a religious community which, as long as it remains that group's living common possession, deserves as much recognition as the unmediated divine one."[6] Therefore, in Frankel's view, no religious reformer had the right, for reasons of rationality, to alter norms the people themselves had not cast aside. However, Frankel claimed, the oral law can still be subject to reinterpretation (but not to reformation).

Frankel favored moderate reform, particularly in the prayer book. He had even gone so far as to institute some reforms in the Dresden congregation where he served as rabbi prior to taking up his new position in 1854, as the head of the Jewish theological seminary of Breslau. He delivered sermons in German and conducted confirmation ceremonies for adolescent boys and girls. He omitted certain liturgical poems and made changes in Velamalshinim in the Shemonah Esreh prayer.[7] Similarly, he favored abolishing the prohibition on eating lentils on Passover and instituting changes in customs relating to circumcision and mourning.[8]

His students at the rabbinical seminary adopted these reforms and even added some of their own, such as omitting the Av Harahamim prayer on the Sabbath, permitting the use of *yayin stam* (wine touched by a non-Jew) and *chalav nochri* (milk from a cow that was not milked by, or under the supervision of, an observant Jew), and carrying objects in the semi-public domain ("karmelit") on the Sabbath.[9] Like their teacher, most of the seminary's graduates were somewhere between Orthodoxy and Reform. Some of them were employed by liberal German congregations, and others were hired by more traditional congregations. While liberal and Orthodox Judaism coalesced into religious societal streams, Frankel's positive-historical Judaism remained a strictly religious school of thought.[10]

The first signs of Orthodox Judaism, which appeared in the second half of the eighteenth century, reflected the struggles of rabbis who regarded themselves as the sole legitimate representatives of Judaism within the Jewish Hasskalah movement, which was beginning to gain momentum, and they identified the danger it posed to tradition. At the beginning of the nineteenth century, this stream began to take shape as a reaction to the early reform communities. The Orthodox movement, perceiving itself as the guardians of pre-modern Judaism, soon came into being in order to negate these modern reforms. Jacob Katz and Moshe Samet indicate that Orthodoxy was a historic renovation, particularly in its tendency to differentiate itself and create separate communities whenever it did not have the upper hand, in its tendency to shun modern education, and in its tendency to impose the rulings of halakha and the adherence to traditional customs.[11]

The important leader of Orthodoxy in its beginning was Rabbi Moshe Sofer (1762–1839) of Bratislava who led the battle against religious reform at the beginning of the nineteenth century. It was he who coined the general rule: "All innovation is biblically forbidden" (Heb. *"Hadash assur min ha-Torah"*). In his view, at a time when the bounds of tradition were being destroyed, it had to be preserved in total. However, his halakhic response to reform was more complex than is commonly thought.[12]

After his death, a unique phenomenon of antimodern religious fanaticism began to spread among some of his students in Hungary—ultra-Orthodoxy. It arose as a reaction to the demand for reforms in education, the synagogue, the order of the prayers, and the growing identification with the Hungarian nation. For the first time, Orthodoxy in Hungary implemented the separation of the community.[13]

Rabbi Samson Raphael Hirsch (1808–1888) was the main Orthodox spokesman against the Reform movement. Hirsch was the founder of neo-Orthodoxy in Germany. Since 1851, he had headed the Adath Yeshurun group in Frankfurt am Main, which counted the Rothschild family among its members. In 1855, he became more influential when he founded *Yeshurun*, an Orthodox journal, which he also edited. In 1876, in the wake of new German legislation, he and his followers broke completely with the general Jewish community to form their own congregation. Regarding this step as a basic and binding religious principle, he urged other Orthodox congregations to do likewise. This aroused great controversy throughout the German Orthodox community. In his refusal to have anything to do with liberal Jews, Hirsch resembled the more radical elements among Hungary's Orthodox Jews.[14] His influence was most greatly felt among the German-speaking Jews of Central Europe, who shared the same living conditions and faced the same spiritual challenges, and in whose language he wrote his theological essays, notably *Nineteen Letters on Judaism* (1836), *Horev* (1838), and his commentary on the Torah (1869–1878).

Hirsch's doctrine contended with the new spirit of philosophy blowing through Europe. He did not reject modernity, acknowledging the value of culture and the positive spirit that pervaded culture in general. He issued a call to renew Judaism through the academic study of the Bible, Hebrew, and exegetical Jewish literature, directed toward understanding the basic worldview of Judaism and its heritage for the next generation. He himself obtained a secular education and even attended university, although he did not complete his studies. The same spirit pervaded the high school he established in Frankfurt, which integrated secular and religious studies, including a high level of Hebrew. Hirsch entitled his method "Torah with *Derech Eretz*," an expression based on the verse in *Pirkei Avot* 2:2: "Beautiful is the study of Torah with the way of the world." Torah must be combined with *Derech Eretz*—appropriate behavior and good character. His school incorporated the newest Western pedagogic methods. He also established a school for girls, something hitherto unknown in the Orthodox world.[15]

Hirsch supported Emancipation and favored Germanic culture. He did not believe that the Jews were a nation in the modern sense of the word, maintaining rather that religion was the unifying factor of the Jewish people. He also claimed that in the past Eretz Israel only served as a means for observing the commandments handed down on Mount Sinai. Therefore, all Jews must take upon themselves the civic obligations of the countries in which they reside, so long as they do not impinge on their religion, the true source of their unity. Hirsch did not abandon the religious hope of a return to Zion, nor did he excise it from the prayer book, but he believed that the messianic return would only come to pass at the end of days through Divine intervention. He acknowledged that it was more difficult to maintain Judaism under conditions of Emancipation, but, unlike the Orthodox Jews of Southern Germany, he maintained that it was essentially positive in nature, capable of helping to assist in bringing about the renewal of Judaism. Nevertheless, he claimed that desirable though it might be, he would not be willing to pay a religious price to attain complete Emancipation, saying explicitly that he would be prepared to forego Emancipation if it harmed Orthodoxy.[16]

Orthodox reactions appeared in Galicia in the mid-nineteenth century, responding to the rise of the local Jewish Hasskalah movement, its educational agenda, and the fear of local adaption of the modern trends in Judaism that had originated in Germany. These reactions were reflected in the establishment of a nationwide charismatic rabbinate, which preceded the Orthodox institutionalized political activity of the 1870s. Orthodoxy in Galicia formally came into being with the establishment of the Machzike Hadath political organization in 1868, a response to the liberal bourgeoisie organization Shearith Israel, which attempted to introduce liberal ideas in Austrian Jewish society and replace the rabbis at the top of the social ladder with professionals. [17]

In Lithuania, however, the first signs of an Orthodox reaction only appeared in the 1870s, after the rise of radical hasskalah and in light of the increasing demands for change in the values of Jewish society. The sense of threat, which was characteristic of the formation of Orthodoxy, grew substantially in Lithuania during the last two decades of the nineteenth century, with the strengthening of socialist tendencies on the one hand and secular nationalist trends on the other. Orthodoxy in Lithuania did not need to separate the community, since at first its reactions were non-political and literary-publicist by nature and they fortified the yeshivah institution as a traditional bastion against modernity. By the end of the nineteenth century, a number of Lithuanian rabbis and activists, swayed by the doctrine and leadership of Rabbi Samson Raphael Hirsch, pushed for the institutionalization of Orthodoxy. This group, led by Jacob Lifshitz of Kovno and Rabbi Eliyahu Akiva Rabinowitz of Poltava, enjoyed media attention and played a significant role in the establishment of Agudath Israel in 1912. The International Orthodox organization was established by neo-Orthodox leaders from Germany, and by Lithuanian rabbis and Hasidic rebbes from Poland, who all opposed the Zionist movement. [18]

The insular and conservative reaction typical of Jewish Orthodoxy emerged simultaneously with the flourishing of modernity, which challenged Judaism and the halakha on many fronts. While in the past, halakha had had to deal with far-reaching changes, as in the case of the printing press revolution,[19] now the changes went deeper and touched on all aspects of life: science, technology, society, and economy.

Scientific progress has posed a number of serious questions for the rabbis. The progress in medical science and the frequent use of cadavers for medical research, while contributing greatly to new life-saving possibilities, raised the question: Does the religious prohibition against profiting from a corpse take precedence over the benefits of autopsies?[20] Modern educational techniques that enable deaf-mutes to attain a high degree of intellectual development, raised the question: Should halakha continue to refer to deaf-mutes as insensible, with no criminal responsibility, and exempt them from religious commandments?[21]

Technological progress in the wake of the industrial revolution gave rise to many halakhic questions: Is it permitted to travel by train on the Sabbath? To use the telephone on the Sabbath? To turn on electric lights or appliances on the Sabbath? Is it possible to perform religious commandments with the aid of automation—matzoth manufactured by machine, tzitzit manufactured by machine, electric lights instead of Sabbath candles? How can we rely on the kashrut of products that were prepared by a mechanized process? Are hormonal contraceptives permitted?[22]

In the personal realm, a compelling issue was the status of civil marriage. With the introduction of civil marriage in some European countries, the question arose as to whether a Jewish couple married by a civil ceremony are really halakhically married and whether the marriage could be severed only by a religious divorce.[23]

Many questions were raised about the proper halakhic attitude toward secular Jews. In the past, many cases of religious delinquency were known and the halakha does not treat them as a single, uniform unit. It differentiated between *mumar le-te'avon*—religious delinquency from utilitarian motives, and *mumar le-hach'iss*—ideological religious delinquency. But these trends were marginalized. However, in the nineteenth century the phenomenon expanded, and in many communities the secular Jews have become the majority. The fundamental question then arose: How should we relate to the phenomenon of secularization? Can we judge it with these traditional tools or must we relate to it differently due to the completely different reality?[24]

Given the rapid growth of capital markets and the modernization of corporations and civil law, which changed the character of ownership of companies and business operations, making partnerships possible through shares to the general public, questions arose regarding the validity of the prohibition against imposing interest on transactions with companies—some of whose owners or shareholders are Jews. Is it then necessary to write a *Hetter Isqa*? And who is responsible for desecrating the Sabbath in a company where some of its owners are Jews? [25]

The mass migration of East European Jews to America and the conscription of Jews in some European countries also raised many halakhic questions.[26] Alongside the conservative trend, which claimed that at a time of religious decline any leniency would have disastrous consequences, a different trend regarded the tendency to make things more difficult as a threat to the continuance of tradition, at a time when alienation from religion was gaining ground and rabbinic authority was being eroded.[27] However, the first tendency prevailed. Orthodoxy's need to distinguish itself from the Reform movement, combined with the fear of a slippery slope, prevailed. Moreover, in Russia—the largest Jewish community in the world—the Masskilim, who opposed the rabbinic leadership, claimed that halakha had stalled and refused to correspond with reality and therefore needed overall reorganization. The Masskilim often attacked the rabbis on this issue.

The controversy peaked in the late 1860s and early 1870s when Moshe Leib Lilienblum called for religious reform in two long essays, which he published in the journal *Ha-Melitz*. Among others, he attacked the contemporary rabbis in Russia: "If only these *rabbis* had truly looked at the Talmudic way, if they had noted that the Talmud is more a guide for how to decide the law than it is for actually teaching it [ . . . ] then they would not have created all these new rules for every moment."[28]

Several of his scholarly colleagues responded, including the poet Yehuda Leib Gordon, eliciting from a number of rabbis reactions that appeared mainly in the pages of *Ha-Levanon*.[29] One of the opponents of Lilienblum was the Orthodox author Yechiel Mikhel Pines. However, he did not categorically reject the concept of reform. He recognized the evolution of halakha and was aware that certain of its elements had been "reformed" over the centuries. He called this process internal reform, as opposed the changes that were externally imposed by those who had no authority to do so. For these views Pines was roundly criticized even by members of his own Orthodox circle.[30]

## NATIONALISM AND ZIONISM

The radical changes in Jewish life that took place in the last two decades of the nineteenth century posed new and fascinating challenges to halakha. The Emancipation, and the successful integration of Jews within the general society which followed, elicited a reaction in the form of modern anti-Semitism, whose spokespersons sought to turn back the clock and cancel the equal rights granted to Jews. This new-old hatred led many Jews to realize that Emancipation had not solved the problems of Jews in the diaspora, and that the solution must be sought in other channels. At that time the majority of world Jewry lived in the Russian Empire and were geographically limited. The economic situation was catastrophic. Moreover, Russian Jews suffered from frequent pogroms. These factors spurred them to leave the kingdom and seek new horizons. The success of the movements of national minorities in multinational empires in Europe, such as Greece and Italy, provided a model for a possible solution.

In the 1880s, after several pogroms in Russian Jewish settlements in the south, a Jewish national movement—"Hibbat Zion"—was founded, promoting immigration to the Land of Israel and the establishment of colonies that would serve as a Jewish national entity. Jews with diverse religious views tried to cooperate: secularists who were deeply rooted in Russian intelligence, radical Hebrew Masskilim who were not observant, moderate Hebrew Masskilim and even Orthodox rabbis. A smaller group of Jews from Romania also joined the movement.[31] From 1882, thousands of Russian and Romanian Jews immigrated to the Land of Israel, spurred on by the realization that Jews had no future Russia and Romania, and harboring a national awareness and a desire to settle the Land of Israel. In the first five years the immigrants established several agricultural colonies in different places in the Land of Israel. The colonies of Rishon Le-Zion, Rosh Pina, Zikhron Ya'akov, Yesud HaMa'ala, Ekron (Mazkeret Batya), Gedera and Wadi Chanin (Ness Ziona) joined Petah Tikva, which had been founded in 1878 by settlers from Jerusalem, to form a new model of Jewish settlement—Jewish agricultural colonies. Until that time, Jews in the Land of Israel had lived mostly in Jerusalem, Tiberius, Safed, and Hebron. By the end of the nineteenth century, Jewish immigrants had doubled the number of Jews in the Land of Israel. The Masskilim of Hibbat Zion agreed that life in the new colonies would be conducted in accordance with halakha, in order to maintain unity within the movement.[32]

However, this national awakening of the 1880s did not penetrate most communities; many Jews were bystanders, waiting to see what would happen next. Even the action plan of Hibbat Zion, for all its practical achievements, did not impel the realization of the vision of generations. The one who redeemed the Jewish national movement from these dire straits, set feasible goals, and outlined a revolutionary new plan of action was Theodor Herzl (1860–1904)—the founder of the World Zionist Organization and its head from 1897 to 1904. Herzl grew up in a liberal Jewish family in the Austro-Hungarian Empire. At an advanced stage of his life he came to the realization that the Jews are a nation, not merely a people sharing a common religion, as liberal Jews in Central and Western Europe had previously thought. He explained the rise of modern anti-Semitism as the result of the rapid emancipation and integration of Jews into general society. Because the Jews are a separate nation, they can never truly assimilate into the nationality of any given state, and their attempts to do so would only meet with rejection and resistance. The only solution to the unnatural situation of the Jews is national-political. Jews must establish their own state. In 1896, he published *Der Judenstaat*, his insight into the Jewish problem and his political plan for its solution. The book opens with Herzl's statement that his is a very old idea—the idea of the rebirth of the Jewish state. Like Hibbat Zion, Herzl recognized the power of generations of longing to return to Zion.

He succeeded in convening two hundred representatives from Jewish communities around the world and thus was established, for the first time, a worldwide Jewish parliament. At the first Zionist Congress, held in Basel in the summer of 1897, the plan "to establish a homeland for the Jewish people in the Land of Israel, protected by international law," was proposed and accepted. The word "state" was omitted from the official brochure in order to not challenge the sovereignty of the Ottoman Empire. The plan of action included extensive diplomatic activities aimed at obtaining recognition from the leaders of the European powers of the Jewish people's right to establish a sovereign state of their own in their ancestral homeland. During his final years, Herzl worked tirelessly on the diplomatic front to achieve the charter. His attempts were unsuccessful and he died in 1904 at the age of forty-four, without achieving significant political recognition. But the organization he founded, as well as the turmoil he caused among the Jews by placing the political demand on the international agenda, were significant legacies. Over the years, they succeeded in realizing the dream of the founder of the Zionist movement.

In 1902, the Orthodox Zionist party, Mizrachi, was founded as a reaction to the establishment of the "Democratic Fraction," a response negating the cultural aspirations of this group. A group of young students, influenced by the path of Ahad Ha'Am, founded the "Democratic Fraction" within the Zionist Organization (1901). Their goal was to harness the Zionist movement to cultural and educational activities in the spirit of modern secular values, and their attempt to place this goal on the Zionist agenda provoked the "cultural debate." At the heart of the debate was the proper nature of national Jewish culture, a debate that they provoked as a response to Herzl's pragmatic-neutral position on this question. Their attitude toward Jewish religion was more extreme than that of Ahad Ha'Am. They considered it to be a phenomenon contrary to modern times, relevant only during exile. In their eyes the new national identity should include the values of progress and science. For this group, the renewed national culture expressed a psychological need for self-determination and offered a manner in which to adapt national existence to the Jewish-Zionist framework. They believed their radical method would be effective in preventing the hegemony of Orthodoxy and in influencing Zionist youth, which had undergone a process of secularization. They sought to head the task of pioneering Hebrew culture.[33]

The official policy of Mizrachi, as stated by its leader, Rabbi Isaac Jacob Reines (1839–1915), was that Zionism is a purely material movement, without any connection to questions of culture. [34] Some of the founders of the Mizrachi, like historian Zeev Jawitz (1847–1924), opposed this view in the belief that the new party must also function in the cultural sphere in the spirit of Orthodoxy. However, when asked to write the first brochure for Mizrachi, he adopted an attitude of compromise between the various opinions. This document also appealed to the Orthodox public, which until now was[35] deterred by the Zionist movement. Jawitz began by declaring that the Zionist ideal had existed from the days of the first prophets, and that anti-Semitism alone is not a reason for Zionism. It is only that many Jews came to recognize, that "in the countries of the Diaspora it is no longer possible for our nation to breathe, that is, it is impossible for us to follow the Holy Torah and to live a life according to the commandments which are the basis of our spiritual wellbeing, and to guard their purity, because the present harsh times force us to attend to our needs."[35] He went on to explain the background to the establishment of the Mizrachi movement, mainly as a reaction to the cultural Zionists' lobbying for secular literature and education. The movement's role is therefore twofold: Firstly, political and practical activity in full cooperation with all members of the Zionist movement. Secondly, cultural and educational activities in the spirit of Orthodoxy, differing from the secular Zionists. "We have not found any other way for our Torah to exist after Zion is rebuilt except by guarding true Judaism in all its aspects and in all its purity."[36] Ehud Luz showed that this position is actually a withdrawal from the religious position of the 1880s, that the Orthodox are the guardians of spiritual matters of the movement. The withdrawal occurred at the turn of the century due to the recognition of the transformation of the public, who supported the Zionist idea.[37]

The new reality of agricultural settlements in the Land of Israel, which reinstated the relevance of biblical commandments pertaining to farmlands, and more importantly, the aspiration of establishing a Jewish state in the Land of Israel that aimed to resume Jewish government, science, and social institutions, provoked intense debate on the question of halakha and the challenges of sovereignty. However, except for the specific debate on the sabbatical year of 5649 (which we will discuss later), there was hardly any serious debate on these new challenges. The political reality of avoiding religious discussions within the framework of the Zionist movement, borne out of a deep rift around religious issues within the movement, led to the denial of the problem altogether, and postponed the discussion.

The secular Zionist leaders had their own ideas on this issue. They were opposed to enforcing halakha as the official law of the forthcoming Jewish state, and they were also opposed to rabbinical influence on the forthcoming Jewish government.

Theodor Herzl wrote briefly about the relationship between religion and state in his book *The Jewish State,* but did so from a non-religious standpoint. Although he believed in the socio-ethical value of the religion, Herzl was opposed to theocracy of rabbinical government and supported a moderate version of separation of religion and state. He supported religious freedom as well as freedom from religion[38] and, much as he respected religion, in his vision for a "Jewish state" he wished to see it kept within certain limits : "We shall know how to restrict them (i.e. the rabbis) to their temples, just as we shall restrict our professional soldiers to their barracks."[39] He made no reference whatsoever to the status of halakha in the nascent Jewish state's law book. His wish was for "good modern" legislation "in the spirit of the times" and in keeping with "the needs appropriate to contemporary society," along the lines of the bodies of legislation found among the developed nations of Europe, to be drafted by "experts in the laws of nations" and not necessarily by experts in Jewish law and tradition.[40]

However, some of them saw the Bible as a source of inspiration and tried to consolidate concrete plans through a free and modern interpretation of its words. Herzl consolidated his socioeconomic concept, among other things, on the idea of the biblical Jubilee. This middle way between capitalism and socialism and between individualism and collectivism, was referred to by Herzl as "Mutuality." He sought to combine free enterprise and social justice. The practical innovation of these concepts, taken from the concept of the Jubilee, is the principle that the starting conditions are equal for all and the land reverts to its original owners in the Jubilee year. However, in contrast to the division of the land during the settlement period, Herzl did not conceive of the land as private property but rather belonging to society as a whole, and leased to its citizens for forty-nine years:

> The Yovel [Jubilee] year is nothing new; it is an ancient institution stemming from our great teacher Moses. After seven times seven years, that is every fiftieth year, all land that had been sold, returned to its former owner, without any payment whatsoever. We have changed this law a little—with us the land reverts to the new society. Moses intended to redistribute the land for the purpose of social justice. You can see that our method serves the same ends. In this way the increase in land value is to the benefit of all, not just the individual owners.[41]

Ze'ev Jabotinsky also consolidated his socioeconomic concept inspired by the biblical commandments: Sabbath, Peah, and the Jubilee. Like Herzl, he regarded his method as an intermediate path between capitalism and socialism. Jabotinsky considered the principle of Sabbath as a source of protective legislation for workers' rights. He considered the principle of Peah as the basis of progressive taxation. And he considered the idea of Jubilee as a caring mechanism, so that modern life would not leave casualties behind in the form of poor people with no chance of getting back on track:

> The concrete measures devised in the Bible to combat poverty and the enslavement of the poor by the rich culminate, as we know, in two institutions: Pea and Sabbath. Pea is the end of the field which must be left ungoverned by the owner so as to provide sustenance to the orphan, widow and the stranger, and is the prototype of all society's social legislation ever enacted throughout history. [ . . . ] Sabbath, on the other hand, is the prototype of all legislative aims at limiting the rights of Capital over Labour—what now call exploitation of man by man.
>
> Apart from these two concrete measures, the Bible also contains the concept of Jubilee year, which is at one and the same time much less and much more than a piece of social legislation. The Jubilee year as described in the Scriptures was to occur once in fifty years, and on that occasion all rural property forfeited owing to debt was to be restored to its original owners. This was less than a piece of social legislation because, as we know, this law has never been really enacted, nor can it be enacted in that naïve form. On the other hand, this is more than legislation—it is a revolutionary vision, grandiose enough to inspire generations and to cleanse the world's social structure. The essence of the Jubilee idea is the assumption that social revolutions are and should be permanent features of humanity's progress. Unlike Socialism, the Jubilee principle does not mean one single final shake-up creating permanent once and for all so as to preclude forever the necessity of further revolutions.[42]

Jabotinsky explained the concept of Jubilee as a socioeconomic revolution, structured in a legal mechanism, which would help return the poor, every fifty years, to a reasonable starting point in "the race of life" and obviate the need for violent revolutions. However, the details of the commandment were of no importance to him; only the principle. For him, this "renewal period" could take more or less than fifty years.

Hayim Nahman Bialik sought to redesign the Sabbath in the Jewish public domain in the Land of Israel as a day of holiness and rest. The halakhic literature was not foreign to Bialik, and even though he belonged to Ahad Ha'Am's school of cultural Zionism, he had no wish to abandon it. He often spoke about the "the vigorous need for a spiritual *Kibbutz Galuyot* [lit. ingathering of the Exiles] and for gathering all the literary works written in the Hebrew spirit during all generations of exile,"[43] including halakhic literature. However, for Bialik, the purpose of this project was a new canonization of the sources of Hebrew culture, according to his view of Judaism as a national culture, in the spirit of Ahad Ha'Am—a canonization, mainly in the historical-literary sense, aiming to make our substantial literature accessible to generations of readers who could not connect with traditional literature due to language barriers.

Bialik himself took the first step, with his monumental work, *Sefer Ha'Aggadah,* an anthology of national values and myths formed over generations by sages and authors. Another project he started was *Mishnah La'Am,* by which he sought to "give the Mishnah to the people as an appropriate book for each Jew who knows Hebrew [ . . . ] in a new form, more appropriate to the contemporary discernments and demands." But when Bialik praised halakha, he was not referring to the halakhic corpus of the *Shulkhan Arukh,* but rather to the principle of halakha, which is different from the principle of aggadah, that is, behavioral patterns as opposed to ideological-literary patterns: [44]

> We are speaking not of this or that particular *halachah* or *aggadah*. Our concern is with *halachah* in general—with *halachah* as a concrete and definite form of actual life, of a life which is not in the clouds, which does not depend on vague feeling and beautiful phrases alone, but has physical reality and physical beauty. *Halachah* in that sense, I assert, is but the inevitable continuation and sequel of *aggadah*.[45]

In this manner he came to redesign the Sabbath. He tried to shape the Sabbath as a day symbolizing national and social values, relying on the central role of the Sabbath in Jewish life throughout history. The highlight of his initiative was the establishment of Oneg Sabbath events in Tel Aviv in his later years, where townspeople gathered for cultural activities of poetry reading and Bible study. Although he believed that the Jewish public should maintain the character of the Sabbath, he did not want halakha to determine how it should look.

More radical redesigning was introduced in the secular Yishuv in the land of Israel, especially among the labor settlements, with regard to Jewish holidays. The ancient holidays and rituals, remodeled according to the needs of the movement, symbolized the past and were aimed at strengthening the attachment to the land. The focus of Shavuot changed from a celebration of the giving of the Torah to a celebration of harvesting the first crops. Kibbutz members innovated the ancient custom of *Bikkurim*—a pilgrimage to Jerusalem to offer the first crops to the priest in the temple—by presenting the first crops of the fields to the participants in the Shavuot ceremony, though Bikkurim has no halakhic significance without the temple. Sukkot, a holiday that traditionally focuses on the four species, was transformed into a harvest festival in keeping with the agricultural calendar. The eighth day of the holiday—Simhat Torah, a festival that celebrates the reading of the Torah, was completely ignored. In new Passover Haggadot, they emphasized the value of national liberation and the spring agricultural aspect of the holiday, replacing the traditional text of the Haggadah.[46]

Actual transformation of secularization of halakhic institute took place with the foundation of the Hebrew Magistrates Court in Jaffa, in 1909. This institution was founded by Arthur Ruppin, who headed the Palestine Office of the Zionist Organization in Jaffa. It was intended as the central institution for arbitration in civil matters, especially monetary and defamation claims. The court was set up as an alternative to the three legal establishments then in existence: Ottoman courts, where bribery was rife; consular courts, which had no authority to judge citizens of other nationalities; and the rabbinical court, which was disqualified by the founders of the new establishment on the grounds that it did not accept the official and binding procedures customarily followed in modern courts of law. This was in line with the process of secularization being instituted for the new Yishuv, some of whose members were not inclined to observe the *mitzvoth* and resented the religious establishment. In the same way that secular Hebrew educational institutions were established in line with the new trend, an effort was also made to establish a secular Hebrew court of law as an alternative to the rabbinical court. This institution gained public support and was funded by the Palestine Office of the Zionist Organization and various local authorities. Well-known public figures, some of whom were not even lawyers, served as judges of the Hebrew Magistrates Court. Among them were: Meir Dizengoff, Arthur Ruppin, Mordechai Eliash, Yaacov Thon, and Mordechai ben Hillel Ha-Cohen. Although it took into consideration sections of the *hoshen mishpat* of the *Shulkhan Arukh*, the court was not committed to halakha, but based its rulings on rational conjecture and universal justice. It regarded itself as the infrastructure of the national secular judicial body in Eretz Israel.[47]

## THE SHMITA DEBATE OF 5649 (1888–1889)

Already in 1888–889,[48] the new Jewish *Yishuv* in the Land of Israel was faced with the challenge of adjusting halakha to agricultural work in the Land of Israel. The year 5649 (1888–1889) was the first sabbatical year since the first Aliyah, during which Jewish farmers worked throughout the Land of Israel. For the first time in many generations, hundreds of Jews were required to refrain from agricultural work for an entire year. On the eve of the sabbatical year 5649, three hundred families were engaged in agriculture in nine colonies: Petah Tikva, Motza, Rishon LeZion, Rosh Pina, Zikhron Ya'akov, Ekron (Mazkeret Batya), Gedera, Wadi Chanin (Ness Ziona), and Kfar Hittim. Even though most of them were supported by Baron Rothschild, this support was provided on condition that a maximal effort be made to succeed in agricultural work. The economic significance of keeping the sabbatical year's commandments represented for them in the short term the loss of income from the crops of the sabbatical year, since normal harvesting is prohibited, and the crops cannot be traded. Moreover, there was a future loss of income from the crops of the eighth year, due to the prohibition on working the land in the sabbatical year. Consequently, those who observed the sabbatical year would also lose the market to those who did not observe it. In the long term this was a test for the new Yishuv and the Hibbat Zion movement: Could Jews establish a productive society that stands on its own and does not need external support on a regular basis? This test was very important to the continuity of the movement. The question was put to the rabbis, who supported Hibbat Zion, on the eve of the sabbatical year 5649. Their decisions were based on halakhic, public, and ideological considerations.

In the Middle Ages commentators were divided on the validity of the shmita commandment for their time. One approach, proposed by Rabbi Yitzhak ben Abba Mari (1120–1190) of Provence and Spain, the author of the *Ittur*, maintained that the validity of *shvi'it* in our time is from the Torah, and all the *halakhot* of the Mishna and the Talmud are binding. Another approach, supported by Rabbis Abraham ben David (1128–1190), Zerachia Halevy (1135–1186), and Menachem Hameiri (1249–1315), who were among the sages of Provence, claimed that shvi'it does not apply at the present time, and anyone who observes it is voluntarily going above and beyond what is necessary, since halakhically it is not obligatory. Both of these were minority opinions, and most of the rabbinical authorities did not accept them. The prevalent opinion in the Middle Ages was that shvi'it was *mid'Rabanan* (ordained by the sages), since in the Torah shvi'it is contingent on the laws of the Jubilee—the fiftieth year, when lands revert to their original owners and Jewish slaves are freed, and this only applies when all Jews live in the Land of Israel (according to Rabbi Yehuda HaNassi).[49] The fact that shvi'it was mid'Rabanan at the time enabled them to seek new ways to remove the prohibition, which would not have been possible in the event that in the accepted view shvi'it was ordained by the Torah.

The controversy arose one year before the 5649 Shmita year (1888–1889), in the summer of 1887. The three chief Gabbaim of Hibbat Zion, rabbis Naftali Zvi Yehuda Berlin (the Natziv 1817–1893), Shmuel Moholiver (1824–1898), and Mordechai Eliashberg (1817–1889) met in the home of Shai Finn, a leader of Hibbat Zion, in Vilna, where they were asked by a farmer from Rishon LeZion how the farmers of Eretz Israel should observe the sabbatical year. The Natziv said they should obey all the laws in full.[50] He later wrote in his halakhic book *Meishiv Davar* that in these times shvi'it is *d'oraita* (a Torah rule) and therefore no leniency is possible. If it is a Torah commandment, the loss will be negligible because the mitzvah has been observed.[51] He claimed that in no way did his halakhic approach go against the situation and it would not incur significant loss because Divine providence would bestow a blessing on the crops during the sixth year, as promised in the Torah. He also assumed that Orthodox Jews overseas would support the new Yishuv, which they regarded as pioneering the redemption of the land. All in all, concluded the Natziv, "Just as the existence of the Jewish nation in the world does not follow the natural order . . . in the same way Eretz Israel differs from all the countries of the gentiles, and depends only on Divine providence according to the commandments, in other words, the provision of *trumot* and *ma'asrot* . . . as well as the observance of the mitzvah of *shvi'it,* as clarified in the Torah." [52]

In contrast, Rabbi Eliashberg of Boisk maintained that when it comes to working the land in the seventh year one should be halakhically as lenient as possible because the future of the new Yishuv depends on successful agriculture in Eretz Israel. Later on he thought that at that time the observance of shvi'it goes above and beyond what is required, because "it is a clear *halakha* that working the land during *shmita* is entirely permissible at this time, it is no more than excessive caution to commemorate the Torah commandment of *shmita* at the time when it was customary,"[53] and therefore work must totally be permitted in a place where the farmers stand to suffer a loss. He also claimed that the fact that Jews overseas voluntarily provide money to those who observe shvi'it does not change the definition of the loss incurred to the farmers because the basic aspiration is not to have to depend upon others. At the same time, it perpetuates the institution of *halukka* (the organized collection and distribution of charity funds for the Yishuv), which was resented by the Hibbat Zion movement.[54] Rabbi Eliashberg's aversion to halukka and his belief in the concept of productive self-help had always been one of his notable characteristics. [55]

Rabbi Moholiver, on the other hand, was undecided. While he agreed that it was possible to find halakhic license to work the land in the seventh year, he felt that there was a political reason why it should not be implemented. Observing the mitzvah "would appeal to the haredim, who would join with us in strengthening the mitzvah of settling the land and would themselves become members of Hovevei Zion."[56] He believed that observance of shvi'it presented an opportunity to convince European haredim that Hibbat Zion does not contradict loyalty to tradition. This was necessary due to rumors about the free lifestyle of some of the new settlers.

The intellectual branch of Hibbat Zion, headed by Leon Pinsker, pleaded with Rabbi Moholiver to help find halakhic license to work the land in the seventh year, as early as 5649 (1888–1889), because they feared the problematic precedent of land lying fallow for an entire year during future Shmita years, and eventually he consented.[57] Together with Shai

Finn and Rabbi Yonatan Eliashberg, the son of the Boisk rabbi, he began working toward finding a halakhic dispensation for farming on shvi'it. His solution was based on the principle of selling hametz to a gentile on Pesach. This temporary sale ensures that during the period of which it is written "it shall not be seen, nor shall it be found," no hametz will be owned by a Jew. During shvi'it, the temporary sale of the land to a gentile is designed to expropriate its holiness for the purpose of mitzvoth that are dependent upon the land. This is because, according to most rabbinical authorities, at this time shvi'it is mid'Rabanan and therefore the status of lands in Eretz Israel, for the purpose of mitzvoth that are dependent on the land, is like the halakhic status of Syria (annexation by an individual), where the sale of its lands to a gentile expropriates its holiness. In other words, in the same way that in Syria, at all times, the sanctity of the land is determined by Jewish ownership and not by its permanent geographic location, so, too, at this time, for lands in Eretz Israel where Torah mitzvoth dependent on the land do not apply, sanctity is determined by the identity of its owners. In accordance with the system whereby shvi'it at this time derives from the Torah, the sale is not useful, because of the rule derived from the Babylonian Talmud, tractate Gittin (47a), that the sale of land in Eretz Israel to a gentile does not exempt it from sanctity for the purpose of mitzvoth that are dependent on the land.

Eventually, Rabbi Moholiver journeyed to Warsaw in February 1888 to meet with Rabbi Israel Joshua Trunk (1820–1893) of Kutno and Rabbi Shmuel Zanvil Klepfish of Warsaw. Together they drew up the wording of the heter. It makes no mention of the status of the shvi'it year at this time, but apparently it was clear that the authors believed, like most halakhic authorities, that it derived from d'Rabanan. The reason for the dispensation appears at the beginning: "If we forbid . . . working the soil and repairing the vineyards the earth will become waste and the colonies will be destroyed, and hundreds of souls will perish from starvation."[58] In other words, the dispensation was based on concern for *pikuach nefesh* and the destruction of the Hibbat Zion enterprise. Further on they mention the temporary sale and the condition that it be executed in a Jerusalem court of law. This condition was necessary because the sale of land is more complicated than the sale of chattels *(hametz)*. After that is written that "it is anyway understandable" that those of means would employ gentile workers in the fields while the poor, who were apparently most of the farmers, and who would do the work by themselves, would do so according to the guidelines of the court. Eventually, Rabbi Moholiver wrote that it was intention to permit the poor to undertake all labors that are forbidden during shvi'it, including those that are d'oraita, but he changed his mind because the rabbi of Kutno demanded that at least labor that is d'oraita must be forbidden, to commemorate shmita.[59] The principle of "commemorating shmita" reflected the rabbis' opinion that the observance of mitzvoth dependent on the land was central to the return to Zion because now it was possible to observe the entire Torah, including mitzvoth that do not apply in the Diaspora. The ideal was to observe all these mitzvoth, including shmita, in their entirety. The dispensation was therefore temporary, until such a time when the Jewish people would no longer need it for economic reasons and would merit to observe shmita as required by halakha. In the end there were two caveats. The first was that the dispensation would only apply to the 5649 (1888–1889) Shmita year; the issue would be discussed again before the next Shmita year. The second stipulation was that Rabbi Yitzchak Elchanan Spektor (1817–1896) of Kovno, who was considered the greatest halakhic authority of Lithuanian Jewry, would join in this decision. In a letter dated 3rd Adar 5638, Rabbi Spector joined the Heter Mechira, which permitted gentile laborers to work the land, but as regards to allowing poor Jews to do the work themselves, he left the door open for further discussion, but eventually he agreed.[60]

One month later, on the March 16, 1888, the rabbis of the Sephardi Edah (community) of Jerusalem also joined the heter—Rabbis Ya'akov Shaul Elyashar (1817–1906) and Refael Meir Fenijel (1804–1893). In a comprehensive halakhic legal opinion, Rabbi Elyashar expanded the halakhic basis for the heter, based on the fact that at this time, most rabbinic authorities accept that shvi'it is mid'Rabanan, and the dispute between the Rishonim as to the number of years of shmita had been abandoned, in other words there was no unanimity regarding precisely when the shmita year occurs. Therefore, one must follow the rule that in the case of doubt, in mitzvoth d'Rabanan, one takes the more lenient view *(safek d'Rabanan lekulah)*. In contrast to the rabbi of Kutno, Rabbi Elyashar permitted Jews to do all their work during shvi'it. He found another solution for the requirement to observe shmita, proposing that one dunam in each field be dedicated to full observance of *hilkhot shvi'it*, in order that the law of shvi'it not be forgotten.[61]

The rabbi from Kutno explained that in the matter of laws of shvi'it that are not observed in the Diaspora, there is no preference for Ashkenazi rabbis over Sephardi rabbis. Thus, Jews who observe Askenazi traditions have no problem accepting the *heter* of the Sephardi rabbis in Jerusalem.[62]

In the summer of 1888, Rabbis Yehoshua Leib Diskin and Shmuel Salant of Jerusalem issued an "open message" to express their opinion that "nobody has a *heter* to plough, to sow, to reap and to plant, either themselves or by a gentile, apart from work on the trees, which is permitted by law."[63]

The controversy over the 5649 (1889) Shmita year elevated the ideological and political arguments among Orthodox Jews in Europe and in Eretz Israel to the level of halakha. Opponents of Hibbat Zion saw no intrinsic value in agricultural settlement that would justify the quest for a new halakhic dispensation that went against accepted practice. Supporters of Hibbat Zion were divided on the issue. Some of them, headed by Rabbi Eliashberg, felt that the material establishment of the Yishuv was of paramount importance for the time being, and therefore they were willing to accept the most lenient halakhic approach, even if it was a minority opinion. They objected to support such as halukka, even as a temporary measure, as a solution to the farmers' distress. They also feared that stringent observance of shvi'it would deter religiously observant Jews from settling in Eretz Israel. Another faction, however, headed by the Natziv and Rabbi Gimpel Jaffe, regarded the religious attitude of Hibbat Zion as a return to observing the mitzvoth that depend on the land, in the sense of "renewing our days as of old." This, they felt, was of paramount importance because it reflected the general nature of the movement, and they were therefore willing to compromise on its economic and societal aspects. Others, led by Rabbi Moholiver and Shai Finn, sought the middle ground to appease both the settlers who feared for their livelihood and the fruit of their labor, and those who were vehemently opposed to the violation of shvi'it. This group searched for a halakhic solution based on a dispensation to work on shvi'it that would at the same time commemorate the seventh year.

In addition, the more stringently observant feared that the heter, which they saw as an evasion, was the beginning of a slippery slope that would end with attempts to bypass other mitzvoth as well. Those who tended toward leniency feared a wider rift between the rabbis and the-Massikilim, or even a total split from the secular farmers as the result of an unshakeable, strict position and the lack of compromise on a vital issue, a dispute that would be endlessly perpetuated through many diverse halakhic questions.

During the following two Shmita years the intensity of the controversy lessened, despite similar dispensations that were granted to the settlers. The establishment and expansion of the agricultural settlements, and in particular the industrialization of the vineyards and the wine making industry, highlighted the size of the losses that would be incurred as the result of not working the land on the seventh year.

The controversy arose again, and with far greater intensity, in the Shmita year 5670 (1909–1910). By that time the new Yishuv had changed in comparison with previous Shmita years. From a societal point of view, the pioneers of the Second Aliya had influenced the secular aspect of the Yishuv, forcing the members of the old Yishuv to come out in sharp defense of their position. Moreover, after twenty-five years of settlement the settlers no longer sought legitimacy from the members of the old Yishuv and they now seized the reins of leadership. From an economic point of view, agriculture was well developed, new agricultural settlements had been established, and Baron Rothschild had long ago rescinded his patronage from the older settlements. Furthermore, the ideal of Jewish labor, so dear to the hearts of settlements, had resulted in the rejection of gentile labor, which had been proposed in previous Shmita years.[64] At that time Rabbi Avraham Yitzhak Kook (1865–1935), the rabbi of Jaffa and the settlements since 1904, drafted a detailed Heter Mechira in *Sabbath Ha'aretz,* his halakhic book, which was accepted by the members of the new Yishuv. It was based on various aspects of the Heter Mechira from a scholarly point of view, while debating the arguments of those who had opposed the heter in 5649. He also proposed a halakhic solution for the use of vines grown by farmers who accepted the heter as well as those who were opposed to it. The solution was known as *otzar bet din*. The problem was that according to those who opposed the heter, fruit grown by farmers who accepted the heter were fruit of shvi'it, and it was forbidden to trade in them. Rabbi Kook proposed that the farmers give the fruit to the bet din, who would, in effect, appoint them as its emissaries to deal with the fruit and sell it. Thus, financial payment for the fruit would not be regarded as its price but rather as payment for services rendered to the bet din.[65] He also summed up the ideological reasons why there was a need for the heter, even adding a touch of his own: a. the danger of not saving a life *(pikuach nefesh)* and the destruction of the settlements, which was the reason for the heter of 5649; b. the fear that imposing shvi'it prohibitions would prevent religious Jews from making aliya; c. the heter would prove to the farmers that there is no contradiction between religion and life, and therefore no reason for them to flout the rulings of the rabbis; d. the fear of unjustified animosity between the members of the old and new Yishuv in Eretz Israel.[66]

Regarding the explicit heter and the halakhic debate it provoked, Rabbi Kook formulated two principles which underlie halakhic rulings dealing with the challenge of sovereignty.[67]

The first principle is that in a time of pressing need, the rabbis can rely on a single opinion, "Anytime there is an opinion on which to rely in such a situation of severe need, it is required to rely on it to rule leniently."[68] To establish this principle, Rabbi Kook stressed his concern for the future of the Yishuv in a time of pressing need:

> For it is clear that the redemption depends on an increase in the number of our brethren, the holy people, in the Holy Land, when we will merit in any case to fulfill all [of the commandments]. And it is similar to "violating one Sabbath [in order to save a person] so that he will be able to observe many Sabbaths". And even though God can hasten the redemption through wonders without any initiative on our part, nevertheless, He in His wisdom decreed that we should initiate the beginning of the redemption. [ . . . ] And since stringency regarding the sabbatical year will impede the settlement, many will be deterred from acquiring land [ . . . ] but when they are informed that there are permits based on the urgency of the situation [.... . . ] because we rely on minority opinions, then many will want to come, and the increased settle-

> ment of the redeemed will increase the heavenly blessing to actualize the redemption.[69]

The second principle is that the population to whom the halakhic ruling is directed is the entire Yishuv—religious and secular Jews alike—and not only Torah observers. The halakhic ruling should therefore enable the entire Yishuv to observe the halakha, and not relate it only to those who have personal religious motivation and willingness to pay a lot of money for it, "but from all those who are unable to do so—and certainly it is impossible for the majority of the population to fulfill it without the permit—we must enact a suspension ]of sanctity] by means of sale."[70]

## NOTES

1. J. D. Klier, "The Kahal in the Russian Empire: Life, Death and Afterlife of a Jewish Institution, 1772–1882," *Jahrbuch des Simon-Dubnow-Instituts*, 5 (2006): 33–50.

2. Jay Berkovitz claims that in France, Jews began to litigate at state courts and secular Jewish courts during the eighteenth century, several decades before the Revolution and the Emancipation. Jay R. Berkovitz, *Rites and Passages: The Beginnings of Modern Jewish Culture in France 1650–1860* (Philadelphia: University of Pennsylvania Press, 2004), 18–21, 24–25, 82–83.

3. Shmuel Feiner, *The Jewish Enlightenment* (Philadelphia: University of Pennsylvania Press, 2004). For example, The Napoleon's Sanhedrin (1806) ruled that while the Bible states, "You shall lend with interest to the stranger and not to your brother" (Deuteronomy 23:21), the Jews of France were not to regard their countrymen as "strangers." On the Enlightenment's values in the halakhic ruling of Napoleon's *Sanhedrin*, see: Berkovitz, *Rites and Passages*, 121–37.

4. On the Reform movement, see: Michael Meyer, *Response to Modernity: A History of the Reform Movement in Judaism* (New York: Oxford University Press, 1988).

5. Ibid., 132–40.

6. Zacharias Frankel, "Anzeige und Prospectus," *Zeitschrift für die religiösen Interessen des Judentums*, Vol. 2 (1845): 15.

7. Andreas Braemer, *Rabbiner Zacharias Frankel* (Hildesheim: G. Olms, 2000), 144–45; Meyer, *Response to Modernity*, 107

8. Meyer, ibid., 88–89.

9. Mordechai Breuer, *Modernity within Tradition —the Social History of Orthodox Jewry in Imperial Germany* (New York: Columbia University Press, 1992), 14.

10. Andreas Braemer, "The Dilemmas of Moderate Reform: Some Reflections on the Development of Conservative Judaism in Germany, 1840–1880," *Jewish Studies Quarterly*, 10 (2003): 73–87.

11. On Orthodoxy, see: Jacob Katz, *Divine Law in Human Hands: Case Studies in Halakhic Flexibility* (Jerusalem: Magnes Press, 1998); Idem, *A House Divided: Orthodoxy and Schism in Nineteenth-Century Central European Jewry* (Hanover, NH 1998); Moshe Samet, *Chapters in the History of Orthodoxy* (Jerusalem: Dinur Centre, 2005); Breuer, *Modernity*; S. C. Heilman, "The Many Faces of Orthodoxy," *Modern Judaism*, 2 (1982): 23–51; Michael Silver, "Orthodoxy," in *The Yivo Encyclopedia of Jews in Eastern Europe*, vol. 2, ed. Gershon David Hundert (New Haven: Yale University Press 2008), 1292–97.

12. Kahana, *From the Noda BeYehuda*, 223–448.

13. Samet, ibid., 106–7; Michael Silber, "The emergence of Ultra-Orthodoxy—the invention of a tradition," in *The Uses of Tradition*, ed. J. Wertheimer (Jerusalem & New York: Jewish Theological Seminary of America, 1992), 23–84.

14. Katz, Orthodoxy, 237–78; Robert Liberles, *Religious Conflict in Social Context: The Resurgence of Orthodox Judaism in Frankfurt am Main, 1833–1877* (Westport, Conn: Greenwood Press, 1985), 201–26.

15. Breuer, *Modernity*, 69–79; Liberles, ibid., 137–64
16. Breuer, ibid., 76–79, 287–92.
17. Chaim Gertner, "'Machine Matzos': The Halakhic Polemic as a Tool for Defining Orthodox Identity," in *Orthodox Judaism—New Perspectives*, eds. Yosef Salmon, Aviezer Ravitzky and Adam Ferziger (Jerusalem: Magnes Press, 2006), 395–426; Rachel Manekin, *The Jews of Galicia and the Austrian Constitution; The Beginning of Modern Jewish Politics* (Jerusalem: Shazar Press, 2015).
18. Yosef Salmon, *Do not provoke Providence: Orthodoxy in the Grip of Nationalism* (Boston: Academic Press, 2014), 85–97; Mordechai Zalkin, "The Question of Orthodoxy's Existence in Nineteenth Century Lithuania," in *Orthodox Judaism*, 427–46.
19. Abraham Berliner, *Ueber den Einfluss des ersten hebraeischen Buch-drucks auf den Cultus und die Cultur der Juden* (Berlin:
20. Breuer, *Modernity*, 257.
21. Ibid., 263.
22. Breuer, ibid., 260–62; Gertner, "Machine Matzos."
23. Breuer, ibid., 252–53.
24. Judith Bleich, "Rabbinic Responses to Nonobservance in the Modern Era," in *Jewish Tradition and the Non-Traditional Jew*, ed. Jacob J. Schacter (Northvale: Jason Aronson, 1992), 37–115; Adam Ferziger, *Exclusion and Hierarchy: Orthodoxy, Nonobservance, and the Emergence of Modern Jewish Identity* (Philadelphia: University of Pennsylvania, 2005).
25. Breuer, ibid., 264–65.
26. In this regard, the *Chafetz Chaim*—Rabbi Yisrael Meir HaCohen of Radin—authored two special books in 1893: *Nidchei Yisrael* for Jews living outside the major Jewish communities and *Machaneh Yisrael* for Jews recruited to the Russian army.
27. Breuer, ibid., 250; Jacob Katz, *The "Shabbes Goy": A Study in Halakhic Flexibility* (Philadelphia: Jewish Publication Society, 1989), 238-–41.
28. M. L. Lilienblum, *Complete Writings of Moshe Leib Lilenblum* (Krakow: Yossef Zeitlin, 1910), p. 37.
29. Shmuel Feiner, *Haskalah and History: The Emergence of a Modern Jewish Historical Consciousness* (Oxford: The Littman Library of Jewish Civilization, 2002), 303-–6; Salmon, *Do not provoke*, 86–94.
30. Salmon, *Religion and Zionism*, 81.
31. On *Hibbat Zion*, see: David Vital, *Origins of Zionism* (Oxford: Oxford University Press, 1975), 65–134; Shimoni, *The Zionist Ideology*, 29–37.
32. Luz, *Parallels Meet*, 33–37.
33. Luz, ibid, 149–76; Steven J. Zipperstein, *Elusive Prophet: Ahad Ha'am and the Origins of Zionism* (Berkeley: University of California Press, 1993), 105–69.
34. On the *Mizrahi*, see: Luz, ibid., 227–55; Shimoni, ibid., 127–36.
35. Ibid.
36. Ibid., 233.
37. Ibid.
38. On this see: J. Adler, "Religion and Herzl: Fact and Fabel," *Herzl Year Book*, 4 (1961–2): 271–303; M. Mautner, "Herzl veHa-Mishpat Ha-Yisraeli (Herzl and Jewish Law)," in *The Jewish State*, eds. A. Sagi and Y. Stern (Jerusalem: Hartman Institute, 2008), 227–50; Luz, *Parallels Meet*, 140–44.
39. Theodor Herzl, *The Jewish State*, trans. H. Zohn (New York: Herzl Press, 1970), 98–100.
40. Ibid. On the different relationships between religion and state in Europe see: K. Medhurst and G. Moyser, *Church and Politics in a Secular Age* (Oxford: Clarendon Press, 1988); B. Neuberger, "The Relation Between Religion and State in Europe," in *The Conflict—Religion and State in Israel*, eds. N. Langental and S. Friedman (Tel Aviv: Miskal, 2002), 336–53.
41. Theodor Herzl, *Old-New Land*, trans. Paula Arnold (Haifa: Haifa Publishing Company, 1960), 95.

42. Vladimir Jabotinsky, *From the Pen of Jabotinsky*, ed. I. Benari (Cape Town: Unie-Volkspers BPK, 1941), 66–68.

43. Haim Nachman Bialik, "HaSefer HaIvri," in idem, *Divrei Safrut* (Tel Aviv: Dvir, 1965), 45–62.

44. Israel Kolatt, "Religion, society, and state during the period of the National Home," in *Zionism and Religion*, eds. Shmuel Almog, Jehuda Reinharz, and Anita Shapira (Hanover, NH: University Press of New England, 1998), 293.

45. Haim Nachman Bialik, *Halachah and Aggadah*. Trans. Leon Simon (London: Education Department of the Zionist Federation of Great Britain and Ireland, 1944), 25–26.

46. Anita Shapira, "Religious Motifs of the Labor Movement," in *Zionism and Religion*, 265–71. On the beginnings of the Hebrew cultural project in Eretz Israel, in the late Ottoman regime, see: Arieh Bruce Saposnik, *Becoming Hebrew: The Creation of a Jewish National Culture in Ottoman Palestine* (Oxford: Oxford University Press, 2008).

47. Paltiel Daykan (Dickstein), *Toldot Mishpat ha-Shalom ha-'Ivri: Megamotav, Pe'ulotav ve-Hesegav* (Tel Aviv: Yavneh, 1964), 23–27; Ronen Shamir, *The Colonies of Law—Colonialism, Zionism and Law in Early Mandate Palestine* (Cambridge: Cambridge University Press, 2000), 30–33; Assaf Likhovski, "The Invention of 'Hebrew Law' in Mandatory Palestine," *The American Journal of Comparative Law* 46 (1998): 339–73.

48. This section is mostly based on Yosef Salmon, "The Origins of the Shemittah Polemic," *Cathedra* 170 (2019): 63–80—an article which I helped prepare.

49. On halakhic opinions regarding the status of the sabbatical year, see: Avraham I. Ha-Kohen Kook, *Sabbath Ha-Aretz* (Jerusalem: Defus Levy & co., 1909), 1–27.

50. Judah Leib Appel, *Be-Tokh Reshit ha-Tehiyya: Zikhronot ve-Ketavim Mi-Yemei Hovevei Ziyyon be-Russia* (Tel Aviv: Gutenberg, 1936), 283.

51. Naftali Zvi Yehudah Berlin (Natziv of Volozhin), *Responsa Meishiv Davar* (repr. Jerusalem, 1968), 15.

52. Ibid.

53. Mordekhai Eliasberg, "Michtav Galuy HaSheni," *Ha-Melitz* 28 (1888): 2727–29.

54. Ibid.

55. Yosef Salmon, "Enlightenment Rabbis as Reformers in Russian Jewish Society," in *New Perspectives on the Haskalah*, eds. Shmuel Feiner and David Sorkin (London: The Littman Library of Jewish Civilization, 2001), 177–78.

56. Appel, *Be-Tokh Reshit ha-Tehiyya*, 283.

57. Menachem Friedman, "On the Social Significance of the Polemic on *Shmita*," *Shalem: Studies in the History of the Jews in Eretz-Israel* 1 (1974): 465.

58. Appel, *Be-Tokh Reshit ha-Tehiyya*, 288–89.

59. Friedman, "Shmita," 476–77.

60. Appel, *Be-Tokh Reshit ha-Tehiyya*, 289–91.

61. Yaakov Shaul Elyashar and Raphael Meir Fenijel, "Devar HaShmita," *HaZvi*, March 23, 1888, 7–10.

62. Yehoshua Trunk, *Yeshu'ot Malko*, (repr. NewYork: 1958), YD 53.

63. Alter Druyanow (ed.), *Ketavim LeToldot Hibbat-Zion VeYishuv Eretz Israel* (Odessa: HaVa'ad Leishuv Eretz-Israel, 1919), 615.

64. Yehoshua Kaniel, *In Transition: The Jews of Eretz Israel in the Nineteenth Century Between Old and New and Between Settlement of the Holy Land and Zionism* (Jerusalem: Yad Ben-Zvi Press, 2000), 390–404.

65. Ibid., 394.

66. Friedman, *Shmita*, 472.

67. Arye Edrei, The Foundations, 833–96.

68. A.Y. Kook, *Mishpat Kohen* (Jerusalem: Mossad Harav Kook, 1966), 128 (translated in: Arye Edrei, "From Orthodoxy to Religious Zionism: Rabbi Kook and Sabbatical Year Polemic," *Dine Israel*, 26–27 (2009–2010): 96.

69. Ibid., 129

70. Ibid., 130.

# TWO

# "Government in the Spirit of the Talmud"

## *The Pioneering Discussion of Zeev Jawitz (1904)*

In his utopian novel *Altneuland*, published in 1902, Theodor Herzl outlines the political, social, economic, and cultural features of the new social order in the Land of Israel as he envisaged they would be in 1923. The foundations of such a social order had been laid not long earlier by European Zionist Jews with a humanist bent.[1] In the novel, Herzl addresses, among other issues, the Jewish dimension of this hoped-for state for the Jews. He describes the freedom of worship, the Seder night celebrations combining the old with the new, the traditional Jewish nature of public life as characterized by the closure of shops on the Sabbath, the institution of a modern version of the biblical Jubilee year, and even the rebuilding of the temple along the lines of a modern Western European "temple" (though without an organ).[2] Completely absent from his description, however, is any traditional Jewish dimension to the new state's legislation or mode of government. Ahad Ha'am and his supporters criticized Herzl's utopian vision, arguing that it was not in fact Jewish but "a European people with European leaders leading a European existence. It has no specific Jewish character whatsoever . . . and I do not think it would be going too far to say that the author would only have to make minimal adjustments to his book for it to be entirely 'Nigerian' in character."[3] Herzl's followers rallied to his support in the face of Ahad Ha'am's fierce criticism. Max Nordau, in a particularly sharply worded article published in the Zionist Organization journal *Die Welt* in March 1903, argues that the humanist and liberal values that would typify the new social order in "the Land of Israel in days to come" are not alien to Jewish culture since

Jews were full partners in the creation of modern Western culture.[4] Among the ranks of both the critics and the defenders of *Altneuland*, the religious Zionist camp was notable for its absence.

Actually, they were in a problematic position in this conflict. On the one hand, they had agreed with Ahad Ha'am's criticism and could not support Herzl. On the other hand, they were Herzl's partners in the war against Ahad Ha'am's influence on the Zionist Organization; he even assisted them in establishing their political party Ha-Mizrachi that year. Therefore, they could not support Ahad Ha'am either.

It would seem, however, that Ze'ev Jawitz's article "le-Atid la-Vo" ("In Days to Come") (*Ha-Mizrach*, 1904),[5] whose title borrowed a phrase from Nordau's article referred to above, provides among other things a reaction to Herzl's vision, even though neither Herzl's novel nor its author is referred to explicitly. The article followed the utopian story *Hadash Maleh Yashan*, which was written by Jawitz, as a direct response to *Altneuland*, but in the end was not published. Actually, it was the first comprehensive religious Zionist discussion on the religious character of the modern Jewish state, such as aspects of the relationship between Jewish Orthodoxy and modernity.

Ze'ev Jawitz (1847–1924) was born in the town of Kolno in northeast Poland. His father was a well-to-do merchant, religiously observant, and well-known for his strong opposition to Hassidism. In 1860, the family moved to Łomża and five years later to Warsaw. Jawitz's father ensured that his son studied the Bible and Hebrew, and even engaged tutors to teach him European languages: French, Polish, and German. Outside the scope of his scheduled studies, Jawitz read voraciously about geography and history and was particularly influenced by the books of Josephus Flavius. He married at the age of eighteen. After his wife died young, he married Golda, the sister of Yehiel Michael Pines. In 1882, he began to publish short essays on Jewish history in the Hebrew periodicals *Ha-Shachar*, *Knesset Yisrael*, *Ha-Magid*, *Ha-Melitz*, and *Ha-Boker Or*. In 1887, he emigrated to Palestine, living in Yehud, near Petach Tikvah. Two years later he was appointed as rabbi and teacher in Zikhron Ya'akov, but after a year and a half of conflict with Baron Rothschild's agents he was dismissed from his teaching position and moved to Jerusalem, where he lived for seven years. In Jerusalem he began to devote his time to a comprehensive historiographic work, *Toledot Yisrael*. Finding it difficult to make a living, he left Jerusalem and Palestine in 1897 and moved to Vilna, where he stayed for eight years. While in Vilna he joined the Zionist Organization, was one on the founders of the Mizrachi movement, and became editor of its journal *Ha-Mizrach*. He left Lithuania for Germany in 1905, living first in Berlin and then in Homburg near Frankfurt am Main. On the death of his wife in 1912 he went to live with his children in Antwerp in Belgium, but with the outbreak of the First World War in

1914 he escaped with his family to England, settling first in Leeds and afterward in London.[6]

His main work was the multi-volume *Toldot Israel* (*History of Israel*, published 1895–1924), which encompasses Jewish history from its beginning—Patriarchs—until the end of the nineteenth century. His historical writing, with its emphasis on internal religious Jewish sources, the unity and continuity of Jewish history, and respect for Orthodox principles, was an alternative to the historiography of the celebrated historian Heinrich Graetz. The alternative that Zeev Jawitz tried to substitute for the *Wissenschaft des Judentums*, the scientific study of Judaism associated with Graetz and others, was influenced not only by Orthodox ideology, which he supported, but also by his nationalist ideology. He regarded Jewish history, as well as the Hebrew language, as a national asset that expresses the Jewish national character. According to him, true understanding of Jewish history is only possible for one who is intimately connected to the Jewish nation and its ancient culture. This point of view resulted from his philosophical perception of the Jewish nation as the Chosen People, with a vast abyss separating it from all other nations both nationally and culturally. In fact, he perceived Judaism as a closed culture that was sufficient unto itself, with all that implies. In his research he tried to produce not only a comprehensive historiography, but also an original Jewish historical philosophy based on his nationalist Orthodox perception.[7]

It would seem that, during the period of national awakening at the turn of the twentieth century, Jawitz was the first writer with a religious outlook to explicitly address in any detail the issue of the relation between religion and state in Judaism. Nevertheless, thinkers had addressed the relation between religion and *nationality* (as opposed to that between religion and *state*) in Judaism and, in doing so, had discussed almost all the possible permutations of their relationship to one another.[8]

## BETWEEN THEOCRACY AND THE SEPARATION OF STATE AND RELIGION

Jawitz presents his article as a response to a friend who is concerned about the mismatch between the halakha as it had developed during the years of Jewish exile and the desire for effective state and governmental structures, or, in his own words: "Can the laws of our Torah coexist with the requirements of national government?"[9] Such a mismatch would raise serious concerns that "our societal arrangements will be inferior to those of other nations."[10] The essence of his response is that there is no need for any such concern since Judaism differs fundamentally from other religions in that it does not focus "exclusively on matters of the soul." Rather, it comprises a body of political law in which matters of state and religion coexist in harmony. He cites Moses Mendelssohn's book *Jerusa-*

*lem* in support of his argument: "Give heed to the words of ben Menachem in his book *Jerusalem* and you will see how these two [state and religion] are cast together like a single piece of metal."[11] Here he has in mind the following statement in *Jerusalem*: "State and religion in this original constitution were not united but identical, not joined together but one and the same."[12] However, Jawitz ignores the subsequent passage in Mendelssohn, which actually casts doubt on his approach: "This constitution existed only once; call it, if you will, by the name of its founder Mosaic constitution. It has disappeared and only the Almighty knows among what people and in which century something similar may appear once again."[13] Mendelssohn in fact espoused the separation of (historical) religion and the state, with the latter based on the laws of natural religion. However, those commandments derived from the historical religion, which was concerned with the relationship between man and the Almighty, were a matter between each individual and his conscience and were in no way connected to the laws of the state.[14]

Jawitz, in contrast, was opposed to any version of a separation of religion and state. Adopting a monistic approach, he sees the relation between state and religion in Judaism as paralleled by that between the body and the soul: "Our nation represents the most fitting body to house its soul, and the Torah is the most fitting soul to be housed in that body; nor do these two merely dwell together but rather they are a single living being . . . "[15] Consistent with this outlook, he uses the following parable to show the dire consequences that, in his view, would follow from a separation of religion and state:

> To what can you be compared? To one who counsels the body to separate from its soul and who presents the body with strong arguments to back his case, for there are many matters—such as evil tidings, fear and worry, sharing in the sorrows of others, striving, thought—which would not trouble the body at all if only it were without a soul. However, since it exists together with a soul, whenever the soul is harmed, so the body suffers too. The body heeded the words of this wise counsellor and cast off its soul. But no sooner had the soul departed than the body also died. Within a few days its old friends could no longer bear the putrid smell; they buried it in a grave; it turned to dust, worms and maggots, and was remembered no more.[16]

Jawitz makes the point that Torah embraces all aspects of life—criminal, civil, international, and religious law—and argues that only the Torah can provide an appropriate basis on which the Jewish people can establish themselves as a sovereign state, seeing as it "embraces and assimilates everything of importance, taking good care of both the people's body and its soul, and recoiling from and rejecting anything harmful, just like all living things instinctively preserve their own existence."[17] On this view, were the Jewish people to adopt any constitution for the state other than the Torah, this would be comparable to transplanting a soul into an alien body, clearly an impossibility. He also argues that Jewish history shows "that for two thousand years the children of Israel [lit. roses] did not fade nor the spirit of Israel fail nor his flesh rot, for the two of them [the Torah and the people] stayed united and they preserved one another."[18] In other words, the survival of the Jewish people on the stage of history was made possible only because the Torah acted as its guide at all times and guarded it in the face of external destructive forces.

Jawitz, therefore, rejects the English model,[19] "which both preserved its religion and established a government to protect it, but nevertheless kept religion and state separate."[20] It seems to me that he specifically chose the English model as a basis for comparison since it is in many ways closest to his perception of Judaism, that religion and nationality are bound up one with the other and are not to be separated.[21] On the one hand, the Anglican Church is in effect a national religion in contrast to both the Catholic Church, which is essentially supranational, and the Protestant Church, which is based more on local communities. On the other hand, at the time that Jawitz was writing, the English were known as a people who both respected their religion and traditional institutions and enjoyed the fruits of enlightened government. The British monarch had to take an oath to affirm the Anglican religion and to declare that he would be "Defender of the Faith." Jawitz points to two significant differences between the English and Jewish paradigms, which prevent the former from providing a suitable model. First, the people of Israel became a nation at one and the same time as they received the Torah, which formed the basis of their religion. From a historical perspective these two occurrences were entirely coincidental. The English, however, functioned as a nation for centuries before adopting their current religion. Moreover, Christianity had existed for many centuries before being adopted by the English. There is thus an inherent difference between the English and Jewish models. Second, religion in England deals with matters of faith and the relationship between man and the Almighty, while the state deals with the relationship between man and his fellow, man and the state, and with international issues. In Judaism, however, the Torah, as has been pointed out above, affects all spheres of life, and is therefore bound to impact on political matters.

Nevertheless, Jawitz emphasizes that the hoped-for Jewish state cannot be a theocracy. In this case he points to the theocracies of ancient Egypt and the Papal States as negative examples, in which the religious authority is identical to the political authority. He reviews the various forms of government that existed in the early days of Jewish history and shows that the monarchy and the priesthood constituted separate authorities and that it was not the priests who were the ultimate rulers: "It was not Aaron but Moses who ruled during the generation of the wilderness, not Elazar but Joshua at the time of conquering and dividing up the

Land, and the names of the High Priests during the days of the Judges have almost been forgotten . . ."[22] According to Jawitz it was only during the Hasmonean Kingdom, a time "of bitterness for faithful Jews," that the priesthood and the monarchy were in the hands of one man. In this regard Jawitz refers to his book *Toledot Yisrael* in which he blames the Sadducees for their theocratic deviation from the traditional Jewish mode of government:

> And in his [Aristobulus's] arrogance he did not place much value on the designation "High Priest,", the title by which his betters who had preceded him had been known. But he heeded his presumptuous counsellors, the Sadducees, and placed the royal crown upon his head, paying no attention to the people. And, unlike Simon and Hyrcanus, he did not listen favourably to the words of the prophets who were unanimous that the Almighty had given the monarchy only to the House of David, and that to the House of Aaron only the priesthood had been given.[23]

Jawitz's opposition to theocracy was very similar to that of secular Jewish leaders such as Leon Pinsker, who regarded "the very idea as a disaster and, even if embarked upon only as an experiment or a trial, equivalent to establishing a Jewish papacy,"[24] as well as to that of Theodor Herzl, who, in his book *The Jewish State*, wrote that "we shall permit no theocratic velleities on the part of our clergy to arise."[25] All the same, Pinsker was in favor of agreed religious reform and of a state whose national driving force would be to unite all factions, while Herzl was in favor of a moderate version of separating religion and the state. In contrast to both, Jawitz favored "government in the spirit of the Talmud."

However, Jawitz's discussion of political theory was incomplete. He did not address the questions, what sort of a government will it be, and who will choose it? The only questions he addressed were, What will be the source of authority for the government's laws and what will be the appropriate way of interpreting these laws?

## RELIGION AND POLITICAL LIFE

As we have seen, one way in which Orthodoxy reacted to the modernizing trends that threatened tradition was to resort to conservatism in halakhic decisions. This Orthodox stance was of concern to some Zionists who feared that the halakha would not accommodate the needs of modern national life and that the rabbis would not be flexible enough to reconcile points of conflict between them.

Regarding the second element in the slogan—"Government in the spirit of the Talmud"—Jawitz argues that, contrary to unjustified concerns, "it is not in the nature [of the Talmud] to be cast in stone."[26] In his view the accepted halakha is sufficiently flexible in all matters related to communal and political life "not to impose constraints on whatever good measures we may wish to import from elsewhere."[27] To support his case he cites a number of halakhot enacted by the sages, which they based on far-reaching interpretations of the Torah to facilitate the orderly conduct of communal life. His examples include: the Sabbath limit (the distance within which one is permitted to travel beyond a town's boundary) of 2,000 cubits in all directions; the permission granted to carry within an *eruv* (a suitable enclosure) on the Sabbath; the rule that "one should not 'afflict' children [to make them fast] on the Day of Atonement";[28] and the form of agreement (*heter iska*) that enables business transactions involving interest. Jawitz seeks in effect to develop a meta-halakhic principle from these examples according to which the sages have the authority to interpret the Halachah with extreme leniency in communal matters. Perhaps the clearest example of this principle that Jawitz finds is the granting of permission "to obtain repayment of loans in the Sabbatical year—an act forbidden by the Torah—through the enactment of the *prosbol* (registration of the loan with the court), so as to ensure a continuous flow of loans to the poor."[29] Jawitz also deals with Hillel the Elder's institution of the prosbol in volume 4 of his book *Toledot Yisrael,* which was written around the same time: "He also set about removing all obstacles that might prevent people making loans and so impede the course of trade and commerce, by making it easier for the owners of capital to extend credit without having to be concerned that the debt would not be repaid."[30]

In this book Jawitz also discusses the importance of economic stability as the underlying motivation for Hillel the Elder's halachic rule. In keeping with Jawitz's concept of Jewish history as an expression of the ongoing immanence of the divine, his aim in the volumes covering the period subsequent to the Babylonian exile was "to demonstrate that all the deeds of our Rabbis from the days of the men of the Great Assembly up until the time of Rav Hai Gaon were in fact a fulfilment of the spirit of the Torah."[31] In this connection he refers his reader to R. Eisik HaLevi's book *Dorot Rishonim* (The First Generations), observing that

> R. Eisik HaLevi proved conclusively that none of the *Tannaim* [the rabbis of the Mishnaic period] nor the sages of the House of Shammai or the House of Hillel, including Hillel and Shammai themselves, innovated anything at all in the Mishnah . . . due to constraints of space we cannot bring here all his cast-iron proofs that the Mishnah in essence originates with the men of the Great Assembly, and we therefore counsel all who wish to delve into this matter to read R. Eisik HaLevi's book.[32]

Thus, he says about Rabbi Akiva, for example, that "he preserved the Law of Moses, expanding its boundaries from within and expounding it in all its detail."[33] He emphasizes that the "expansion" that Rabbi Akiva propounded was solely "from within," meaning that he did not invent new laws, in contrast with Graetz's approach, which emphasized the innovative nature of Rabbi Akiva's method.[34] He, therefore, did not view the interpretive methodology described above as entailing any halakhic reforms whatsoever; rather, he saw it as a mechanism that had been an established part of accepted tradition from days of old. And just as he did not consider that Hillel the Elder or Rabbi Akiva or their colleagues had departed from traditional halakha, so neither would the sages of his generation be departing from traditional halakha when they ruled leniently in political matters.

For Jawitz, there was no need for the rabbis of his generation to be ordained in the same way as the *Tannaim* had been for the above meta-halakhic principle to retain its validity.[35] In his view this principle was also being applied to some extent in the Middle Ages, despite the criticism of the medieval rabbinic authorities that "they paid no attention to the demands of everyday life and merely piled one stringency on top of another."[36] He cites in support of his case the example of the ruling that, "while making a fire by a non-Jew for heating on the Sabbath was forbidden at the time of the Talmud, the rabbis of the Middle Ages permitted it when they realized that the communities in the cold lands of Europe would not be able to tolerate this prohibition."[37]

He also cites the permission granted by the Rema (Rabbi Moses Isserles) to extinguish a fire on the Sabbath as well as the rulings that permit Jews to engage in battle on the Sabbath, and, in particular, the ruling of the Shulchan Aruch (the authoritative sixteenth-century code of Jewish law) that nowadays Jews in all places are permitted to bear arms against their enemies on the Sabbath, even in a dispute concerning only monetary matters.[38]

Jawitz was also asked a pointed question about the use of new technologies (electricity and the telephone) on the Sabbath. No definitive halachic rulings had yet been made at the time about these inventions, although the Orthodox tended not to use them on the Sabbath. Jawitz penned two important responses to this question. The first, which, according to Jawitz, touched on "all those matters without which the nation would not be able to establish itself on its land," stated that "this upright and vibrant nation, which will always find the correct path, will manage to accomplish its goals in these matters as well, without detracting in any way from its holiness."[39] In this response he bases himself on Hillel the Elder's words to the B'nei Beteira (the religious heads of the Sanhedrin at the time): "Leave it to Israel; if they are not prophets, yet they are the children of prophets!"[40] meaning that the wisdom of the community will decide in these matters. The second response states: "Were it the case, God forbid, that we would not be permitted to light our streets with electric lights on the Sabbath, or if we were not permitted to use the telephone on the Sabbath," then it would be preferable to be in the Land of Israel even if it meant "returning for the entire (Sabbath) day to the confused state of affairs that prevailed in Paris and in London thirty years ago" rather than "to remain in the Diaspora and have to witness the troubles and suffering of your brothers by the light of the electric lamp, and to be able tell your friends over the phone about the latest harsh decrees enacted against your people."[41] That is to say that Jawitz was aware that in the hoped-for state there were certain red lines, which, from a halachic point of view, could not be crossed. In his view, however, these would at most cause only some temporary discomfort and they in no way provided a reason to abandon the idea of the Jewish state. Jawitz sums up the subject in the following words:

> In sum, I truly believe that, to the extent they are able, our leaders will enact leniencies to the full extent permitted by our Torah, since this is the nature of the oral law which states "the power of leniency is to be preferred." However, if, despite all their efforts, they are unable to permit some matter which has until now been forbidden, we hope that men of culture, having to forfeit some small pleasure in order to fulfil the commandments of our perfect Torah, will not hold it in any less honour than the honour generally found among the nations of the world when one of them forfeits a great pleasure so as to preserve their ways and customs.[42]

It would seem that his halakhic approach is similar to the first step of the Jewish reform in Germany in the nineteenth century, where the goal was to establish their reforms on halakhic precedents. However, he definitely revoked their motivation completely and referred to it as an unacceptable external motivation.[43] In truth, he followed in the footsteps of his brother in law, Yechiel Michal Pines, who claimed that reforms are legitimate only if borne as a result of an internal exigency.[44]

## RELIGION AND SCIENCE

In the last quarter of the nineteenth century, popular-scientific literature became widespread in central Europe, and the impression it gave was that the new scientific discoveries in various disciplines—cosmology, Assyriology, biology (Darwinism), and so on—were proving materialistic and atheistic thoughts and ridiculing religion and tradition. The Orthodox leaders in German Jewry initiated an apologetic response, which clarified that there is not any contradiction between science and Judaism.[45] Jawitz was required to deal with this issue, too, during his study on the forthcoming Jewish state.

The next issue that Jawitz tackles is the possibility of establishing, from a religious viewpoint, a modern Jewish university with a view to fostering objective scientific research. An anonymous friend argued "that it is impossible to establish a scientific institute as long as we adhere to our Torah, because any expert who came and spoke about the theories of Darwin and Haeckel[46] would, together with his audience, be considered heretics and atheists for denying the order of creation as handed down to us in the Torah."[47] In fact the question of establishing a Jewish university in Jerusalem had been on the agenda ever since the establishment of the Zionist Organization. The proponent of this idea was Professor Zvi Herman Shapira, founder of the Keren Kayemet (Jewish National Fund) and lecturer in mathematics at the University of Heidelberg.[48]

The idea of the university had two important implications from a national perspective. First, it would help foster national values via scientific research into matters of national importance such as knowledge of the land, language, literature, and history. Second, through the development of the applied sciences, it would lubricate the wheels of economic growth in agriculture, industry, and medicine with a view to establishing a strong Jewish presence in the Land of Israel.

Opposition to the idea from the religious camp was principally directed at the method of teaching Jewish studies. The wealthy businessman Ze'ev Wissotzky, who was one of the supporters of Shapira's idea and donated 10,000 roubles toward it, conditioned his support on the requirement "that these funds will not be used to print any book that debases the holy writings of Israel, or that speaks evil of the Talmud, or that desecrates our faith, or that insults the Jewish people, nor will such an author receive any fee."[49] Jawitz argues against the anonymous friend, asserting that the Torah permits the study of every area of knowledge, including "heretical belief systems whose practices are absolutely forbidden to us."[50] In support of his position he cites the exegesis of the sages on the verse "you shall not learn to do after the abominations of those nations" to the effect that "you shall not learn in order to do but you may learn in order to understand and to teach."[51] He also brings support from the medieval Jewish philosophers—Rabbi Sa'adiah Gaon, Rabbi Yehuda Ha-Levi, R. Moses Maimonides, R. Levi ben Gershon, Rabbeniu Behaye, and R. Yosef Albo—all of whom studied Platonism and Aristotelianism, including the theory of the eternity of the universe, which stands in contradiction to the Torah's creation story, and who taught these ideas to their students, and all this without being accused of heresy.[52] He emphasizes that they did this "even though the Jewish people did not then dwell in its own land and so have a responsibility to establish institutions of learning (i.e., universities) with professorial chairs occupied by scholars from around the world."[53] Jawitz thus revealed his own personal stance, which was in favor of opening such a university.

Jawitz goes on to try to show that the ongoing progress of the natural sciences was always close to the hearts of the sages. He argues that the sages of Israel, in contrast with the Catholic priesthood, not only did not oppose the scientific method of Copernicus and Galileo "but even strove to find support for the method in the Talmud and the Zohar.[54] And one of the leading scholars of our generation, known for his great piety, in the introduction to his commentary on the Torah is full of praise for Darwin."[55] Jawitz does not, however, name this pious scholar, perhaps for fear that he would be attacked for his daring stance.[56] He adds that Judaism is not opposed to the dissection of corpses in the teaching of medicine; indeed "eighteen hundred years ago Rabbi Yishmael's students dissected a corpse in order to confirm the number of bones it had."[57]

In his autobiographical story of 1893, *Haravot leltim* (Swords into Ploughshares), Jawitz—in the guise of the character Otniel giving advice to his son Yehudah, who was about to start studying at the Mikveh Yisrael agricultural school—recommended "studying the laws of nature in general and the science of plants in particular,"[58] and paying special attention to the writings of Linnaeus, Liebig, Schleiden, and Humboldt.[59] This was based on his belief that these sources of knowledge were prerequisites for the settlement and development of the land.

Jawitz believes there to be no real conflict between Judaism and science. He adopts the "interpretational" approach according to which any apparent conflict lies in a misunderstanding of either the biblical or the rabbinical texts. [60]

For instance, Jawitz adopted conclusions from modern research according to which the period of the Persian Empire extended for more than two hundred years, as opposed to the Midrash Tannaim "Seder Olam,", which states that "the Persian Kingdom [existed] during the time of the Temple thirty-four years"[61] to a total of fifty-four years. He claims that there may have occurred an exchange of the letters *beit* (second letter of the alphabet) and *lamed* (twelfth letter of the alphabet) in the words of Rabbi Yossi, and notes that the correct phrase is "the Persian Kingdom [existed] before the Temple thirty-four years."[62]

In conclusion, Jawitz argues that many of the medieval Jewish sages, while remaining completely faithful to their tradition, were at the same time active in the forefront of science and culture: "Are there many peoples who, even without the restrictions imposed by the law, could boast of philosophers like Maimonides and Rabbi Abraham ibn Ezra, of poets like Rabbi Solomon ibn Gabirol and Rabbi Yehuda Ha-Levi, mathematicians like R. Yitzhak Ha-Yisraeli, philologers like ben Janach and Efodi?"[63] In addition, he cites the German researcher Schleiden's observation that

> it was the Jews who, by translating the works of the Greek and Roman scientists into Arabic, enabled the spread of knowledge throughout the world . . . and, once these works had become established among the Arabs, particularly in the fields of medicine and nature, and once the pre-eminence of the west began to decline, they performed the complementary service of translating the wonderful works of Arab writers

> into Latin for the nations of Europe, works which formed the foundation of science as we know it today.[64]

Furthermore, Jawitz argues that not only the Jewish sages in Spain but also those in Germany and France, who were "oppressed and wearied by the heavy yoke of exile which destroyed the peace of mind necessary for scientific speculation,"[65] made great contributions to scientific method. In his view, the Ba'alei Ha-Tosafot (the authors of a medieval commentary on the Talmud) were the fathers of comparative literary criticism, and in their literary analysis were the first "to compare sources with one another, to find the common denominator between them and reconcile them, and dovetail them together, reflecting as they did the spirit of one people . . . "[66] Here he is alluding to the myth of Sephardi superiority, which was current among members of the Jewish Enlightenment, providing them with legitimacy for their modern approach to religion. According to this view it was the golden age of Spanish Jewry, which embodied the spirit of cultural openness, philosophical reasoning, and aesthetic appreciation, in contrast with which Ashkenazi Jewry was culturally more inward-looking. Following this approach, they sang the praises of the great names of Sephardi Jewry, such as Shmuel Ha-Nagid, Rabbi Solomon ibn Gabirol, Rabbi Abraham ibn Ezra, Rabbi Yehuda Ha-Levi, and Maimonides.[67] Jawitz supports the Jewish-Sephardi model, but at the same time does not reject the Jewish-Ashkenazi model. In his view, there is also much to learn from the wonderful intellectual achievements of "our humble Rabbis who lived in the dark exile of Lunel and Orleans," despite the harsh circumstances under which they lived.

## RELIGION AND LIFE

Another argument that Jawitz strove to refute was that Judaism was antithetical to joy, beauty, and physical prowess. From its very beginning the Zionist movement promoted all forms of Hebrew artistic creativity: plastic, literary, and theatrical, as well as physical achievement. This was seen by many as a necessary condition for the return of a people to a normal life in its land.[68]

In 1895, an argument broke out between the old Yeshuv and the new Yeshuv regarding a theater performance in Rehovot. Eliezer Ben Yehudah and Yosef Klauzner expressed their support for a Hebrew theater in their essays on *Ha-Zvi*. They emphasized the necessary of the "joy of life" for the development of the new Yeshuv. At the same time, the *Habazeleth* published essays completely revoking this idea, calling for those looking for the "joy of life" to emigrate to Paris.[69] In this period, Jawitz was much involved in the new settlements' life and intimately familiar with this debate.

In his book *Altneuland,* Herzl also talks about theaters and opera houses in the Land of Israel staging original Jewish works. The novel's heroes attend a performance in Haifa of the new opera *Sabbatai Zvi,* which tells the story of the life of the seventeenth-century false messiah.[70] And in 1906, the Bezalel Academy of Arts and Design was established in Jerusalem in recognition of the need for a national dimension of aesthetic creativity as part of the nation's process of rebirth. Art was thus perceived as an essential form of national expression, side by side with literature, history, and language.[71] At the root of these developments was the understanding that, apart from political, practical, and spiritual initiatives, the national rebirth would also need a mental transformation. It seems that Jawitz was much preoccupied with the idea that pride in physical achievement and natural rejoicing in life were essential ingredients in the return of the Jewish people to its land. In a letter written in 1892 to his son, Yehudah Leib, he had already highlighted the idea of the "joy of life" (Heb. *messos ha-hayim*), arguing that it is in no way conflicted with tradition.[72]

Jawitz took on the challenge of the Enlightenment critique that "religion" and "life" are in conflict with one another,[73] arguing that Judaism is not opposed to any of these things. He realized that these activities were essential if the citizens of the state were to lead fulfilling lives, and he cited traditional sources in their support.[74] Thus, he emphasized that "in their [the Talmudical sages'] eyes beauty, strength and stature were required characteristics for the High Priest."[75] And he cited their saying: "The Divine Presence rests upon man not through gloom but through joy."[76] To provide further legitimization for the development of aesthetic sensibilities, Jawitz pointed to "the small drawings appearing in the manuscript *siddurim, machzorim* and Pesach *haggadot* that are preserved in the ancient book depositories, many of which experts testify to be the handiwork of artists."[77] He also argued that "the later authorities placed clear limitations on the prohibition against making sculptures."[78] And he cited the *Shulhan Aruch* (*Yoreh Deah,* 141, 7), which rules that the prohibition "You shall not make a graven image nor any manner of likeness"[79] does not apply to making a sculpture of a man's head, nor of a body without a head.

Furthermore, in his story "Swords and Ploughshares" the character representing Jawitz praises physical prowess: "Who can deny that strength and courage are the splendour of youth and the honour of men . . . and in the times of our prophets was it not an honour to be known as a mighty man of valour; and army service was a school for heroes where they learned of might and courage."[80] In this he preceded R. Kook, who saw the establishment of the Bezalel Academy of Arts as meeting the natural desires of a people aspiring to sovereignty,[81] and the physical exercise "and gymnastics that Jewish youth engage in" as a way of bolstering the nation's courage.[82]

Nevertheless, Jawitz is only prepared to recognize the value of joy, beauty, and physical prowess in areas where they "are either of some practical use or a source of legitimate pleasure"; they are to be opposed if they break the bounds of "the pure morality of the Jewish Torah" and "the Jewish spirit": "As long as the Jewish people remains true to its spirit, and does not pretend to be something it is not, then it surely cannot yearn for the love of victory or the beauty of physical power, for conquest or subjugation, for the desire of the eyes or the delusions of the senses, for dances of the stage or the athletic stadium, for the heroism of the hunt or for the protracted war, for drink or sensuality."[83] It is in these very matters that Jawitz finds one of the significant differences between, on the one hand, Jewish culture and, on the other, Hellenistic culture, which, in his opinion, in turn influenced Aryan culture, Europe's leading culture. Jawitz's approach to the understanding of history, which had been particularly influenced by R. Yehudah Ha-Levi, R. Nachman Krochmal, and Samuel David Luzzatto, made an important distinction between Jewish national character and its cultural foundations, on the one hand, and those of other nations, on the other, in keeping with Rabbi Yehudah Ha-Levi's notion of the "uniqueness of the Jewish people"[84] and Luzzatto's dichotomy between Judaism and Hellenism.[85] In a letter that he wrote at the end of 1893 to Moshe Leib Lilienblum, he proclaims his agreement with Luzzatto's approach, "which stresses the enormous gulf between the teachings of Judaism and those of the Greeks and their followers."[86] In this article he also bases himself on Luzzatto as well as on Moritz Lazarus (1824–1903) and Heymann Steinthal (1823–1899), the originators of the notion of "national psychology."[87] According to this idea, just as the psychology of the individual analyses personality as an expression of a person's emotions, imagination, and spirit, so there exists a psychology of nations which provides an understanding of national character as an expression of each nation's literature, laws, morals, arts, and institutions. A nation is thus a collective entity, which has created a unique culture.[88] In Jawitz's view, the conclusion of all three of these writers is "that Greek wisdom is the polar opposite of the pure morality of the Jewish Torah; it is totally different from it and in fact liable to destroy it."[89] In his opinion, therefore, other cultures must not be blindly mimicked, and should be drawn upon only after their benefit to the original Jewish spirit and their compatibility with it have been assured.

Jawitz's article "le-Atid la-Vo" (*Ha-Mizrach,* 1904), in which he set out his concept of "government in the spirit of the Talmud," was a pioneering attempt to place these issues on the agenda of the religious Zionist camp. Nevertheless, by his detailed argument that the religious Zionist camp had no interest in setting up a "Jewish papacy," he was able to somewhat dampen the fears of the secular Zionists that the state would be religious Catholic-style. In effect, in the article Jawitz offers an Orthodox response to the challenge of modernity in the following areas: the relationships between state and religion, between religion and science, and between "religion and life." He emphasizes that in these areas religion does not stand in opposition to human understanding or the changing demands of life.

However, although Jawitz was the first to deal with these topics, his article did not contain practical proposals for moving forward on them. While he did indeed address some specific questions, such as the possibility from a religious perspective of establishing a Jewish university, the article mainly deals with overarching rules and principles, such as outlining a framework for the debate about the legitimacy of either theocracy or the separation of religion and state. He concludes that the rabbis are permitted to interpret halakha leniently when it comes to communal and political questions. He cites historical precedents for all these matters. But for most topics of contemporary concern he refrains from delineating a detailed policy. Thus, he does not come down one way or the other on the question of the use of electricity on the Sabbath; nor does he make any mention at all of the issue of milking cows on the Sabbath. Furthermore, he does not discuss the topic of the sale of land to non-Jews in the sabbatical year; nor does he cite this example in support of his case for lenient rulings, possibly because (like his esteemed brother-in-law Yehiel Michael Pines and the latter's rabbinical authority Mordechai Gimpel Jaffe) he took the view that such a land sale is invalid and that the land should indeed not be worked in the sabbatical year. Similarly, he ignores a number of important topics, both procedural and substantive, relevant to his theme, which both his predecessors and others coming after him did address. These include topics such as the nature of the governmental regime and the method of selecting the leadership, the relationship between the religious and the secular sectors, relationships with non-Jews, and so on. Nor in the field of aesthetics does he set out halakhic limits for theatrical performances or for the plastic arts.

Actually, Jawitz's discussion focused on the negative way—the Jewish tradition revokes theocracy such as separation of church from state, while it does not revoke modern science, technology, and joy of life. He did not open a positive discussion about designing the social, economic, and political character of the forthcoming state, in inspiration of the Jewish tradition and with an obligation to it.

Jawitz interest in the character of the forthcoming Jewish state relates to his attempt to create a national Jewish culture, without causing a rift with the past, as in the framework of the Ha-Mizrachi party, which was dedicated to the continuity of the Jewish tradition. The attitude of the movement's leader, Rabbi Isaac Jacob Reines, was juxtaposed with that of Jawitz. He believed that Ha-Mizrachi had to focus on consensual, practical, and diplomatic activity and leave cultural activity to a later time. Jawitz failed to advance his attitude in the framework of the political movement, and after the Pressburg conference (late 1904) he resigned from leading the movement. Since then, his influence on its agenda has reduced.

## NOTES

1. D. Penslar, "Herzl, Zionism and the Origins of Jewish Social Policy," in *Theodor Herzl, Visionary of the Jewish State*, eds. G. Shimoni and R. Wistrich (Jerusalem: Magnes Press, 1999), 215–26; S. Avineri, "Herzls utopische Vision," *Internationales Theodor Herzl Symposion* 5 (2004), 25–35; S. Feiner, "Humani nil," 709–31.
2. T. Herzl, *Old New Land*, trans. L. Levensohn (New York: Wiener, 1987), 122–23, 185–91, 247–54.
3. Ahad Ha'am, "Altneuland," in idem, *The Collected Writings of Ahad Ha'am* (Jerusalem: Dvir, 1961), 319. See also S. Laskow, "The 'Altneuland' Controversy," *Ha-Tzionut* 15 (1991): 35–54; Y. Goldstein, *Ahad Ha'am and Herzl: The Struggle for Political and Cultural Nature of Zionism in the Shade of Altneuland Affair* (Jerusalem: Dinur Centre & Shazar Centre, 2011).
4. M. Nordau, "Ahad Ha'am on 'Altneuland,'" *Zionist Writings*, Volume 2: *Speeches and Articles* (Jerusalem: HaSifria HaZionit, 1960), 110–19.
5. The significance of this article has been recognized by G. Bat Yehudah under the entry "Ze'ev Jawitz," in *The Encyclopaedia of Religious Zionism*, vol. 2, ed. Y. Rafael (Jerusalem: Mossad Harav Kook, 1960), 506–7.
6. A. S. Hirschberg, "The Life of Rabbi Ze'ev Jawitz: On The Completion of Ten Years since His Death," in Z. Jawitz, *Toledot Yisrael*, vol. 14 (Tel Aviv: Achi'ever, 1954–62), 123–61; R. Michael, *The Writing of Jewish History* (Jerusalem: Bialik Institute, 1993), 424–65.
7. A. Yedidya, *Criticized Criticism: Orthodox Alternatives to Wissenschaft des Judentums 1873–1956* (Jerusalem: Bialik Institute, 2013), 197–221.
8. On the topic of religion and society in religious Zionism, see Y. Salmon, "Tradition and Nationalism," in *Essential papers on Zionism*, eds. J. Reinharz and A. Shapira (New York: New York University Press, 1996), 94–116; I. Kolatt, "Religion, Society, and State during the Period of the National Home," in *Zionism and Religion*, 273–301.
9. Z. Jawitz, "In Days to Come," *Ha-Mizrach* 1 (1904), 323.
10. Ibid.
11. Ibid.
12. M. Mendelssohn, *Jerusalem and other Jewish Writings*, trans. A. Jospe (New York: Schocken Books, 1969), 99. The passage is a quotation from the German, which reads as follows in the original: "Staat und Religion war in dieser ursprünglichen Verfassung nicht vereiniget, sondern eins; nicht verbunden, sondern eben dasselbe."
13. Ibid., 102.
14. A. Altmann, "Moses Mendelssohn's Political Philosophy," *The Solomon Goldman Lectures* 3 (1982), 31–38; E. Schweid, "Religion and State in the Works of Spinoza, Mendelssohn and Strauss," in *Religion and State in Twentieth Century Jewish Thought*, ed. A. Ravitzky (Jerusalem: Israel Democracy Institute, 2005), 149–58; R. Sigad, "Moses Mendelssohn, Judaism, Theocratic Politics and the State of Israel," *Da'at* 7 (1981), 93–103.
15. Jawitz, "In Days to Come," 331.
16. Ibid., 332.
17. Ibid., 331.
18. Ibid.
19. S. V. Monsma and J. C. Soper, *The Challenge of Pluralism: Church and State in Five Democracies* (Lanham, MD: Rowman & Littlefield, 1996); J. A. Backford, "Great Britain," in *The Encyclopedia of Politics and Religion* (London: Routledge, 1998), 307–11; idem, "Politics and Religion in England and Wales," *Deadalus* 120 (1991): 179–201.
20. Jawitz, "In Days to Come," 332.

21. Z. Jawitz, "Unity," *Ha-Mizrach* 1 (1903): 10–17.
22. Jawitz, "In Days to Come," 324.
23. Z. Jawitz, *Toledot Yisrael*, vol. 4 (Vilna, 1900), 185. To substantiate his case, Jawitz refers there to Josephus Flavius's book *Jewish Antiquities*, XIV, 3, 2. See a similar criticism of the Hasmonean Dynasty by Nachmanides in his *Commentary on the Torah*, Volume 1: *Genesis*, (Jerusalem: Mossad Harav Kook, 1976), 269. On the separation of powers in the Jewish tradition, see also A. Shapira, *Primitive Democracy in the Bible: Ancient Foundations of Democratic Values* (Tel Aviv: Hakibbutz Hameuchad-Sifriat Poalim Publishing Group , 2009); Stuart A. Cohen, "The Concept of the Three Ketarim: Their Place in Jewish Political Thought and Implications for Studying Jewish Constitutional Theory," in *Kinship & Consent: The Jewish Political Tradition and its Contemporary Uses*, ed. Daniel Judah Elazar (New Brunswick, N.J.: Transaction Publishers, 1997), 47–76.
24. Letter from Y. L. Pinsker to Rav Dr Isaac Rülf, 30.1.1884, in *Y. L. Pinsker: Herald of the National Rebirth: Auto-Emancipation and its Critics: Open Letters, Speeches and Correspondence*, trans. M. Yoeli (Jerusalem, 1960), 153.
25. Herzl, *The Jewish State*.
26. Jawitz, "In Days to Come," 325.
27. Ibid.
28. Ibid.
29. Ibid.
30. 30 Jawitz, *Toledot Yisrael*, vol. 4, 54.
31. Ibid., vol. 6, viii.
32. Ibid., 212–13 n. 3.
33. Ibid., 131.
34. H. Graetz, *Geschichte der Juden*, IV (Leipzig: Oskar Leiner, 1908), 51.
35. The line of classical rabbinical ordination, which claimed to trace its line of authority back to Moses, seems to have died out in the fourth or fifth century CE.
36. Jawitz, "In Days to Come," 325.
37. Ibid.
38. *Shulchan Aruch*, Orach Chayyim, 329, 7.
39. Jawitz, "In Days to Come," 327.
40. *bPesaḥ*, 66a.
41. Jawitz, "In Days to Come."
42. Ibid., 333.
43. Jawitz, *Toledot Yisrael*, vol. 13, 201–19.
44. Y. M. Pines, *Children of my Spirit*, vol. 2 (Mainz; Defus Yechiel Brill, 1872), 35–40.
45. Breuer, *Modernity*, 203–13: M. Ascher, *Kein Widerspruch zwischen Judentum, Wissenschaft und Leben!* (Neuchâtel: H. Itzkowski, 1908).
46. Ernst Heinrich Haeckel (1834–1919), German zoologist and philosopher and one of the founders of Darwinism.
47. Jawitz, "In Days to Come," 326.
48. H. Shapira, *Zionist Writings* (Jerusalem: Defus Zion, 1925), 9–16. See also I. Kolatt, "The Idea of the Hebrew University in the Jewish National Movement," in *The History of the Hebrew University of Jerusalem: Origins and Beginnings*, eds. S. Katz and M. Hed (Jerusalem: Magnes Press, 1997), 3–74.
49. K. Z. Wissotzky, *Collected Letters* (Jerusalem: Yad Beb-Zvi Press, 1981), 8.
50. Jawitz, "In Days to Come," 326.
51. Ibid.
52. Actually, he probably knew, at this point in time, that Maimonides was indeed accused of heresy, as he wrote later in *Toldot Israel*, but preferred ignoring this fact. Jawitz, *Toldot Israel*, 12, 76–80.
53. Jawitz, "In Days to Come," 326.
54. These include R. Judah Loew ben Bezalel ("the Maharal of Prague"), David Gans and R. Yosef Shlomo Rofeh of Candia. On this see, A. Nehar, *David Gans and his Times* (Jerusalem: Rubin Mass Ltd., 1982), 309–17; D. Ruderman, *Jewish Thought and*

*Scientific Discovery in Early Modern Europe* (New Haven: Yale University Press, 1995), 78, 83, 124.

55. Jawitz, "In Days to Come," 327. He may have been referring to R. Samson Raphael Hirsch, who had already argued in 1873 that it was permissible to accept the theory of evolution as it led to an appreciation of the unity of creation, the handiwork of the one Creator; see S. R. Hirsch, "The Educational Value of Judaism," in idem, *The Collected Writings*, vol. 7 (New York and Jerusalem: Feldheim, 1992), 263–64.

56. For Jewish reactions to Darwin's theory of evolution, see Y. Shavit and J. Reinharz, *Darwin and His Kind* (Bnei Brak: Hakibbutz Hameuchad-Sifriat Poalim Publishing Group , 2009).

57. Jawitz, "In Days to Come."

58. Jawitz, "Swords into Ploughshares," in *The Grape Basket: Stories from the Land of Israel at the Time of the First Aliyah*, ed. G. Yardeni (Jerusalem: Bialik Institute, 1967), 77.

59. Carl Linnaeus (1707–1778), Swedish botanist and zoologist, laid the foundations for the scientific classification of plants and animals; Justus von Liebig (1803–1873), German chemist, specializing in agricultural and biological chemistry; Matthias Schleiden (1804–1881), German botanist and early developer of cell theory; Alexander von Humboldt (1769–1859), German naturalist and explorer.

60. On the ways of resolving contradictions between Judaism and Science, see S. Rosenberg, *Torah and Science in Modern Jewish Thought* (Jerusalem: Ministry of Education, 1988).

61. *bAbod. Zar.* 9a.

62. Z. Jawitz, *Toldot Israel*, vol. 3 (Berlin, 1910), 31.

63. Jawitz, "In Days to Come," 328.

64. Ibid.

65. Ibid., 329.

66. Ibid.

67. I. Schorsch, *From Text to Context: The Turn to History in Modern Judaism* (Hanover, NH: Brandeis University Press, 1994), 71–92; Graetz, *Geschichte der Juden*, vol. VI.

68. On the debate concerning the introduction of the plastic arts into the revival of Hebrew culture, see A. Holtzman, *Art Work: The Revival of the Nation – Hebrew Literature in the Light of Plastic Art* (Haifa: Kinneret Zmora-Bitan Dvir, 1999); E. Baram Eshel, "A Rootless Hebrew Writer Interprets the Second Commandment: An Inquiry into Reuven Breinan's Novella *Notes of a Hebrew Artist*," *Moed* 19 (2010): 160–70. On the physical prowess, see T. S. Presner, *Muscular Judaism: The Jewish Body and the Politics of Regeneration* (London: Routledge, 2007).

69. G. Yardeni, *The Hebrew Press in Eretz-Israel 1863-1904* (Tel Aviv: Hakibbutz Hameuchad Publishing House,1969), 264–66.

70. Herzl, *Old New Land*, 95, 103–6.

71. M. Olin, "The Search for a Jewish Art in Palestine: Bezalel 1906–1948," *Das Jüdische Echo* 48 (1999): 375–89; B. Jo-Kim, "Schatz's Bezalel: Zionist Icon and Hebrew Art," *Historia veTeoria* 5 (2007).

72. Letter from Ze'ev Jawitz to his son Yehudah Leib, 14 Marcheshvan 5653 (4 November 1892), The Jawitz Collection, New York Public Library, item 95.

73. Sholem Ya'acov Abramovich, better known as Mendele Mocher Sefarim, was particularly critical of what he perceived as Judaism's tendency for abstinence from the natural joy of life. In his story "Ha-Nisrafim" ("The Burned," 1896), for example, he observes that in the spring, when "creation in all its beauty and splendour" makes its appearance, Jews are forbidden to rejoice, being shrouded in the mourning of the days of the Omer (which always fall at that time of the year).

74. On the place of art in Talmudic and Jewish thought, see D. Cassuto, ed., *Art and Judaism* (Ramat Gan: Bar Ilan University Press 1989), 83–164.

75. Jawitz, "In Days to Come," 330.

76. Ibid., 331.

77. Ibid., 329.

78. Ibid., 327.

79. Ex. 20: 4.
80. Jawitz, "Swords into Ploughshares," 69.
81. A.Y. Kook, *Collected Letters of Rav Kook*, vol. 1 (Jerusalem: Mossad Harav Kook, 1943), 203–6.
82. A.Y. Kook, *Orot* (Jerusalem: Mossad Harav Kook, 1950), 80.
83. Jawitz, "In Days to Come," 330.
84. Yehudah Ha-Levi, The Kuzari: in Defence of the Despised Faith, trans. D. Korobkin (Northvale, NJ: Jason Aronson, 2010), 16–17. For more on this concept, see S. Rosenberg, "Heart and Uniqueness: The Idea of Chosenness in the Thought of R. Yehudah Ha-Levi and in Modern Jewish Philosophy," in *The Philosophical Thought of R. Yehudah Ha-Levi*, ed. Haya Schwartz (Jerusalem: Ministry of Education, 1978), 109–18.
85. S. D. Luzzatto, "Judaism Versus Atticism: S.D. Luzzatto's Song for his Generation," *Zion*, vol. 1 (Frankfurt am Main, 1841): 81–93. See also S. Feiner, "Critique of Modernity: Samuel David Luzzatto and the Counter-Enlightenment," in *Samuel David Luzzatto: Two Hundred Years since His Birth*, eds. R. Bonfil, Y. Gottleib and H. Kasher (Jerusalem: Magnes Press, 2004), 146–65.
86. E. Segal, "The Historical Thought of Ze'ev Jawitz" (M.A. thesis, Bar-Ilan University, 1992), 49. In the spirit of Luzzatto, Jawitz also made a distinction between "the intellectual and value systems derived from the teachings of Moses and those derived from the teachings of Greece"; Z. Jawitz, "Transitory Worlds and an Enduring World," *Sefer ha-Shana* 1 (1900): 43–54.
87. Jawitz, "Transitory Worlds."
88. On this, see E. Schweid, *A History of the Philosophy of the Jewish Religion in Modern Times*, 1–3 (Tel Aviv: Am Oved Publishers , 2003), 105–13; I. Belke, ed., *Moritz Lazarus und Heymann Steinthal—die Begründer der Völkerpsychologie in ihren Briefen* (Tübingen: Mohr Siebeck, 1971).
89. Jawitz, "In Days to Come," 329.

# THREE

# The Balfour Declaration and the Pioneering Debate on Halakha and the Challenge of Sovereignty (1917–1921)

The changes engendered in the Jewish world in the wake of World War I reached their climax with the Balfour Declaration and the conquest of Eretz Israel by the British Army. The combination between the two events, which complemented each other—the theory and the possibility of fulfilling it—created a unique moment in Zionist history and consciousness. With the issuance of the Balfour Declaration in London on November 2, 1917, the British government expressed its support for the establishment of a national homeland for the Jewish people in Eretz Israel. It seemed that after decades of political Zionist activity, the longed-for charter had finally been granted and Zionism had attained its hitherto greatest achievement. The leaders of the Zionist movement interpreted this statement as sanctioning the program drawn up in Basel and recognizing the Jewish people's right to establish a sovereign state in the Land of Israel. They took advantage of the Balfour Declaration to conduct a propaganda campaign promoting Zionism. This suited the interests of Britain, who hoped that the declaration and the practical possibility of its realization would garner the support of American Jews for their country's continued involvement in the war alongside Britain.[1] At that time, the interpretation of the term "national home," in the sense of Jewish autonomy under the United Kingdom or "The Seventh British Dominion," was not as widespread in Zionist circles and pro-Zionist British circles as it would be a decade later.

Among the religious supporters of the Zionist movement were those who regarded the declaration as heralding the Redemption and on this basis some of them even sought to draw up a practical strategy. While the

Zionist leadership made plans for renewed momentum that would encompass mass immigration, extensive settlement, and even the establishment of national institutions in Eretz Israel, several religious leaders also began to express their opinions and question the place of halakha in the future Jewish state, in light of the incredible opportunity that had suddenly opened up for the Jewish people to return to Eretz Israel. Two concurrent Zionist initiatives made it clear that a serious discussion of the issue was imperative, otherwise the secular Zionists would establish facts on the ground that went against the spirit of tradition. The first initiative was the establishment of the university in Jerusalem. The First World War had disrupted the activities of the committee, headed by Chaim Weizmann, that was entrusted with implementing this resolution. In July 1918, some six months after the British gained control of Jerusalem, the cornerstone of the Hebrew University was laid on Mount Scopus. The founders, who made it clear that the university would be the spiritual and cultural center of the Jewish people, went so far as to apply the biblical phrase: "Out of Zion shall go forth the Law." This attitude was a matter of concern for Mizrachi (the religious Zionist party), which regarded the Torah and its institutions as the spiritual wellspring of the Jewish people.[2]

Another, and even more worrisome endeavor was that instigated by Mordechai ben Hillel HaCohen, to convert the Hebrew Magistrates Court to the main judicial body of the Jewish Yishuv (the Jewish community in Palestine). At the first constituent assembly of the Jewish Yishuv held in June 1918 in British occupied territory, the attending rabbis were insolently informed that the laws of *hoshen mishpat* (the fourth section of the *Shulkhan Arukh,* which treats with civil and criminal law), in their existing format, had no relevance in a modern judicial system.[3] In a memorandum submitted to the British administration by the Palestine Office of the Zionist Organizationin 1919, the writer termed this institute "The Jewish Court of Peace" instead of "The Hebrew Court of Peace" and presented it as a central national institute.[4]

Another extensively researched episode, which contributed to the sense that the traditional character of the Yishuv was under threat, focused on whether to permit women to vote for local institutions while the Yishuv was preparing for the British Mandate in Eretz Israel.[5] The rabbis were divided on this issue. While some even refused to regard it as a halakhic question, it nevertheless added fuel to the general debate on the subject of halakha and autonomy.

For the first time there was an in-depth discussion stemming from very real considerations about the place of halakha in a modern, autonomous Jewish state. The physical return to Eretz Israel, the spread of secularization in Jewish society, and technological and scientific advances raised new halakhic issues that had hitherto not been dealt with. The hoped-for autonomous reality glimmering on the horizon had also given rise to an essential difference in the nature of halakhic questions, which had now changed from questions about the individual and the community to questions relating to the state and its people. Halakha, which had been formulated during the long years of exile, had no precedent for the diverse new topics now on the agenda. And halakhot dating back to the ancient sovereignty of the nation stood in stark contrast to the prevalent international legal reality and could not be resuscitated.

The discussion, which began after the Balfour Declaration, was more detailed than the general discussion of Jawitz. Zionist rabbis, especially Mizrachi members, who were excited by the declaration and its political meaning, took part in it.

The discussion was started by Rabbi Pinkhos Churgin (1893–1957). He was born in Russia, a graduate of Volozhen yeshiva and Yale University, he specialized in Bible translations. At the time of the declaration, he was living in the United States and was a member of the Mizrachi movement.[6]

His article *LiShe'elat HaRegah* (The Question of the Moment), was published in *HaIvri* in 1918 together with his recognition of the "value of this great moment in the life of our nation"[7] and his call for mass immigration and considerable monetary investment in land development. The article begins with his misgivings due to the fact that secular Zionists were establishing facts on the ground that would determine the character of the Yishuv:

> We can already predict that the intellectuals in the Zionist camp will voice their opinion that the time has come to realize their spiritual ideal, to create a "spiritual center." We have already heard this uttered by one of our *gdolim* [respected leaders], who is considered to be a member of our opponents' camp, so it will come as no surprise to hear the same thing formulated as a demand by the Zionist camp itself. But there is no greater danger facing the Yishuv than the attempt to affix this seal on Eretz Israel.[8]

Churgin regarded the attempt to imbue the Yishuv with secular characteristics as coercion of the minority as opposed to the will of the majority. It imposed an alien, artificial character on the natural, cultural, and spiritual nature of the Jewish people:

> We must now appeal to the entire nation, to the multitudes, in their wide boulevards, to fan the flames of their great love of the land, but the people do not know this spiritual center, they do not wish to know: their soul has been twisted away from this spirituality to one that others are creating for them, that others are amending for them. The nation dreams of a spiritual center, it aspires to the destiny that "from Zion will go forth the Law, and the Word of the Lord from Jerusalem." This is the natural dream to which its soul yearns. It must not be exchanged for alien theories, gleaned from outside.[9]

That same year, in another article entitled *Binyan Olam* (An Everlasting edifice) published in *HaIvri*, Churgin stipulated that life in the national Jewish homeland in Eretz Israel should be conducted in accordance with Jewish tradition and Jewish life as it had been lived in ancient times. "Eretz Israel of the future must conform with Eretz Israel of the past."[10] In this article he also enumerates the areas in which the religious Jewish character of the national homeland would find expression:

> There is no doubt that it is of paramount importance to restore the crown of religion to its rightful place. Religion shaped the life of our people, forged its unique nature and its national identity. Religion must be widely shown and expressed in general life. Sabbath must be a national day of rest, with no compromises or concessions. [ . . . ] Sabbath rest must be total and complete: a respite from commerce, factory work, on land and sea, in the postal and telegraph services. This is a religious Sabbath. It is only this Sabbath that can stamp its imprint on our lives. It contains the splendor of the past and the glory of the future.
>
> The legal establishment is our second conduit from the past. The ancient Jewish justice that never ceased, even in exile, that embodies all the beauty and purity of our lives, demands absolute control of our future lives in the land. Any attempt to alter our ancient judicial system in the courts of law will negate the special nature of our lives and widen the chasm between past and future. In the future, too, the Talmud and its armor-bearers must serve as the sole wellspring for laws of society and statehood. [ . . . ]
>
> Alongside the legal establishment there is also place for the agricultural establishment, for which religion has a special interest. The laws of *shmitta* and *yovel* must be reinstated. The renewal of the *yovel* in particular has special value because it provides a solution to a thorny economic problem, that of land purchase.[11]

In the matter of "restoring religion to its rightful place" Rabbi Churgin shared the same vision as other rabbis who participated in the debate. However, this vision clashed with the plans of secular Zionist thinkers. It raised new questions about the compatibility of halakha with the sovereign reality, which it did not recognize. These questions encompassed diverse topics. They were both general and specific, theoretical and practical. They covered criminal, civil, and public law. They even touched on matters between man and God. The opinions expressed, while grappling with the challenges posed to halakha by modern sovereignty, offered several directions for contending with these challenges.

## AGAINST THE SEPARATION OF RELIGION AND STATE

First and foremost, the rabbis who participated in the discussion negated the possibility raised among some in the secular camp of separating religion and state in the nascent national homeland.

Theodor Herzl had already written briefly about the relationship between religion and state in his book *The Jewish State*, but he did so from a non-religious standpoint, as we have seen.[12] After the Balfour Declaration several Zionist thinkers expressed themselves in a similar vein, provoking strong reactions from the Zionist rabbis. Chief among them was Rabbi Meir Berlin (Bar Ilan 1880–1949), the Russian born youngest son of the Netziv of Volozhin and president of the Mizrachi organization in the United States at the time. In his article entitled *Lish'elat Atidenu beEretz Israel* (Questioning our Future in Eretz Israel) that appeared in 1918 in *HaIvri*, the newspaper he edited, he sought to undermine Herzl's proposal for the separation of religion and state, an idea that was gaining ground in secular Zionist circles. First and foremost, he maintained that the lives of Jews in their own country must be formulated in line with its unique national spirit, they must be connected to Torah "as a flaming ember" rather than in imitation of other countries.

> With all our heart we aspire not to be like the gentiles. The land of the Jews will not be like the land of the Serbs or even like the United States, for they are divided only by their language, their interests, and their political life. Our great men desire a religious spirit to pervade our land, the spirit of our tradition and our Torah. Otherwise we will lose more than we gain. Although we will heal ourselves, we will dwell peacefully, no longer tasting the flavor of exile, and we will be entirely free, nevertheless we will not heal our souls. Because instead of continuing to weave historic threads as the Chosen People, in our own eyes and to a great extent also in the eyes of the rest of the world, we will suddenly cut the thread and we will be a small, simple, poor nation, like dozens and hundreds of others in the world. We will acquire the earth under our feet but there will be no heaven above us.[13]

He was aware of the huge challenge that sovereignty posed to Jewish halakha and referred to the pressing need to contend with this issue and prepare for its realization:

> When we live in our own land and conduct our own affairs, there will certainly be rules and regulations, laws and precepts, customs and proprieties—and the stipulations of other states will cause them to differ from what we had two and three thousand years ago. How will we adapt our opinions and outlook to real, everyday life? Many are now asking: what will be the relationship between religion and state? In other words, how will we solve the questions of church and state that other nations are debating. Many seek to determine our view, the view of Orthodox Jews, on religious questions that affect public life. Al-

> though until now we exempted ourselves from discussing these issues, we are no longer entitled to remain silent. [ . . . ] Can it be that the time has come first of all to determine for ourselves the nature of our spiritual life in our land, in conformity with our written Torah and oral tradition?[14]

He went on to reject the possibility of separating religion from the Jewish state. He claimed that the political and religious lives of other nations are in no way similar to the Jewish nation. In other countries political life is secular, its laws formulated by man. The church is not supposed to impact on political life, only on the religious world of the individual. The relationship between various religions and politics is imprecise, without concrete rules of conduct. In principle the two bodies are separate. It is only man's desire to control and rule that engenders rivalry. Therefore, the solution of separating religion and state is natural. But this is not the case in Israel. Political and religious life are nurtured from one and the same source—the Torah:

> Not only does our Torah encompass matters relating to political and public life, it also contains laws and precepts for the state and public life. These laws are the very body of the Torah and religious commandments. Those same chapters wherein are written and repeated matters concerning the individual and his soul, and between man and God, contain regulations and details about political conduct and public life, our relationship with other nations, how to fight them and how to make peace with them.[15]

Therefore, we do not have two separate authorities, but different branches of one entity that has functioned harmoniously throughout Jewish history. Any attempt to separate them is irrelevant. To do so would be analogous to slicing up the Torah. He believed that through education and literature it would be possible to influence the Jewish Yishuv and its aspirations, in order that they themselves would desire to conduct their political life according to the Torah, out of a deep inner understanding. Only in this situation could a supreme national religious establishment, accepted by the public, succeed in guiding in the spirit of the Torah and dealing with the challenge of sovereignty.

Rabbi Pinkhos Churgin also confronted this issue. In his article entitled *Knesiah, Dat, Umemshala* (Church, Religion, and Government), which appeared in *HaToren* in 1919, he rejects the idea of separating religion and state in Israel, based on a political review of various regimes throughout history. Like Rabbi Berlin, he regards this concept as a kind of imitation of other countries, "the same absolute enslavement to the world of opinions, viewpoints and concepts, but, because we do not cleave to them, we cannot become refined and shaped in their furnace."[16] This idea was the result of historical circumstances in countries such as the United States and France, but it did not suit other countries that did not share their circumstances, and definitely not Israel. He linked this concept in particular to the universal nature of Catholic Christianity, which perforce had to become separate when it encountered the national state. A country like England, with its own national church, had no need for such a separation. In Israel, where "first of all the Jewish religion developed along with the Jewish government, halakha itself hints at the impossibility of a battle between religion and state."[17] Like Berlin, Churgin regarded religion and state in Israel as two sides of the same coin, indivisible, rather than two separate entities. He concluded that halakha and sovereignty could be made compatible through a gradual process of development, "the rule of our future lives must be delivered into life itself. It will shape our lives and determine their boundaries."[18]

## RESTORATION OF THE SANHEDRIN

Rabbi Bar-Ilan and Rabbi Churgin did not offer practical suggestions for how halakha should deal with the challenge of sovereignty. They both believed that gradual development and religious education would eventually obviate the conflicts between religious and secular and between halakha and the sovereign state. However, the other participants in the discussion offered practical suggestions for solving the problems caused by modern sovereignty.

One was Rabbi Chaim Tchernowitz (1870–1949), known by his pen name "Rav Tzair" (Young Rabbi). He was born in Russia and had a traditional upbringing. In 1896, he received ordination from Rabbi Yitzchak Elchanan Spektor. In 1897, he moved to Odessa where he was appointed rabbi and head of the yeshiva. In Odessa, he became familiar with Ahad Ha'Am's circle and began to publish articles in the journal *HaSchiloah*. In 1911, he left Odessa. After a short visit to Eretz Israel he settled in Germany and completed his studies for a doctorate degree at the University of Würzburg. During the First World War, when he was forced to leave Germany due to his Russian nationality, he moved to Switzerland. In 1923, he emigrated to the United States.[19]

In the article *Merkaz Dati* (Religious Center), whicht appeared in *HaIvri* in 1920, Tchernowitz dealt with questions about the religious character of the future Jewish state. He sought to do so from a historical point of view: "When we come to build our national institutions we must obey the dictates of history, in order to ensure that our institutions endure forever, because anything that is not erected in accordance with history's plan is built in vain and will ultimately fail."[20]

Tchernowitz maintained that history has proved that Jewish national existence is based on the covenant between God and Israel. God bestowed upon them the land and they undertook to observe the Torah and mitzvoth. Jewish history is an indivisible union of nationalism and religion. Nationalists who are not religious and religious people with no nationality are alien creatures, foreign to historical Judaism. A national edifice that does not rest upon the foundations of the covenant cannot succeed:

> A return to Zion without the God of Zion—is a contradiction. It is a new form of Judaism, it is not historical Judaism. This will not be Israel's return to its historical holy land but the colonization of wandering Jews from the land of Syria. It will not represent the continuation of Jewish history and the natural aspirations of the Jewish people throughout their years of exile, neither will it provide spiritual fulfillment for all the tribulations we have suffered for thousands of years. Nor will it provide a satisfactory answer to the eternal question of the Jewish vision.[21]

He was aware that halakha, as formulated during the years of exile, would require adjustments in order to contend with the challenge of sovereignty, but he thought it should be done gradually, in step with the national revival. In the meantime, we must refrain from adopting a legal system that is alien to Judaism, and preserve halakha as the national Jewish body of law.

> It is impossible for one nation to acquire fixed statutes and legal procedures from another nation without making changes, stripping it of its former shape and imparting a new shape. Because jurisprudence is the consequence of custom and custom is the consequence of the national psyche. In the same way that the values of nations differ, so too their jurisprudence is not the same. For example, is it possible for us Jews to accept a long-standing duel as the foundation of our legal system and say: if a man prevails over his fellow by strength it is a sign that he is right? All Jewish sensibilities would oppose it! A Jew declares that one who beats his fellow is evil. In his eyes, the victim is always right. [ . . . ] Is it possible to eradicate from the heart of a Jew the prohibition against fraudulent dealing? No such injunction exists among merchants of other nations. On the contrary, he who cheats more is praised and regarded as a good merchant. All trade is based on fraudulent dealing.[22]

Tchernowitz believed that religion had the power to adapt itself to the new sovereign reality and rejected the criticism leveled by slanderers that it was irrelevant. "Judaism is not ghetto-like because it existed in the ghetto, but because it preserved the Jews in the ghetto. Once the nation is freed it too will become free."[23] He completely rejected the possibility of separating religion from state in Israel, claiming that such a rash action would destroy both nationalism that is sanctified by religion, and religion that would become a state within a state and would challenge the authority of the government: "If religion is abandoned under duress, then a cadre of priests will rise up to defend it and constantly do battle against the state. And eventually its power will be greater than that of the state."[24]

Nevertheless, he took pains to explain that his attitude toward the relationship between religion and state differed from theocracy. Religion does not exert control over the life of the individual and his beliefs. It is only public life couched in state laws that includes a social order that will endure in accordance with halakha. The distinction between maintaining Jewish life in public and the lack of coercion to observe Judaism in one's private life developed into the widespread dissimilarity among mainstream religious Zionists after the establishment of the state.

The option of applying halakha in matters pertaining to the individual and those pertaining to the general public, and its compatibility with sovereign reality, would come about through a process similar to the process that Judaism experienced in the early days of the Second Temple, by way of an establishment parallel to the Sanhedrin (Great Assembly) in the days of Ezra:

> You may ask who will decide this matter? Who will tell us what pertains to belief and what pertains to religion? When the state comes into being we will need a new assembly of the Sanhedrin, that will convene all the religious literature in order to proclaim the national and political commandments and the principles of religion that will be protected by the state, as did the men of the Sanhedrin in their time, when they came together to strengthen the Torah and the known *mitzvoth*. We need a *Shulkhan Arukh* wherein the most important *mitzvoth* relate to the land and the establishment of the state.[25]

Tchernowitz brought example of laws which, in his opinion, needed to be reexamined, "matters that people regard as prohibitions, but were not prohibited in a quorum. Those who taught Torah were not in general agreement on these matters,"[26] although he refrained from expressing his own opinion as to whether they should be prohibited or permitted. Among other things, he enumerated the prohibitions on traveling by train and making use of electricity, the telegraph, and the telephone on Sabbath, as well as modern methods of combining agricultural species. Finally, he maintained that these new problems could not be solved by ordinary rabbis but only by rabbis who were also political scholars, in other words, those who also understood the diverse constraints and needs of the state. Only they could decide which halakhot could be discarded for "the sake of the public."[27] These men, who would constitute a supreme rabbinical institution, would be vested with the power wielded by the Sanhedrin in its time. "The Sanhedrin will serve as a religious center in which will be concentrated all the power of Torah and Jewish knowledge. From them Torah will issue forth to all of Israel, they will differentiate between the sacred and the profane, between pure and impure. Every religious question, whether it applies to the state, the general public, or Diaspora communities—will be resolved in this center. There will be no other authority than this one."[28] In his article *LeHidush haSan-*

*hedrin Ubeit Din HaGadol* (Reinstating the Sanhedrin and the High Rabbinical Court), published in 1925, he even drew up a detailed and practical plan for the restoration of this establishment.[29]

Another rabbi of the time who proposed to establish the *Beit Din HaGadol* (High Rabbinical Court) in Jerusalem was Ben-Zion Chai Uziel (1880–1953). He was born in Jerusalem and had a traditional upbringing. From 1911–1921, he served as the Hakham Bashi of Jaffa. During World War I, he was deported from Eretz Israel for a short period. After the war he returned to Jaffa, and in 1921 he was appointed rabbi of Salonika. In 1923, he was appointed rabbi of Tel Aviv. In 1939, he was elected as the Sephardi Chief Rabbi of the Eretz Israel, a position he continued to hold until his death. Rabbi Uziel supported Zionism and was a member of the Mizrachi movement.[30] He regarded the Balfour Declaration and the British conquest of Eretz Israel as a unique opportunity to reestablish the Jewish state and "return to fulfill the Torah law of Israel."[31]

In 1919, he published an article in *HaDvir* entitled *Chok Umishpat beYisrael* (Law and Justice in Israel), wherein he rejects the halakhic possibility of establishing legal proceedings for appeals like those conducted in other countries. He proposed restoring the Bet Din Hagadol (High Rabbinical Court) as the supreme religious body, to be entrusted with restoring the laws of the Torah in the era of national revival:

> First and foremost we must restore our ancient laws and establish a High Rabbinical Court in Jerusalem which will issue instructions to all Israel, from which will be appointed judges and rabbis for the land, and to which all of Israel will submit their legal questions. They will also be consulted on the matter of the revival of the nation and the land, and political and national conduct.[32]

In fact, Rabbi Uziel proposed bringing together seventy-one rabbis to establish a High Rabbinical Court made up of the finest sages in Israel who would wield extensive halakhic authority. There were precedents for an establishment of this nature because some rabbinical courts were recognized as being superior to others due to the prominence of their members. He claimed that such an establishment no longer existed and therefore there was a need to reinstate it. Nevertheless, at this stage he was not referring to an institution like the Sanhedrin, but of somewhat lesser stature. In any event, it would play a cardinal role in dealing with the challenge posed by sovereignty.[33]

Actually, fourteen years before the Balfour Declaration, this idea was conceived by Rabbi Aharon Mendl Hakohen (1866–1927) of Cairo, in the context of struggling with modernity and secularization. He came to the conclusion that only the restoration of the Sanhedrin—a unified authoritative rabbinical institution, could properly meet the modern challenges halakhically. He tried to convince his colleagues about the necessity of this idea but remained a lone voice.[34]

However, also according to Rabbi Abraham Isaac HaCohen Kook (1865–1935), the halakhic flexibility demanded by political exigencies depended on the reestablishment of the Sanhedrin. In an article published in 1904 in the periodical *Ha-Peles*, just before he emigrated to Eretz Israel, he wrote:

> For the public and national good, we hope for the return of our judges as at first and our counsellors as at the beginning; and once they have restored our glory as in days of old, then Torah will once again come forth from Zion and the Great Sanhedrin (which, as explained by the Rambam and as agreed by all, is the keystone of the Oral Law) will be re-established in all its splendor and majesty; and then all will be made ready (in accordance with the Torah, the source of life, and in keeping with the religious aspirations of earlier generations) for that exalted religious authority, "the Great Bet Din in Jerusalem," to enact more lenient rulings for the community in those matters where leniencies are available in accordance with the Torah.[35]

After the Balfour Declaration and with the commencement of the British Mandate for Palestine, Rabbi Kook participated in the establishment of the Chief Rabbinate of the Land of Israel in the hope that a Great Sanhedrin would emerge from it in the future.[36] However, he did not believe it would be possible because there were many controversies among the sages of Israel.[37]

## DEMOCRACY AND HALAKHIC REFORMS

The restoration of the Sanhedrin or the High Rabbinical Court was an extremely complex project, requiring practical initiative, public agreement, and major rabbinical accord. In fact, the solution depended entirely upon rejecting the detailed examination of specific halakhic questions that had already been raised in the context of administering the state. The man who devoted himself to a detailed examination of these questions was Rabbi Haim Hirschensohn (1857–1935).

He was born in Safed and had a traditional upbringing. His father, Rabbi Jacob Mordechai (1822–1899), was influenced by the proto-Zionist rabbi Elijah Guttmacher and supported the Hibbat Zion movement. In 1866, the family settled in Jerusalem. After his marriage, he tried working at several small factories with little success. During the years 1887–1889, he edited the journal *HaMisdarona*, a literary platform for traditional *Wissenschaft des Judentums*. He was Eliezer Ben Yehuda's partner in reviving spoken Hebrew and one of the founders of the Safah Beurah (Clean Language) association. Due to his involvement in cultural and educational projects in Jerusalem, he was banned by Rabbi Disskin and his wife Sonia. In 1896, he left Eretz Israel for Constantinople where he took over the directorship of two Hebrew schools. He was an early member of the

Zionist Organization, and several years later he was among the first to join the Mizrachi movement. In 1904, he was appointed rabbi of the Orthodox community in Hoboken, New Jersey, a position which he held until his death in 1935.

Apart from his rabbinical duties he served on the Education Committee of the Rabbinical Council of America and the American Zionist Federation. His extensive Torah writings also date from this period. They include essays on the Oral Law, the Bible, Jewish education, Jewish philosophy, and the genre of responsa.[38]

In 1919, after the Balfour Declaration, Rabbi Hirschensohn published his book *Malki BaKodesh* (Holy King), the first of six volumes of responsa dealing with "the conduct of the Israeli monarchy in accordance with halakha." In the preface to his book Rabbi Hirschensohn acknowledged Israel's historical change "from one period to another. From a time of exile and subjugation by kings to a period heralding the beginning of Redemption and the coming of the Messiah."[39] He also presents two practical questions that were posed by a participant at the 21st Conference of the American Zionist Federation, regarding the application of halakha to the structure of the hoped-for state as an additional reason for writing his book, noting that: "To reinstitute these practices would make us appear ridiculous."[40]

Unlike Rav Tzair, Rabbi Hirschensohn believed that it would only be possible to reinstate the Sanhedrin after the Jewish people were all incorporated into one unified group,[41] but the challenges of sovereignty should be met halakhically without delay, using all available means. In the same way that Rabbi Kook ordained the *heter mechirah* (a halakhic mechanism whereby agricultural lands in Israel are sold to non-Jews, allowing the lands to be cultivated and vegetables grown during the Shmitta year) for the year 5660, Rabbi Hirschensohn utilized two basic principles in his halakhic ruling relating to Jews in Eretz Israel: his ruling was addressed to the entire Yishuv, not only those who were religiously observant. Whether it was "the beginning of the Redemption," in religious terms, or preparation for Jewish sovereignty, in political terms, the current time demanded daring arbitration and deviation from rulings and traditions of the Diaspora.[42]

Nevertheless, in his rulings he went far beyond Rabbi Kook. Not only did he respond to practical questions, he also anticipated questions that could arise in the future. He did not restrict his innovations to situations which the Yishuv and the state would be unable to accept according to traditional halakha, but also instances which it would be difficult to abide by. In addition, he sought to adjust halakha to conform to political and legal principles in line with the amended constitutions of other nations.

In the introduction to his book Rabbi Hirschensohn clarifies that this was no ordinary book of responsa, but one that touched on questions that applied to the nation as a whole. These were matters that had to be attended to without delay: "These questions are of interest to every Jew who is prepared to do some constructive thinking along Jewish lines in order to determine the form of the new Jewish life in the new Palestine."[43]

In other words, he was not providing halakhic answers to specific questions relating to explicit cases. This was a halakhic work dealing with timely questions affecting the nation as a whole, presented in the form of responsa literature. Why did Rabbi Hirschensohn choose this particular genre, one that was better suited to individual cases than a pioneering halakhic presentation for the entire nation? I believe his reasons for so doing were firstly, the desire to show that these questions are not merely theoretical but in fact actual questions unlike any others, that the rabbis must address without delay, no less important than the private queries that regularly arrived at their doorsteps; and secondly, a desire to demonstrate that his method was anchored in age-old rabbinical tradition and did not challenge it.

In his opinion, the halakhic response to the challenge of sovereignty had failed. He believed that Jewish sovereignty would not succeed for long if national life was not governed by the Torah:

> For political redemption came to our people through the political power of Cyrus, Darius, Artaxerxes, or in our own days through the Declaration of the British Government, which has been approved by so many of the allied nations. Nevertheless the persistence of the Eternal People has depended less on such externals than on adherence to the Law and its interpretation through the Halakha. It is the Law which has ensured our survival, and it is only on the basis of the Law that we may hope to assure our future in the Land of Israel.[44]

This view is consistent with Hirschensohn's attitude toward the relationship between religion and statehood. Like other religious Zionist thinkers he originally believed that, unlike Christianity, Judaism has a monistic identity of religion and nationalism: "religion and nationalism are one and the same."[45] After closer familiarity with American Jewry and the phenomenon of secularity spreading through the Jewish people, he amended his opinion and began to regard the relationship between religion and Judaism as dualistic, similar to that between the soul and the body.[46] In his opinion, nationalism could stand alone without religion, but religion could not endure without an affinity to nationalism: "The truth is that the Jewish religion is a national religion, but there is no Jewish nationalism except for religious nationalism. Religion is only one of the conditions of the life of a people; it preceded the people and helps its moral progress and enhances it through spiritual enrichment, but it is not nationality, just as wealth is not life, even though it sustains and brings life."[47]

Nevertheless, secular nationalism is empty, it is like a body without a soul and thus cannot endure over time and lead the nation to its eternal destiny. Therefore, the nation must sustain its life according to the Torah. This dualistic relationship finds expression in two concepts coined by Rabbi Hirschensohn: *Brit Am*—the covenant made between individuals to become one nation, and *Brit Eloha*—the covenant made between individuals or a nation and the Almighty, to maintain and observe the words of the Torah.[48]

A large portion of his thesis deals with the desired method of governing the long-awaited Jewish state. He rejects the possibility of establishing a monarchic regime. Seemingly, this would be the most desirable regime in Judaism, as was customary during most of the biblical period and the time of the Second Temple. The Torah commandment to the people to appoint a king was obeyed for generations, in the words of Maimonides (Sefer HaMitzvot, *mitzvoth aseh 163).* But Rabbi Hirschensohn claims that from a halakhic point of view, there is no commandment to appoint a king in our time:

> I wish to clarify that according to Go-d's word this is halakha, to show first of all that now there are no *mitzvoth* at all relating to the appointment of a king, even after we return rejoicing to Zion and the first kingdom is established in Jerusalem. Therefore Israel did not observe this *mitzvah* even after the building of the Second Temple, because they were not commanded to do so according to law and halakha. Those kings ruled through their own strength and heroism, like the Hasmonean dynasty, or through the power of Rome, like Herod and Agrippa, but they were not appointed by reason of the *mitzvoth*.[49]

Similarly, Rabbi Hirschensohn does not accept the prophecies relating to the Messianic king as the final stage of the Redemption, when society will change and there will be no need for a regime to rein in the selfish desires of human beings. If at all, the purpose of the Messianic king will be restricted to the realm of spiritual leadership.[50]

After rejecting the obligation to appoint a king at this time, and the model of monarchic rule, Rabbi Hirschensohn arrived at the type of regime which, in his opinion, is the best and most logical, according to "the moral recognition that time has taught us through much experience, wisdom, and studies of political economy."[51] This is the republican-democratic method with which he was well acquainted, one that he had come to admire during his years in the United States.

Apart from drawing on experience, Rabbi Hirschensohn found a democratic aspect in Jewish tradition that pointed toward the adoption of this regime. He explained the commandment to appoint judges (Deuteronomy 16:18) as not only as an injunction to appoint religious judges, which "is only an explanation of half the commandment," but also a commandment that applies only in Eretz Israel, to appoint "the heads of the people, its leaders, lawmakers, counselors, and those who fight its battles."[52] These appointments must be made democratically, with the people electing their leaders.

Rabbi Hirschensohn believed that the most significant aspect of democracy in Jewish tradition can be found in the principle of the Covenant. Israel's acceptance of the Torah with its concomitant acceptance of the statutes was not done under duress but through the free will of each individual, who by so doing drew up a pact with the Almighty:

> In my humble opinion, this is the underpinning for one of the great principles of Jewish faith—of its religion and nationality; it is the pillar of the entire Torah and the commandments. It is one of the basics of our faith that the Holy One, Blessed be He, did not set Himself up as a tyrant over His creatures, and just as He does not want one man to rule over another except for his good, so He would not want to force anyone to observe the commandments against his will nor to enter the Covenant at Sinai and the desert of Moab unless these commandments were accepted willingly. [ . . . ] The result of this is that our obligation to the Torah and to every one of the Divine commandments is grounded in this Covenant and is not by virtue of the authority of the nation's wise men, Judges and elders. For if the Torah had been forced on the people, then it would have been a decree from above rather than a voluntary act of acceptance of the Law, in accordance with God's will. Only after the nation was united by entering into the Covenant and willingly promised to observe the Law did the people choose judges and elders from among themselves to ensure the guardianship of their oath, as is the case whenever any nation accepts a constitution *ab initio,* only afterwards delegating authority to judges and officials of the people. This was the rule not only at Sinai, but everywhere and at all times in Jewish history.[53]

Democracy is the underpinning of the link between the people and the Torah and between religion and nationality, and its derivative is that the power of government lies in the nation. It is the nation that inspires its leadership. Thus, in accordance with this principle, a democratic regime is required.

This approach echoes that of Rabbi Kook, who maintained that the source of halakhic authority was not decreed by our sages but rather by the nation's acceptance of halakha as a binding set of rules. In his book *Eder Hayakar* (published in 1906) Rabbi Kook elaborated on this principle:

> Many have thought that the principle of the foundation of the existence of the Oral Torah was only what was accepted by the nation of the greatness of the Sages and their holiness. Therefore, according to a well-known desire, [there were those who] began to take on airs to criticize (with a critique that was, of course, insolent and full of radical leanings) those heads of [all coming] generations, patriarchs of the world—thinking that in this way they would weaken the force of obligation of the practical foundation [halakha]. And these [critics] didn't

> know that the great value of the Sages, and their elevated sanctified [lit. "Divine"] status, is a truth unto itself, and [though] it can also add something [lit. "spice"] to make it more pleasant and to improve the tendency to follow in their [the Sages] ways; but the [true] eternal foundation [of the Oral Torah] is simply the [fact of] the acceptance of the [Oral Torah] by the [Jewish] nation, in its ways of life. And indeed we see, for example, that the decree of Rabbenu Gershom Meor haGolah—in the places in which it took hold—is just as strong and secure in the heart of the nation as any other Torah prohibitions, even though he was not a Sage of the Mishnah, nor a Sage of the Gemarah, because the approval of the whole nation attached [itself] to it [the decree] (at least in the course of [future] generations), "and whoever does not include himself in the community has withdrawn himself from the body of Judaism."[54]

This principle was also expressed by Rabbi Kook with regard to the proper form of government for this time, when it is not possible to appoint a king. In his opinion, the power of government lies in the hands of the nation as a whole.[55]

At the end of 1915, Rabbi Kook, in a responsum to a question from his friend Rabbi Zalman Pines, wrote concerning the prerogatives of kingship that "at a time when there is no king, because the prerogatives of kingship also have a bearing on the general state of the nation, then these rights revert to the people in general."[56]

As we have already seen, Rabbi Hirschensohn also believed that in our day, too, governmental power is in the hands of the nation. It did not end when the state of the Jewish people was destroyed and they were exiled from their land. Unlike other nations who are committed to their constitution only as long as they live in their own country, or as long as their state continues to exist, the commitment of the Jewish people is total and continuous even during their exile, because the Covenant sealed in the wilderness of Sinai and the plains of Moab is independent of geographical and political realities, although it is directed at national political life in Eretz Israel.

To bolster his support for a democratic regime, Rabbi Hirschensohn discussed the two relevant issues: the status of women and non-Jews in the future Jewish state. As a result of widespread mobilization in warring countries during the First World War, women began to take the place of men on the home front, and therefore they were frequently required to fill roles to which they were hitherto not accustomed. This new reality heightened the demand for equal rights for women. In response, after the war the world powers granted women the right to vote in Russia, Britain, Germany, and the United States. At the same time an intense debate was raging in Eretz Israel regarding the right of women to vote in elections for Yishuv institutions. The laborers and civilian factions were in favor of granting rights to women. However, the Sephardim and the Ashkenazi members of the old Yishuv were opposed on the grounds that it went against the essential role of women, since "all the glory of the king's daughter is within,"[57] a reference to her modesty and the private confines of her family. The attitude of the Mizrachi faction was inconsistent because they tried to mediate between both sides in order to avoid weakening the Yishuv. Many rabbis, too, came out against granting voting rights to women.[58]

Rabbi Hirschensohn maintained that halakha does not discriminate against women. In principle, the status of women is equal to that of men. He explained that halakhot that actively discriminate against women are the result of how the Torah related to social and ethical realities in ancient times. The Torah does not come to change this social reality but to guide toward just and righteous conduct. That being said, social and ethical conditions in ancient times cannot serve as the yardstick of halakha, "for we do not learn *halakha* from ancient situations."[59] This interpretation accords with his tendency to seek the historical and cultural contexts underlying the mitzvoth and halakhot in order to thoroughly understand them and consequently deduce how to adapt them to modern day reality. Thus, for example, he explains the mitzvah of selling one's daughter into slavery. Although this practice existed in ancient times, the Torah restricted it as much as possible out of concern for the daughter's honor. Today, however, this practice does not exist in the civilized world and therefore there is no license to observe it. Halacka promotes the development of moral and ethical humanity; it certainly does not oppose it. Therefore, the rights of women in a Jewish state, including the right to vote and to be elected, must be equal to those of men. From the point of view of obligation to specific mitzvoth, Rabbi Hirschensohn explains the halachic differences as religious differences, like those between a Cohen (priest), a Levite, and an Israelite. They are definitely not civil differences:

> Different laws exist for women and men but it is not because in principle they are of lower status and have no rights. The differences are theological and religious, in the same way that there is a difference between an Israelite, a Cohen and a Levite. The tribes of Israel are not of lesser value, nor do they have fewer rights than those of the Levites, since among our people no man is elevated above another due to his birth. Even a learned *mamzer* takes precedence over an uneducated Cohen. But the customs of religion, like those of the people, obligate a division of labor, some for men, some for women, some for Cohanim, some for Levites, whereas all the congregation are holy and the Almighty resides within them.[60]

The underpinnings of the halakhic attitude toward the civil status of gentiles had already been formulated in halakhic discourses conducted in Europe in the eighteenth century, the era of emancipation. In his book *Exclusiveness and Tolerance* Jacob Katz expounds on the halakhic-societal attitude of German rabbis toward Christians from the eleventh century to the beginning of the nineteenth century, when Napoleon convened the "Sanhedrin." He points out that initially the rabbis viewed Christians as idolaters, as is ordained in the Talmud, with all that implies regarding the moral double standard toward Jews and toward Christians. At the same time, for practical reasons this attitude was tempered in certain cases so that Jews could profit from trading with their Christian neighbors.[61] Katz also cites the unusual and relatively unknown stand taken by Rabbi Menachem Me'iri, who lived and worked in Provence in the second half of the thirteenth century. According to him, Christians and Muslims were "nations fenced in by religion" rather than idolaters, and therefore they should not to be discriminated against in the Talmud as regards the strictures between man and his fellow man. They are "like Israel in all these things . . . with no prejudice whatsoever."[62]

At the end of his book Katz mentions two aspects of the change that came about in the halakhic social attitude toward Christians during the enlightened era of the eighteenth century. The first was elucidated in the teachings of Moses Mendelssohn and his followers, who extolled the virtue of enlightened religious tolerance and the principle of common humanity, based on the fact that we are all rational human beings with natural rights.[63] The second was expounded on in the writings of German rabbis such as Yair Bachrach and Jacob Emden, followers of Rabbi Moshe Ravkash (1591–1671), who wrote his religiously tolerant *Be'er Hagolah*, an exegesis on the *Shulhan Arukh*, in Amsterdam in the 1660s. Like Me'iri, he claimed that contemporary Christians were not the idolaters of the Talmud but rather, in common with Jews, they had a religious tradition as regards "their interpretation of the world, the Exodus from Egypt, and various religious principles."[64] These rabbis maintained this open-minded attitude as much for reasons connected to the more spiritual nature of Protestant Christianity and the more tolerant winds beginning to blow through Central and Western Europe as for reasons of apologetics. Nevertheless, they never sought to break down the barriers between Jews and Christians or to legitimize Christianity, since to them the supremacy of Judaism over Christianity was patently obvious. This trend was perpetuated among Orthodox rabbis in Germany and Bohemia all through the nineteenth century.[65]

In fact, the whole topic of the strictures between man and his fellow man, as well as the claim of a double ethical standard regarding halakha in this context, had no practical significance as regards the difference between the two approaches. All agreed that there is a halakhic prohibition against stealing from Christians or defrauding or deceiving them, in the same way that there is a halakhic obligation to help Christians in distress and to restore their lost property. The difference lay in the theoretical question of attitude toward non-Jews belonging to non-monotheistic Eastern religions, and, more importantly, in the validity and sanctity of Talmudic precepts dealing with the attitude toward idolaters.

In fact, Rabbi Hirschensohn adopts the first approach regarding common humanity—"the sons of Noah are our brethren according to the religion of Israel,"[66] This ordains the inclusion of non-Jews into the brotherhood of commandments between man and his fellow man. He does not distinguish between "gentiles who are restricted by the ways of religion" and those who are not. He also makes no distinction between the commandments that apply to "your fellow creature" and those that apply to "your brother," unlike the Orthodox rabbis who preceded him. His basic premise was that nowadays gentiles observe the seven Noahide laws and therefore they are included in the definition of a *ger toshav* (a non-Jew living in the Land of Israel who accepts upon himself the seven Noahide laws and the Israeli sovereignty). Consequently, every gentile in the Jewish state must have civil status, equal to that of Jews in every respect. The differences explicitly enumerated in the Torah, such as in the phrase *lenochri tashich*, which permits the loan of money with interest to a gentile, as opposed to the prohibition on taking interest from a Jew, he restricts to business loans, explaining that the distinction applies to religion, not status. He further explains that as regards civil rights, there is no difference between gentiles and Jews, but there are several differences in the religious sphere, such as the prohibition to loan money to Jews with interest, including business loans, "this type of prohibition and permission is a matter of justice and mercy, unlike the situation that applies to prohibited foods, which have absolutely nothing to do with justice and mercy."[67]

Furthermore, Rabbi Hirschensohn asserts that international law, or "the laws of civilization," as he calls them, are binding because they are the Noahide laws of morality and justice, which we share. There is a kind of alliance of all of humanity to preserve these laws, an alliance to which the Jewish nation is also committed. In this context, he acknowledges the validity of international treaties, maintaining that we have a duty to uphold them, just as we must uphold individual agreements because to breach them would be a desecration of God's name. He reinforces his argument with the story of the Gibeonites in the Book of Joshua, from which we learn that international treaties must be respected even if they are obtained by guile, unless they are breached by the other party.[68]

Rabbi Hirschensohn also discusses what would be the most desirable economic system, based on the Torah. After Russia's Bolshevik revolution, the debate intensified on which economic method to adopt. Socialism challenged the Western system of capitalism, that was so deeply rooted in the American way of life. On the one hand it revered private property and free enterprise, but on the other hand, it failed to contend with the vast social gaps between the bourgeoisie and the proletariat, and the masses who were unsuccessful in adapting to the rigors of life. In the

Zionist movement the ideas promulgated by socialism were growing in popularity, and among the immigrants to Eretz Israel the members of the socialist movements soon became the dominant group. When the American Zionist Council convened in Petersburg in 1918 they proposed that the socialist economic model be adopted in Eretz Israel.

Rabbi Hirschensohn believes that we should aspire to social justice, but he rejects Marxism. First of all, he maintains, a true social revolution cannot come about as the result of bloodshed, "for the world cannot be genuinely restored through destruction. All the empty claims of historians who chronicle humanity's slaughter in the world, the claims that every war results in progress, are nothing but emptiness. They are useless. Do not believe them."[69] Secondly, he has serious doubts about the efficiency of a system that stifles private initiative, which is the motor that powers economic activity. "It is questionable whether its theoretical underpinnings can survive in the real world."[70] Rabbi Hirschensohn seeks to establish a Jewish economic system based on halakha. He argues that halakha supports free enterprise and competition, while at the same time it promotes intervention in economic activity if unnecessary damage is incurred by one of the parties. "It would appear that our sages were in favor of trade restrictions so that the laborers and the people would not be harmed through profiteering. But they did not agree to restrict competition because free competition would not harm the laborers. On the contrary, it brings about progress and development in the world."[71] One such example of intervention is the prohibition on profiteering over and above one-sixth of the market price.

He maintains that halakha also regulates exploitation of laborers by their masters and establishes a suitable rate of overall profit. After reviewing the laws alluding to workers, he comes to the conclusion that in the opinion of our sages, the workers' portion of profit for the finished product, in other words for their work, comes to one-third of the overall profit, with the other two-thirds going to their employer for his initiative, funding, and equipment. The relationship between workers and their employer is defined as a partnership, not a master-servant relationship. Since in his opinion it was halakhically the ideal method, Hirschensohn hoped to apply it in Eretz Israel before state custom (a binding halakhicconcept) would determine a different one in practice. He also deals with the right to go on strike. After a halachic discussion he concludes that people have the right to go on strike, based on the ruling that "a worker can reconsider, even halfway through the day,"[72] unless the employee will suffer losses that go beyond cessation of production.[73]

Hirschensohn, like Jawitz, dealt with issues involving halakha and science. His interest in the subject began when preparations were underway for the Hebrew University in Jerusalem. A practical question focused on the permissibility of carrying out autopsies in the interests of medical science. In American and European medical faculties, autopsies were regarded as essential to the study of medicine. We have seen that Jawitz, who believed they were permissible, cited the Babylonian Talmud to support his argument, showing that Rabbi Ishmael's students performed an autopsy for the sake of learning. The response of Rabbi Yehezkel Landau in his book *Noda BiYehuda,* marked a precedent. He wrote that an autopsy is permitted only if it can save a life right now—in other words, if the autopsy can save the life of a patient who is seriously ill at this time. His ruling, forbidding autopsies to be carried out, even in the interests of furthering medical science, and even if they can save lives in the future, is based on the prohibition on desecrating the dead [*Nivul HaMeth*] that overrides the concern for saving lives in the future, but permits lives to be saved at the present time. After deliberating with doctors, Rabbi Hirschensohn concluded that autopsies for the sake of research and study are essential for medical progress. "By examining and studying dead bodies doctors have learned more in the last century than has been learned in the past two thousand years."[74] Therefore, he maintains that it is out of the question for the Faculty of Medicine of the Hebrew University in Jerusalem to refrain from carrying out autopsies, even if the rabbis express the opinion that it is forbidden. "This will mark the official breach between religion and action. Our opponents will say it is impossible for the people of Israel to live in Eretz Israel according to the Torah of Israel, because they believe the Torah forbids something that medical theory cannot do without."[75]

From his halachic deliberations Rabbi Hirschensohn concluded that the prohibition on desecrating the dead stems from respect for the living, who want to avoid humiliation after death, and not from respect for the dead. Thus, in a situation where desecration of the dead is for the benefit of the living and for medical progress, it certainly meets this requirement. There is no disrespect of the dead and no prohibition. This applies only to autopsies for the sake of ascertaining the cause of death or preventing or healing similar cases in the future. "It certainly cannot be done by others because not everyone suffers equally and dies from the same illness."[76] However, in the interests of medicine, because it is possible to use the bodies of non-Jews, since enough people have been executed or have willed their bodies to science, it is not permitted to specifically use the bodies of Jews.[77] His opinion on the matter of autopsies for medical study correlates with that of Rabbi Kook, who also maintained that bodies of non-Jews should be purchased for this purpose, and not those of Jews.[78]

On each of these topics he strives to provide a lenient halakhic answer, in order to deflect possible conflict between halakha and modern sovereign reality, even going so far as to employ methods of halakhic reasoning that were not customary in his day.[79] In order to contend with the challenge of sovereignty he was prepared to institute far-reaching halakhic reforms. He introduced into the system of halakhic considerations those political and societal values that Western countries regard as essential, for they are common to the universal humanity to which Judaism belongs.

In terms of the method of ruling he in fact renewed the reasons why specific mitzvoth are necessary, in order to adapt halakha to modern-day reality and the challenge of sovereignty. This method, controversial even in the time of the Tannaim, was hardly ever applied by rabbinical Jewish authorities during the course of history. Yet Rabbi Hirschensohn was forced to adopt it in order to arrive at the optimal outcome from his point of view—significant reform that would facilitate the observance of halakha in the modern, sovereign era. He maintained that if such a reform was not instituted, either halakha would be rejected by the non-religious, or else sovereignty would be rejected by other nations—two disastrous results from the point of view of the Jewish people and their ever-increasing aspiration to attain sovereignty.

In his efforts to embark on a rabbinic dialogue covering all the points he had raised, Rabbi Hirschensohn sent his book to dozens of rabbis around the world. Many of those who responded criticized his basic premises and his method of ruling, claiming that halakhically he had gone too far. For example, Rabbi Kook wrote that in several places he came to erroneous conclusions, because "he is not inclined to suspect that absolute values in today's society, such as morality and justice, are often nothing more than pottery overlaid with silver waste."[80] And Rabbi Zvi Pesach Franck (1873–1960) of Jerusalem accused him of showing a lack of respect toward the Rishonim.[81]

## MISHPATEY HAMELUCHAH—THE PROPOSAL OF A SEPARATE MONARCHICAL LEGAL SYSTEM

Another rabbi who dealt with specific halakhic questions was Reuben Margolies (1889–1971). He was born in Lvov and had a traditional upbringing. Although he received ordination from Rabbi Meir Arik of Buchach, he did not serve as a rabbi but devoted his life to the study of rabbinic literature. He was a member of the Mizrachi movement. In 1934, he immigrated to Mandatory Palestine and settled in Tel Aviv. He held the position of director of the Rambam library in Tel Aviv until his death.

In 1921, he published his book *Kavei Or* (Lines of Light): Halakhic Studies of Political Settlement in Eretz Israel. He dedicated his book to "His Excellency the President of Israel Eliezer ben Menachem, also known as Sir Herbert Samuel, the Commissioner of Eretz Israel."

In his introduction, he expressed his excitement at the great changes the Balfour Declaration and the mandate had generated among the people, and described how he viewed the task it imposed upon the intelligentsia, in tandem with the concrete task of building up the Yishuv:

> Due to Divine Providence this generation finds itself in an era of great outcomes, an era in which the cornerstone is being laid for Jewish life in Eretz Israel. Through its efforts the Jewish nation has shaken itself free of the dust of the Diaspora that annihilated both body and spirit, and has adjusted to the natural life of a nation in its own land, a life that is suited to its spirit, the spirit of Israel. Now, at the birth of our world, a voice has issued forth from God's mountain that was destroyed, calling upon all the people to help build the land and create a spiritual center for the Jewish nation and its Torah. This immense enterprise requires the assemblage of the entire people, for its sons shall be its builders, some with their currency and others with their Torah. Together they will lay its economic and spiritual cornerstone. [82]

He was well aware of the great challenge of introducing halakha into the modern categories of law and government. It was clear to him that a great deal of work was required, and that it could not be done superficially, certainly not by imitating another country. Wide ranging theoretical study was needed in order to reestablish the national institutions in accordance with halakha:

> Today we stand at the threshold of a new era in the life of the Jewish people in their land. We must organize our political way of life in Eretz Israel and create public institutions. As we delve deeper in order to describe these institutions and their characteristics (because we must think on the end before we begin) we will not find adequate answers to the essential questions in our minds, and we will be unable to think of the essential features of these institutions, since we have no suitable, fixed and specific plan of our own. How can we choose a political plan according to the laws and procedures of other countries, since our way of life is regulated by the laws of the Torah. Therefore every institution must be established in accordance with the spirit of the Torah and Judaism. This is a new creation. [83]

In his opinion, the reestablishment of national institutions in accordance with the Torah should only be achieved through historic Torah study, "because only then will we know how to connect the thread of history to its continuation in accordance with the Torah and life." [84]

The first problem he raises is that of the status of non-Jewish minorities in a legal system that functions according to halakha. While attesting to "the integrity of its logic and the adaptations of our laws to the requirements of global justice" [85] in relation to the Hoshen Mishpat , he is nevertheless aware that we must take reality into consideration. There are non-Jewish minorities in Eretz Israel who cannot be discriminated against: "Therefore it is incumbent upon us, who demand justice for the minorities in all the lands of our dispersal, to be exemplary in extending rights to the people who dwell in our land. We must also consider their opinion." [86]

The examples he brings of possible discrimination include the prohibition on appointing non-Jewish judges and the invalidation of the testimony of non-Jewish witnesses in a court of law. After a historic perusal of halakha, Rabbi Margolies came to the conclusion that throughout the time of Israel's sovereignty during the period of the First and Second Temples, the king maintained a separate legal system with its own law courts alongside the laws of halakha, to contend with problems that could not be resolved by halakha, particularly because of the difficulty of condemning and punishing according to the Torah with regard to the laws governing evidence. For example, he elucidated the judgment of King David in the story of the poor man's lamb, whereby the rich man deserved to die and was also sentenced to pay fourfold for his robbery, despite the fact that according to halakha only a thief pays fourfold or fivefold, not a robber. He found recognition of a separate monarchical legal system (*Mishpatey HaMeluchah)* in the writings of Maimonides (*Hilchot Melachim*, chapter 3, halakha 10 and *Hilchot Rotzeach*, chapter 2, halakha 14), who acknowledges the possibility that the king or the law court could mete out the death sentence, despite the fact that there was not sufficient evidence according to halakha, in order to ensure that justice was done. He even came to the conclusion that the monarchical legal system was not only the prerogative of the king, but of every leader appointed by the people. Nevertheless, since there was no structured monarchical book of laws, at certain times monarchical courts of law deviated from justice and honesty, and the prophets rebuked them for so doing. He came to the conclusion that:

> From this historical study we learn that the Torah permitted the nation's leader when preparing to institute a regime to establish courts of the people who would pass judgment and issue punishments on behalf of the rulership. But we have also seen the shortcomings that ensued from the lack of an authorized book of law that would serve as a guideline. Therefore, now that we must establish those institutions that are necessary for political life, the Supreme Court must establish, apart from legal penalties, a new book of general laws, lucid laws in a logical sequence. Of course these will not be the laws of the Roman tyrants but the laws of Israel, which incorporate the spirit of justice and morality of the ancient Jewish people and its Torah, and those Torah laws will be the state laws of Eretz Israel.[87]

In these courts of law non-Jews can also serve as judges, and their testimony will be as acceptable as that of Jews. The purpose of monarchical law was not to authorize secular legislation when it was not consistent with halakha, as was the case in retrospect after the establishment of the state, following the Talmudic precept of *dina d'malchuta dina* (the law of the land is binding), but to facilitate religious rulings on a halakhic track that bypassed the existing halakhic codex, in order to contend optimally with the challenge of sovereignty.[88]

Rabbi Kook was also of the opinion that monarchical law touched on many aspects of Jewish life, and that it was possible to deviate from case law. In a letter to Rabbi Zalman Pines he elaborated on the subject:

> Everything that affects the nation, including the amendment of a temporary order, as a hedge against injustice, it governed by monarchical law, for the king has the right to conduct himself as he pleases, even if it is not seemly and is not to his benefit, as long as it is for the benefit and the honor of Israel. As Maimonides writes in *Hilchot Melachim* chapter 13, halakhah 10: "Anyone who kills without undisputable evidence". . . the king has the right to kill him and do whatever is required in order to thwart evildoers; thus monarchical law is much more far reaching than the honor and rights of the king himself.[89]

Alexander Kaye claimed that Margolies represents a pluralistic attitude to law. He maintains the idea that Jewish sovereignty may have within it a plurality of legal regimes and a plurality of legitimate sources of legal authority. This position had the advantage that it was able to preserve a distinction between current halakha and the state, thereby avoiding the imposition of current halakha on people who did not recognize its authority and preventing the imposition of radical modifications on halakha in order to engineer its accommodation with the requirements of modern law.[90] Indeed, we saw that most of the rabbis, in those years, had practical ideas of how to solve this problem by keeping legal centralism, which maintained that all legal authority in the state must derive from a single source of authority—the current halakha and its ordained commentators. The solution may come by way of modification or expansion of the halakha itself, whether evolutionarily (moderate halakhic reforms) or revolutionarily (restoration of the Sanhedrin), or by combining the two—rulings of the sages.

Rabbi Margolies also discusses autopsies for the purpose of medical science. After delving into the halakha, he concludes from the words of *HaMagen Avraham* (*Yore De'ah*, 330, 19) that "even if it is not certain to save lives it is possible to desecrate the dead. Everyone is obligated to suffer in order to save his fellow man" because autopsies are permissible for the sake of medical science, which is essential to advance medicine and save lives."[91] In contrast to Rabbis Kook and Hirschensohn, he did not impose restrictions regarding the bodies of Jews.

## NATIONAL ACCEPTANCE OF HALAKHA

Another American rabbi of the time who expressed his opinion on the place of halakha in Jewish political life was Rabbi Bernard Drachman (1861–1945). He was born in New York and had a traditional upbringing. He attended Colombia University, and in the early 1880s he was sent by Temple Emanuel to study at the Jewish theological seminary of Breslau.

He also studied at the universities of Breslau and Heidelberg. After returning to New York he served as a rabbi in several Orthodox communities. He was among the founders of the Jewish Theological Seminary of America in 1887, teaching Bible, Hebrew, and Jewish philosophy. In 1908, after being dismissed from the seminary, he took up a teaching position at the Isaac Elchanan Yeshiva (later Yeshiva College). He died in 1945 in New York. Rabbi Drachman supported the Zionist movement and was one of the founders of the Mizrachi movement in the United States.

In his autobiography he describes the enthusiasm with which many American Jews, himself included, greeted the League of Nations' acceptance of the Balfour Declaration and the decision to promote the establishment of a national homeland for the Jews in Eretz Israel:

> Words cannot describe the wave of emotion which swept over the Jewish masses, over all Jews who had preserved Jewish feelings and Jewish thoughts in their hearts and minds, when these world-stirring announcements became known to them. It seemed to them that the apparently unending Jewish exile had finally reached a glorious termination, that the sufferings and persecution and misery which had seemed the inevitable accompaniment of Jewish history and now vanished into the abyss of the past. It seemed, indeed, that the days of the Messiah had arrived. [ . . . ] I understood those feelings and felt them myself.[92]

In March 1920, he published an article in *HaToren* entitled *HaGalut Betoch HaGeulah* (The Exile Inside the Redemption),[93] dealing with the issue of halakha and the challenge of sovereignty. He began by describing Hibbat Zion as a movement of religious national revival, striving to restore the national assets to their rightful place, "and the most elevated and precious of all is our holy Torah and the religion we love more than life itself."[94] He goes on to express his rancor when he sees how prominent Zionist leaders relate to the Jewish religion and their plans to establish secular courts of law in Eretz Israel that are not bound by halakha, "as if we had not law and judgment in our Written and Oral Law and in the *Hoshen Mishpat*."[95]

He claims that the establishment of a secular Jewish state in Eretz Israel is illogical, unjust, undemocratic, unhelpful, and goes against "the spirit of our nation and its character, as they have become clarified through our history."[96] He also maintains that religion and nationality in Israel are indivisible, "for our holy Torah is the foundation of Israel and a part of its soul that cannot be separated without utterly destroying and losing it."[97] It is therefore impossible to talk of separating state and religion.

The main problem, in his opinion, is to ensure the acceptance of halakha as the basis for Israeli law by the secular public, who no longer feel bound to halakha in their daily lives. He proposed that we regard Jewish halakha as the national constitution, arguing that halakha had served as the state's constitution during the times of the First and Second Temples and "it has endured for two thousand years in a condition of being stopped,"[98] and therefore, when the Jewish state is reborn, halakha must be incorporated as its law. Whether a Jew is religious or secular, he is culturally and historically bound to observe halakha as the national law of the Jewish people. Judaism, unlike Christianity, does not force anyone to observe principles of faith that his reason rejects. Man is judged by his deeds, not by his beliefs:

> There is no logical reason why an enlightened, intelligent Jew, even if his ideas do not conform with the accepted beliefs of the nation, should not observe the laws of Judaism and live in accordance with them once they become the laws of the nation to which he belongs, if he wishes to remain among them. He will not have to trouble himself and delve into the study of the Torah. He can look upon the Torah as the statutes of the Jewish people that every Jew who is faithful to his people is obliged to observe. Judaism, for its part, will be satisfied with this and will not inquire into his motives.[99]

This proposal requires that the secular Jew ignore the aspects of holiness imbued in the Torah and halakha and relates to them as secular-national law, amended by the founding fathers many generations ago, in the same way that citizens of the United States relate to the American constitution. Naturally, the supreme religious council will be charged with examining the demands of reality, changing or amending ordinances as required, but the basis of the constitution will remain accepted Jewish halakha:

> When four or five million of our people live in Eretz Israel according to policies that are in line with ancient ways and they feel a need to change them, it will be possible to obtain these changes in the proper manner. There is no doubt that the elders and rabbis will recognize and acknowledge the needs of the people and they will do what is needed for the good of the people as they have always done.[100]

Rabbi Drachman also expressed his confidence in the power and authority of the *poskei* halakha (adjudicators) to adjust halakha to meet political needs, but he postponed this to a later stage in the development of the state, once four million Jews would be living in Eretz Israel. Rabbi Drachman did not seek to downplay the cultural achievements of the nation, but rather to measure them against the yardstick of the Torah in such a way that it would be quite clear that the Torah is the central source of authority and the cultural achievements of the people are secondary:

> I do not intend to alienate the general culture. That would be great folly. But we must do as Rabbi Meir did, according to the Talmud: he ate the inside and threw away the shell. We must hold onto whatever is good and useful in the general culture but we must give preference to

> the true culture of our nation. As Maimonides said: "Torah wisdom is a fine lady while other wisdoms are cooks and apothecaries."[101]

This approach is of course much more moderate than that favored by Rabbi Hirschensohn, who, basing himself on the principle of joint humanity, regarded the culture of other nations as a binding precedent for Judaism. As far as Rabbi Hirschensohn was concerned, the issue was not one of rationally adopting something that developed outside of Judaism, but human achievement that developed within human society, of which Jews are a part just like any other people.

Rabbi Drachman's ideas and his proposal were strongly opposed by Rabbi Kook, who had recently been appointed Chief Rabbi of Jerusalem. When Rabbi Drachman's article was reprinted in Jerusalem in 1920 in a separate pamphlet, Rabbi Kook expressed great reservations. He felt that Rabbi Drachman was proposing a superficial and temporary solution to a deep and serious problem. He maintained that it is impossible to sever faith from action, regarding it as self-deception and "gratifying heresy, by saying that we are handing over the concept of the soul, to do with as they please, while not even demanding the imposition of religious practices."[102] If the observance of mitzvoth becomes the perfunctory acts of people who are merely going through the motions, and the dimension of holiness is removed from the system of commandments, it goes against the spirit of Judaism, "At this time, when we are laying the foundations for the nation, how can we bring in such a deceptive element, saying it is enough to observe *mitzvoth* in a mechanical fashion, we must do so because of the constitution, or as a national "fixture," not because it is the word of God and His Torah, but rather the *mitzvoth* of people going through the motions—how can such a thing be?"[103]

He believed the solution would come when we realize the utopian vision of resurrected holiness that will complement the material building of Eretz Israel.[104] This resurrection of holiness will deal with the spiritual aspect of deeds, with the soul, and thus there will be no severance of faith from action. It will deal radically with the rift that appeared during the period of Enlightenment between religion and everyday life, and between faith and action. Rabbi Kook was not willing to compromise on the overall vision and arrive at a state of status quo. He believed wholeheartedly that the complete resurrection would come, and it would include holiness, whereupon the phenomenon of secularity would vanish. He sought to postpone the discussion to a later time when all the nation would be together in Eretz Israel, out of a conviction that on the one hand, most of them would want their lives to be guided by the Torah,[105] and on the other hand, the generation's sages would then be authorized to institute the regulations required to contend with the new challenge of sovereignty. The necessity of maintaining unity between all the camps was his guideline for halakhic rulings, but in cases where confrontation was inevitable, the unity of observant Judaism was more important to him. Actually, his writings contain echoes of most of the proposals that were raised in this debate, but his desire to also include Haredi Jews caused him to blur his personal stance and he only intervened in practical instances that could not be delayed, such as the Heter Mechira.[106] He did, however, express his willingness to institute necessary general regulations in the framework of the chief rabbinate,[107] "so long as most of the rabbinical authorities are in agreement and are thereafter accepted by the public, they will have the power of a *din Torah* (matter of litigation)."[108] But in actual fact the only ruling that was introduced was the establishment of the Court of Appeal, which was the condition set by the British regime for recognizing the institution of the chief rabbinate.[109]

The Balfour Declaration and the conquest of Eretz Israel by the British Army sparked lively and significant debate about adapting halakha to deal with the challenge of sovereignty. Those who took part in the debate were rabbis who supported the Zionist idea, most of them members of the Mizrachi movement. They were guided by the premise that there could be no separation of religion and state because they were two sides of the same coin. Therefore, religion and halakha must be expressed in the character, constitution, and rules of the future Jewish state. For a Jewish state, separation of religion and state is not an option. Similarly, most of the Jewish nation were not in favor of halakhic authority and therefore every effort should be made to resist facts on the ground that go counter to what they want. This assumption prevented them from suggesting compromises to the secular Zionists, such as some ideas that were put forward during the time of the British Mandate, when it became absolutely clear who held political power in the Zionist movement and the institutions of the Yishuv.

The assumption of the religious Zionist rabbis, that the Jewish state's laws should be in accordance with halakha, was common to those who shared a realistic messianic ideology and to those who set a divide between Zionism and redemption.[110] The former believed efforts should be made to advance the vision of messianic redemption, both materially and spiritually. The latter wished to preserve halakha as the only proper Jewish way of life, both on the communal and on the national levels.

Various opinions were put forward on the question of what steps should be taken to adapt halakha to the challenge of sovereignty and how to obligate the secular public to observe halakha. Rabbis Berlin and Churgin argued that such adaptation should be achieved through gradual development, as it became necessary. At that time, all that could be done was to inspire the public through information and education, in order for them to want a Jewish state constitution that rests upon a halakhic foundation.

Others maintained that a more activist, unusual approach should be adopted in order to suit halakha to the new reality.

Rabbis Tchernowitz and Uziel maintained that adapting halakha to the reality of sovereignty should be attained by reinstating the Sanhedrin or Bet Din Hagadol, which had the requisite authority for interpreting halakha and Torah requirements. Only such an establishment could successfully undertake this mission. Rabbi Hirschensohn argued that reinstating the Sanhedrin is not a practical option for our time. He maintained that halakhic reforms should be achieved through lenient rulings and creative interpretations of halakha that required an explanation of the phrase's reasoning and clarifying which principles should be preserved. He demonstrated this by means of several new halakhic issues that had cropped up. Rabbi Margolies believed following a supplementary track for the halakhic codex, similar to the institution of monarchical law, which had the jurisdiction to make rulings and amend regulations as required by changing needs.

Another branch of the discussion centered on the halakhic obligations of secularists. Rabbi Drachman claimed that halakha should be the fixed constitution of the state and in any event such a commitment would be national and civil, not religious. But Rabbi Kook pointed out that a commitment to halakha must be made out of conscientious religious awareness and such awareness would only come in the wake of the all-encompassing national spiritual resurrection that would accompany the material national revival.

Whereas rabbis in Eastern Europe and Eretz Israel based their proposals on institutions and historic halakhic precedents—renewing the Sanhedrin, establishing a legal system parallel to royal laws and the rulings of the sages—American rabbis turned to the modern concepts upon which the American system of government is based in an attempt to anchor them in Jewish sources: the idea of the social treaty—the Sinai covenant; commitment to humanity common to all human beings and its expression in international law; and practical commitment to the constitution adopted by the founding fathers. In this way, they claimed, halakha would be accepted as the foundation of the legal system of the Jewish state, even by secular and liberal Jews.

Ultimately, it was the situation in Eretz Israel, which was based on a secular Jewish majority with decisive political clout, that partially dictated the system of agreements, compromises, mutual arm-twisting, and capitulations that shaped the conduct of the national institutions and public space of the nascent state. Disputes on the place of religion and halakha in the national homeland focused on laws of personal status, Sabbath observance in public, and kashruth in kitchens that catered to the public.[111] The general debate that was initiated in the wake of the Balfour Declaration faded away during the 1920s, only to be reignited in the eve of the establishment of the state.[112]

## NOTES

1. James Renton, *The Zionist Masquerade: the Birth of the Anglo-Zionist Alliance 1914-1918* (New York: Palgrave Macmillan, 2007), 149–55.
2. Kimmy Caplan, "Reaction of Five Orthodox Rabbis of the Hebrew University of Jerusalem," *Contemporary Jewry* 10 (1996): 139–63.
3. Mordechai ben Hillel HaCohen, "Mishpat HaShalom (Magistrate Court)," *HaOlam*, 9 (1920), vol. 17-19; Amihai Radzyner, "Rabbi Uziel, the Tel-Aviv-Jaffa Rabbinate and the Rabbinical Court of Appeal: A Play in Four Acts," *Bar-Ilan Law Studies* 21 (2004): 139–46. On the Rabbis' feeling of threat, see ibid., 149–53.
4. Shamir, *The Colonies of Law*, 30–31.
5. On this, see: Margalit Shilo, *Girls of Liberty: The Struggle for Suffrage in Mandatory Palestine* (Waltham: Brandeis University Press, 2016).
6. For biography of Churgin see the introduction to Leivy Smolar and Moses Aberbach, *Studies in Targum Konathan to the Prophets* (Baltimore/Hoboken: Baltimore Hebrew College/ Ktav, 1983).
7. Pinkhos Churgin, "*Lishe'elat Haregah* (The Question of the Moment)," *HaIvri* 8 (1918), vol. 2, 4.
8. Ibid.
9. Ibid.
10. Idem, "binyan Olam (An Everlasting edifice)," *HaIvri* 8 (1918), vol. 31, 3–4.
11. Ibid.
12. On this, see chapter 1.
13. Meir Berlin, *Bishvilei HaTechia* (Tel Aviv: Hapoel Hamizrachi, 1940). 77.
14. Ibid., p. 78.
15. Ibid., p. 80.
16. Pinkhos Churgin, "*Knesiah, Dat, Umemshala* (Church, Religion and Government)," *HaToren* (1919), vol. 35, 3.
17. Ibid., 4.
18. Ibid., vol. 44, 8.
19. Zeev Gries, "Nationalism and Religion in the Writings of 'Rav Tzair' (Rabbi Chaim Tchernowitz)," in *Jewish Thought and Jewish Belief*, ed. D. J. Lasker (Beer Sheva: Ben-Guryon University Press, 2012), 191–247.
20. Chaim Tchernowitz, "Merkaz Dati (Religious Center)," *HaIvri* 10 (1920), no. 20, 3.
21. Ibid., no. 21, 4–5.
22. Idem., *BeSha'arei Zion* (New York: Schulsinger Brothers, 1936), 160.
23. Ibid., 163.
24. Ibid., 165.
25. Ibid., 170–71.
26. Ibid., 172.
27. Ibid., 173
28. Ibid., 172.
29. Ibid..
30. On him, see: Marc Angel, *Loving Truth and Peace: The Grand Religious Worldview of Rabbi Benzion Uziel* (Northvale, N.J.: Jason Aronson, 1999).
31. B. C. Uziel, *Mikhmannei Uziel* (Tel Aviv: Hapoel Hamizrachi, 1939), 437 .
32. *HaDvir*, 5 (Tishrei 5620): 27.
33. Radzyner, "Rabbi Uziel," 161–64.
34. Gershon Bakon, "The Rabbinical Conference in Krakow (1903) and the Beginnings of Organized Orthodox Jewry," in *Let the Old Make Way for the New*, eds. David Assaf and Ada Rapoport-Albet (Jerusalem: Shazar Cente, 2009), vol. II, 201*–02*.
35. A. I. Kook, "Streams in the South," *Ha-Peles* 4 (1904): 138–44; repr. in *Otzrot HaRaAyah*, vol. 2 (Sha'alabim, 1988), 776.

36. On R. Kook's halakhic approach, see N. Gutel, *Both New and Old* (Jerusalem: Magnes Press, 2005); A. Rozenak, *The Prophetic Halakhah* (Jerusalem: Magnes Press, 2007).
37. Cohen, *The Talit*, 58–59.
38. David Zohar, *Jewish Commitment World: R. Hayyim Hirschensohn and His Attitude Towards the Moderna* (Tel Aviv: Hakibbutz Hameuchad-Sifriat Poalim Publishing Group , 2003), 17–30.
39. Chaim Hirschensohn, *Malki BaKodesh*, vol. 1 (St Louis: Moinester Printing Co., 1919), 7.
40. Ibid., IV
41. Hirschensohn, *Malki BaKodesh*, vol. 2, 30–45.
42. Edrei, "From Orthodoxy," 90–145.
43. Hirschensohn, *Malki Bakodesh*, vol. 1, III
44. Ibid.
45. Chaim Hirschensohn, *HaMisdarona* 1 (1887): 253.
46. Eliezer Schweid, *Democracy and Halakhah* (Lanham, MD: University Press of America, 1994), 7–22; Zohar, *Jewish Commitment World*, 93–105.
47. Hirschensohn, *Malki Bakodesh*, vol. 4, 244 (trans. In Schweid, *Democracy*, 14).
48. Schweid, *Democracy*, 47–56; Zohar, *Jewish Commitment World*, 169-171.
49. Hirschensohn, *Malki Bakodesh*, vol. 1, 23.
50. Ibid., 36.
51. Ibid., 8.
52. Ibid., 39.
53. Hirschensohn, *Malki Bakodesh*, vol. 3, 80–81 (trans. In Schweid, *Democracy*, 49–50).
54. Abraham Isaac Kook, *Eder Hayakar* (Jerusalem, 1906), 39. The concept "the nation's acceptance," as a binding concept, existed already in the Maimonides introduction to Mishneh Torah: "But whatever is already mentioned in the Babylonian Talmud is binding on all Israel. And every city and country is bound to observe all the customs observed by the sages of the Gemara, promulgate their decrees, and uphold their institutions, on the ground that all these customs, decrees and institutions mentioned in the Talmud received the assent of all Israel." And in Rabenu Asher's Responses (43, 8): "One sage was in our country and his name was Gershom. He instituted good ordinances about divorce in the Gaonim Period. And his ordinances and decrees are constant and steady like they were given from Sinai, because they (the collective) received them and transmitted them to the next generations." See more in: Rosenak, *The Prophetic Halakhah*, 295–96.
55. Hagi Ben-Artzi, *The New Shall be Sacred: Rav Kook as an Innovative Posek* (Tel Aviv: Miskal, 2010), 81–86.
56. A.Y. Kook, *Mishpat Kohen* (Jerusalem: Mossad Harav Kook, 1966), 357.
57. Ps. 45: 14.
58. See Shilo, *Girls of Liberty*.
59. Hirschensohn, *Malki Ba-Kodesh*, vol. 2, 192.
60. Ibid., 12.
61. Jacob Katz, *Exclusiveness and Tolerance: Studies in Jewish-Gentile Relations in Medieval and Modern Times* (Oxford: Oxford University Press, 1961), 24–36.
62. Ibid., 115–18. See also Novak and Halbertal, who followed in the footsteps of Katz. David Novak, *The Image of the Non-Jew in Judaism* (Portland: The Littman Library of Jewish Civilization, 2011), 195–99; Moshe Halbertal, "'Ones Possessed of Religion': Religious Tolerance in the Teachings of the Me'iri," *Edah* 1, 1 (2000).
63. Katz, ibid, 169–81. See also Novak, who explained this change philosophically: ibid., 206–12.
64. Katz, ibid., 164–68.
65. Ibid., 193–94. Yosef Salmon surveyed different rabbinic attitudes regarding Christians and Christianity in the nineteenth century but focused on the geographic region of the Austro-Hungarian only. His conclusion, that after the Hamburg Temple

controversy (1819) the intolerant approach reappeared, as a reaction to the Reform and its assimilational trends, is invalid for the German geographical context. Yosef Salmon, "Christians and Christianity in the Responsa Literature from Late Eighteenth century to the Second Half of the Nineteenth Century," in *By the Well*, eds. Uri Ehrlich and others (Be'er Sheva: Ben-Guryon University Press, 2008), 635–51.

66. Chaim Hirschensohn, *Eileh Divrei HaBrit*, vol. 1 (Jerusalem: HaIvri, 1926), 5–6.
67. Idem, *Torat HaHinnukh HaYisraeli* (Seini: Defus Jacob Wieder, 1927), 160
68. Zohar, *Jewish Commitment World*, 192–93.
69. Hirschensohn, *Malki Ba-Kodesh*, vol. 3, 46.
70. Ibid.
71. Ibid., 44.
72. bB. Mesi'a. 10a.
73. *Zohar, Jewish Commitment World*, 247–48.
74. Hirschensohn, *Malki Ba-Kodesh*, vol.3, 9.
75. Ibid., 7.
76. Ibid., 149.
77. *Zohar, Jewish Commitment World*, 259.
78. Kook, *Daat Cohen* (Jerusalem: Mossad Harav Kook, 1942), section 199.
79. Schweid, *Democracy*, 77–90; Zohar, *Jewish Commitment World*, 236–60.
80. *Malki BaKodesh*, vol. 4, 9.
81. Ibid., 38–40.
82. Reuben Margolies, *Kavei Or* (Lvov: Praca, 1921), III.
83. Ibid., 41.
84. Ibid., 3.
85. Ibid, 41.
86. Ibid.
87. Ibid., 51.
88. Eliav Shochetman, "The Halakha's Recognition of the Laws of the State of Israel," *Jewish Law Annual*, 16–17 (1990–1991): 417–500. □
89. Kook, *Mishpat Kohen*, 335. See more, Gutel, *Both New and Old*, 144–47.
90. Kaye, "The Legal Philosophies," 74–80.
91. Margolies, *Kavei Or*, 64.
92. Bernard Drachman, *The Unfailing Light: Memoirs of an American Rabbi* (New York: Rabbinical Council of America, 1948), 381.
93. On this article Rabbi Kook's criticism of it, see: Rivka Schatz Uffenheimer, *The Messianic Idea from the Expulsion from Spain* (Jerusalem: Magnes Press, 2005), 239–42.
94. Dov Drachman, *HaGalut Betoch HaGeulah* (Jerusalem: Defus Shi"sh, 1920), 1.
95. Ibid., 4.
96. Ibid., 5.
97. Ibid., 16.
98. Ibid., 6.
99. Ibid., 15.
100. Ibid., 9.
101. Ibid., 16–17.
102. Ibid., II.
103. Ibid.
104. On this, see: Yehudah Mirsky, *Rav Kook: Mystic in a Time of Revolution* (New Haven & London: Yale University Press, 2014), 149–52.106 This is what he wrote at the height of the controversy on giving voting rights to women: "I think that this time it is our modern brethren who must act leniently and give up their new demand. Then, when it is in our power to bring the nation together, it will become apparent how they all feel about it. This is after all a simple matter. No nation in the world is forced to accept cultural mores against their will."
105. Abraham Isaac Kook, *Ma'amarei Hare'ayah* (Jerusalem 1984), 193–94.
106. Edrei, "From Orthodoxy."

107. For historical and legal review of the Sages' Regulations, see: Menachem Elon, *Jewish Law: History, Source, Principles: Ha-Mishpat ha-'Ivri*. trans. Bernard Auerbach & Melvin J. Sykes (Philadelphia: Jewish Publications Society, 1994), 643–65, 780–879.

108. Rabbi Avraham Isaac HaCohen Kook addresses the Conference of the Chief Rabbinate in Eretz Israel. In A. Morgenstern, *Ha-Rabbanut ha-Rashit le-Erez Yisra'el: Yissuda ve-Irgunah* (Jerusalem 1973), 180.

109. Radzyner, "Rabbi Uziel," 132–37.

110. On those terms and positions, see: Jody Myers, *Seeking Zion—Modernity and Messianic Activism in the Writings of Tsevi Hirsch Kalischer* (Oxford: The Littman Library of Jewish Civilization, 2003), 177–82; Aviezer Ravitzky, *Messianism, Zionism And Jewish Religious Radicalism* (Chicago & London: The University of Chicago Press, 1996), 10–39, 79–144; Salmon, *Religion and Zionism*, xiii–xxvii; Shimoni, *The Zionist Ideology*, 139–51; Dov Schwartz, *Religious-Zionism: History and Ideology* (Boston: Academic Press, 2009), 10–18, 27–33.

111. Kolatt, "Religion," 273–301; Yossi Katz, "Religion and Zionism in the Yishuv Era: The Sabbath Observance Clause in Lease Contracts between the Jewish National Fund and the Agricultural Settlements," *Zion* 68 (2013): 207–36.

112. In fact, the debate reverberated into a brief episode, following the recommendations of the Peel Commission for the partition of the land of Israel into two states, in 1937.

# FOUR

# The Age of Jurists (1918–1948)

## JEWISH LAW AS ZIONIST LAW

During the Mandate period, secular Zionist jurists and activists contended with halakha and the challenge of sovereignty by seeking to establish a national Jewish legal system in Eretz Israel. They had no interest in the overall corpus of halakha, only those sections that corresponded to civil, public, and criminal law. After the Balfour Declaration and the British conquest of Eretz Israel, they sought to harness the institution of the Hebrew Magistrates Court and the pioneering academic field of the study of Jewish Law to create a Hebrew national law, distinct from the law of other nations and based to some extent on the Jewish legal tradition embedded in Tannaic and Talmudic literature. Since they belonged to the cultural Zionist school of Ahad Ha'am and were influenced by the historical school of law, these jurists and activists did not believe that the legal system was created by a universal rational arbiter but rather that it was created by the people through a long and unconscious process that reflects the spirit of the nation. "Thus the nation testifies that history is the original source from which flows good conduct, and the main form in which this creation is clothed."[1] Therefore, every nation must have its own unique legal system, and no nation can adopt the legal system of another "because if we live according to an alien law and we are dependent on the values of strangers, our entire national existence will be defective and faulty. It will not contain the kernel of revival to bring about total freedom and complete redemption."[2] They maintained that, in line with the revival of Hebrew as the national language, Jewish Law, too, must be revived as the national legal system.[3]

Initial signs of this trend had already appeared even before the First World War, with the first appearance of the Jewish Magistrates Court in

Jaffa, but they did not fully develop into a significant innovation. A vestige of the application of Jewish Law from that time has been linked to the dispute between the settlement committee of Hadera and the landowners who lived abroad. The settlement committee was forced to expend a great deal of money to preserve the rights of every landowner in the settlement because of claims made by their Arab neighbors. The committee argued in court that landowners who lived abroad were also obliged to share these expenses and requested that the court permit them to sell a percentage of their lands for a sum exceeding their portion of the general expenses. After repeated advance notices in the Jewish press both in Eretz Israel and abroad, an assemblage of the court, headed by Rabbi Kook, authorized the claim of the village committee, based on the Talmudic ruling "Hefqer Bet-Din Hefqer,"[4] meaning that the court has the power to expropriate Jewish money regardless of Jewish sovereignty.[5]

When the Hebrew Magistrates Court was revived in 1918, the group dealing with the study of Jewish Law consolidated, in line with the trend toward suiting traditional Jewish law to modern sovereign reality. Toward the end of 1918, the Jewish Legal Society was established in Moscow by two jurists, Samuel Eisenstadt and Paltiel Dickstein (Daykan). A deliberate distinction was made between the terms "Jewish Law" and "halakha" for two essential and complementary reasons. First of all, the topic of Jewish Law limited to those sections of halakha that corresponded to other legal systems, such as the Hoshen Mishpat and parts of Even Ha'ezer, rather than the entire corpus of halakha. Secondly, the aim was to differentiate it as much as possible from the religious aspect of halakha, leaving the "secular" aspect intact, in other words, separation of religion and law.[6] The steps taken by the new Zionist association were swiftly curtailed by the new Bolshevik regime and as a result many of its members moved to Eretz Israel. They were integrated into the Jewish Magistrates Court system and the Jewish Law Society established in 1920 in Jerusalem. However, Amihai Radzyner maintains that the society established in Jerusalem was not the true successor of the Moscow Society.[7]

The Jerusalem Society, founded by Dr. Yehuda Janowitz, formerly a founder of the Moscow Society, brought together scholars and jurists of diverse religious outlooks. They included Norman Bentwich, the first attorney general of Mandatory Eretz Israel; Gad Frumkin, member of the Eretz Israel Supreme Court; Professors Asher Gulak and Simcha Assaf, members of the Institute of Jewish Studies in the Hebrew University; Rabbi Ya'akov Berman, supervisor of Mizrachi schools; religious attorney Mordechai Eliash; Dickstein and Eisenstadt. Since the members of the society harbored different perceptions regarding the novel concept of "Jewish Law" and the proper way to revive it, disputes arose around the editing of the society's scientific journal, *HaMishpat HaIvri* (The Jewish Law).[8]

The regulations of the society required its members to transmute Jewish Law into national law by utilizing the academic tools of *Wissenschaft des Judentums* and the study of law.[9] Although the members of the society embraced very diverse opinions as to how they defined "Jewish Law," their most dominant members believed there was a real connection between this concept and the corpus of traditional halakha. Thus, for example, founder Yehuda Janowitz wrote the following in his introduction to Simcha Assaf's book *Ha-Onshin Ahare Hatimat ha-Talmud* (Penal Law in the Post-Talmudic Period) published in 1922 by the Law Library of which Janowitz was the chief editor: "Our great rabbis and sages, the authoritative rabbinical judges who are with us today, and those who come after us, all face one of the supreme historical goals since Israel became a nation—to revive and renew Jewish Law and create a bridge that will unite the old with the new, traditional law with scientific law."[10]

Janowitz and the other religious members of the society related to halakha as a binding religious-national legal system whose every change required rabbinical consent and negated the far-reaching freedoms that Magistrates Court judges had taken upon themselves. In contrast, Eisenstadt, Dickstein, and the other secular members approached halakha as a legal system that was essentially secular. "The religious covering should not hide the healthy core of Jewish Law"[11] that can be and in fact must be updated in light of modern legal perceptions that have become entrenched in the public and support the prevailing policy of the Jewish Magistrates Court.

One example of their use of halakhic tradition when dealing with practical legal problems is Dickstein's article on the question of fraud in the Hebrew Magistrates Court. According to halakha one can cancel a sales transaction if the price is over or under one-sixth of the market price, or the market range of prices. Dickstein cited several cases where the Hebrew Magistrates Court judges had reason to refer to the Talmudic laws governing fraud, contrary to the norm "in contemporary European law as well as in the official laws of Eretz Israel."[12] Nevertheless, in some cases the court relied on the ethical concept underlying the laws of fraud, while ignoring halakhic law. This was evident in the case of a contractor who undertook to build a house while taking a price cut. Apparently, the law of fraud did not apply to him because of the Talmudic ruling that there is no fraud regarding land, according to the explanation "but regardless of what the *halakhic* ruling is on this complicated question according to accepted rabbinical teaching methods, our legal views also obligate us to act in the matter of building contracts according to the laws of fraud."[13] Dickstein praised this legal approach, accepting "the authority of the *Shulhan Arukh* only in its general spirit and fundamental views," and the non-subjection "to the details of its laws, when they do not suit the conditions and requirements of the time."[14]

A main area of dispute concerned the status of women. Secular members, who espoused the concept of equality of the sexes, sought to change the laws pertaining to women in matters of inheritance, legal status, and public appointments. They frequently criticized the rabbinical courts for ruling according to tradition on family law.[15] In 1930, Gad Frumkin, the president of the society, proposed convening a world conference of rabbis to institute regulations promoting the legal equality of women with regard to the situation of *agunot* ("anchored" women), *get* (halachic divorce) refusal, and inheritance. He expressed his fear of Orthodox opposition to any halakhic change and called upon the rabbis to respond to his initiative:

> The difficulty is that certain orthodox Rabbis are opposed to the idea of having a body with legislative power of any sort, one of the reasons being that the right to legislate, which was given to Moses and by him to Joshua, was handed on until it reached the men of the Great Synagogue, and then it stopped with the destruction of the Temple.
> Not at this stage, and not by a humble layman like myself, can this controversy be resolved or even argued, but I feel that the duty falls mainly upon orthodox Rabbinical and communal authorities to discover the means of supplying the remedies for hardships of the nature described, so that the honour and purity of Jewish family life which has played not a small part in carrying Israel through their 2,000 years of sufferings in the Diaspora may be preserved.
> Perhaps the time has come for responsible Rabbis and influential communal leaders to form themselves into a Committee to consider the possibility of convening the long-needed Assembly.[16]

That same year Eisenstadt and Dickstein sought to convene a world conference on Jewish Law to consolidate practical proposals for adapting Jewish Law to modern day sovereign reality. They raised the following topics:

a. 1900 years after the exile of the Sanhedrin, the possibility of its renewal in our generation, or establishing a Great Assembly (Knesset Gedolah), Bet Din Gadol, or any other central institution for issuing Torah, *halakha*, and legislation for all of the Jewish people.
b. Rabbinical court in Eretz Israel and abroad.
c. Marriage and divorce laws, the problems resulting from the contradiction between Israel's laws and the secular State law; obstacles regarding Levirate marriage: *yibum* (Levirate marriage to a brother-in-law), *halitza* (removal of shoe—traditional method of preventing such a marriage), and *agunah* (an abandoned wife who is "chained" to her missing husband); marriages of minors and polygamy among oriental Jews.[17]

Ultimately, the conference failed because it was very poorly attended. This was largely due to the fact that it was boycotted by the religious members of the society, either because they were personally opposed or because the rabbis, led by Rabbi Kook, had instructed them not to participate, despite the announcement by the organizers that they had no intention of passing any practical resolutions, unlike the conference of Reform rabbis in the nineteenth century. They merely intended to raise suggestions, and above all they wanted to keep the peace between all factions.[18] The opposition to the conference brought to the surface a dispute between religious and secular society—Who had the authority to render halachic innovations or amendments? In Rabbi Kook's manifesto against the conference, he wrote:

> In reply to the honored Rabbi's question as to whether to attend the world conference on Jewish Law which is soon due to take place, my reply is as follows: This conference is not authorized to deal with the matter of the supreme Bet Din of all Israel. It is not entitled to deliberate and argue about religious matters concerning matrimony etc. Such a conference, whose organizers are secular and have no authority in such matters, cannot provide answers to the questions they have raised. Therefore it goes without saying that there is absolutely no reason for you to attend.[19]

While the secular members of the society argued that the authority for innovation was granted to jurists who are scholars of Jewish Law, the religious members maintained that practical authority was strictly the purview of the rabbis. The scholars were expected to assist by bringing forth further aspects of the issue under discussion. The attitude of the religious members was also that of the Mizrachi members, who understood the extent to which sovereignty challenged halakha, but nevertheless objected to the viewpoint projected by the secular members of the Jewish Law Society and the Hebrew Magistrates Court. Their objections centered on two cardinal points, apart from the question of authority: the separation of religion and law and the character of halachic enactments and amendments. The approach that rejected the separation of religion and law was rooted in a religious Zionist perception that did not separate religion from nationhood. Thus, they were opposed to any separation between religion and national institutions such as the law or the state.

If opposition to the first issue necessarily stemmed from a religious Zionist outlook, opposition to the second issue arose from the Orthodox fear of new reforms and which was wary of halakhic changes. In an editorial marking the second conference of the national council of the Hebrew Magistrates Court, Rabbi Yehuda Leib Fischman (Maimon), head of Mizrachi in Eretz Israel wrote: "Jewish Law cannot and should not be born and created, in the same way that the Hebrew people cannot and should not be born and created. The Hebrew people, the most ancient people to exist, never lived a moment without a national law."[20]

This distinction between revival and creation in effect delegitimizes the opinion of Eisenstadt and Dickstein, comparing them to the members of the Reform movement in Germany who also claimed the continuity of tradition while adapting it to the reality of modern times.

## ENACTMENTS, NOT AMENDMENTS

Members of the Mizrachi movement and religious members of the society declared that changes in halakha can only be made through *takanot hahamim* (religious regulations) by a supreme rabbinical body, such as the Chief Rabbinate. As we have seen, the first enactment by the Chief Rabbinate was to establish a court of appeal, but the Orthodox camp objected to this. In his book *Bate ha-Din ve-Sidrehem Ahare Hatimat ha-Talmud* (Courts and Procedure in the post-Talmudic Era), Simcha Assaf justifies this enactment. He did so not by means of the modern legal reality of civilized nations, as did Rabbi Haim Hirschensohn, nor through the coercion of the British government, as did Rabbi Kook, although he agreed with both these arguments, but by historical research that proved the existence of this institution among various Jewish communities throughout history. He regards this as going counter to the direction of the secular members of the society and the members of the Hebrew Magistrates Court:

> In the Middle Ages our secular courts of law tended not to oppose the ancient legal tradition. On the contrary, they always strove to approximate them, frequently asking the advice of the rabbi or expert *dayanim*. [ . . . ] They did not aspire to create a new law. [ . . . ] However, when the magistrates court was established its proponents devised the theory of innovating Jewish Law which, in their opinion, was not suited to modern life and contemporary viewpoints. This "innovation" would be carried out purposefully and with foresight by scholars who would review the *Hoshen Mishpat* and select what was good and fine in their eyes. [ . . . ] The purpose of [the Magistrates Court] was not to assist our accepted court of law but rather to oppose it. Never in previous centuries had such a thing been thought of in Israel.
>
> Anyone who thinks this through will clearly see that this is not the way to solve the legal problem facing us. We must not create new legal establishments which have no connection with our legal tradition, or introduce new laws, but rather we must develop what we have and maintain the golden chain of our noble past.[21]

In his introduction to his previous book, *Ha-Onshin Ahare Hatimat ha-Talmud* (Penal Law in the Post-Talmudic Period), Assaf dwelled on the importance of the institution of enactments by the Sages, the intelligent manner in which it was applied throughout the years, and the legitimacy of considering the legal situation of other nations as the basis for enacting regulations:

> We are accustomed to thinking that after the Talmud was sealed, creativity ceased to exist and innovation ended in the school of Jewish Law, but this was not the case. Creativity and innovation did not end but continued, albeit more slowly and with measured steps. Naturally Jewish Law rests on the Talmud, but frequently we encounter Talmudic rulings that, under the influence of the times and the particular situation, acquired new shadings, new comments. Sometimes we find temporary orders, regulations enacted by outstanding rabbis of the generation and community leaders which do not originate in the Talmud—and sometimes they even seem to contradict Talmudic law—because even in the Middle Ages our sages deemed it a virtue and even an obligation to enact regulations to reform world order as required by the pressing needs of the hour. These enactments are many in number. Some of them were enacted under the influence of the general law and accepted customs of the citizens of the land.[22]

As examples of later enactments by the Sages that took into account local law, either due to the needs of the hour or ethical criticism of the existing halakha, Assaf refers to an enactment by the Sages of Spain that required a witness to take an oath before giving testimony; the enactment by Rabbenu Tam and the Toledo community restricting a man from obtaining his wife's inheritance in the early years of their marriage, or if his wife has children from a previous marriage; and a further enactment by Rabbenu Tam regarding testimony from relatives, wives, and minors, in cases of fights and injuries and other matters.[23]

In their research, the secular members of the society focused on halakhic literature up to the finalization of the Talmud. Their reasoning was that since this body of literature was mainly created during an early period of sovereignty, it would serve as a fitting basis for the revival of national law in the new sovereign reality. Post-Talmudic literature came into being during the time of exile and therefore was not suited to the new sovereignty. Assaf, however, focused his research on post-Talmudic literature as the basis for contemporary Jewish Law, both because he wished to emphasize legal continuity and the commitment to previous generations and as a living example of the enactment of regulations in the generations following the finalization of the Talmud.[24]

Chief Rabbis Isaac Halevi Herzog and Ben Zion Meir Hai Uziel made extensive use of enactments of the Sages. They enacted a large number of regulations on various topics. In 1943, they published important procedural regulations for rabbinical courts[25] and in 1944 and 1950 they published new regulations dealing with family law.

In 1944, the Chief Rabbinical Council enacted three rulings: to require a father to pay child support for his children up to the age of fifteen because of new nineteenth-century Western regulations that required all children to attend school up to the age of fifteen; to obligate a *yabam* (the brother of a deceased childless husband) who refuses to release his sister-in-law to pay for her support until he lawfully sets her free; and to increase the minimum amount in the *ketuba* (Jewish marriage contract) from ten to fifty lirot, in light of the erosion of its monetary worth over the years and its incompatibility with the main purpose of the ketuba.[26]

## ABRAHAM CHAIM FREIMANN

The practical deliberations in the issue were rekindled in the 1940s in anticipation of the establishment of a sovereign Jewish state. Prominent among them were the opinions of two Orthodox German Jewish jurists, both well versed in modern jurisprudence and the sovereign challenge facing halakha, who nevertheless followed separate and opposing paths that represented the polar extremes of how Orthodoxy contended with this issue. Abraham Chaim Freimann and Isaac Breuer were both of distinguished lineage: Freimann was the great-grandson of Rabbi Jacob Ettlinger (1798–1871) and Breuer was the grandson of Rabbi Samson Raphael Hirsch (1808–1888). They formulated the outlines of a Jewish political system according to halakha.

Abraham Chaim Freimann was born in Holeszów, Czechoslovakia, in 1899. His family moved to Posen and then to Berlin, where his father, Jacob Freimann, was appointed Av Beit Din (head of the rabbinical court) and a member of the board of trustees of the Orthodox rabbinical seminary founded by Rabbi Esriel Hildesheimer. Freimann studied law in the universities of Frankfurt and Marburg, specializing in Jewish jurisprudence, and then served as a district judge in Königsberg. As he wrote to Gershom Scholem in the winter of 1927: "I enjoy working in the courts of law. Here I am truly a free man, like my name, not subservient to anyone—which is very important to me."[27] In the same letter he writes of his desire to make aliya to Eretz Israel and the difficulties of finding work in his field, which leads him to the following rumination: "I have despaired of the return to Zion, and yet my heart tells me that my place is there, therefore I will try."[28] When the Nazis gained ascendancy in 1933, he was dismissed from his position and made aliya. In 1943, he was appointed lecturer in Jewish Law at the Hebrew University. In 1948, he was killed on his way to work when a Hadassah convoy came under attack.

While still in Germany Freimann began researching the families of the *Rosh* (Rabbi Asher ben Yehiel) and Maimonides, and published works on the Rishonim. His studies were based on the democratic foundation of halakha, in other words, the principle of public acceptance of authority. In the second part of his study of the Rosh and his descendants, published in 1920, he wrote:

> The unity of the Jewish people is based on the unity of its Torah, that is, the existence of a book of law that is recognized by the entire nation. Once the greatest scholars were in agreement, the *mishna* was recognized as a parliamentary binding book of law. The authority of the Babylonian Talmud is based on its absolute acceptance by the entire Jewish community. The *halakhic* writings of the Geonim and their rulings came forth from the Babylonian *yeshivot*, which were, in their time, the supreme Jewish authority.[29]

This principle was expressed throughout Freimann's life in his main field of research—Jewish Law.

Shortly after his arrival in Eretz Israel, he composed a memorandum of guidelines for the study of Jewish Law. His purpose was to create "a guide to the legal reality of our times," with the emphasis on the post-Talmudic period.[30] He wanted to establish an enterprise that would bring together all the laws, customs, and regulations that had been generated in Jewish communities up to the present time.[31] This was in fact an applied science project that aimed to facilitate the adaptation of halakhic rulings to modern sovereign reality.

The general idea behind this project was similar to that of the *Otzar HaGeonim* project of Benjamin Menashe Levin, who, by collecting commentaries of the Geonim on all tractates of the Babylonian Talmud, saw a kind of spiritual ingathering of exiles, which would ultimately lead to the restoration of the one and only center of Torah authority in Eretz Israel. [32]

Freimann, too, in a later study, regarded "the dispersal of the sources of Israel's laws as the dispersal of the nation itself, and therefore gathering them together would be a kind of ingathering of exiles." He maintained that "it is the duty of the scholar of Israel's laws to bring forth from this scattered, dispersed material the legal creative expression of various eras, its roots and its absorption—not only in the sense of the study of antiquity, but as a guide to the legal existence of our time, paving the way for the future of the law in our land."[33] He viewed rabbinic literature and that of the communities of the Middle Ages and the beginning of the new era as a living, evolving legal method, one that was largely dismembered when legal autonomy was abolished in the nineteenth century. Freimann believed that the way to ensure its continuity lay in bringing together the vast amount of legal material that had accumulated up to the present time. His unique initiative proposed that the exiled legal sources be collected for the purpose of applying halakhic rulings, against the background of various traditions of rulings that had crystallized in the new era, and within the framework of the main precedents of halakhic rulings taken from the broad geographic range of the arbitrator.

One such example can be seen in his discourse regarding the halakhic obligation to provide sustenance for a child born out of wedlock. According to the Shulkhan Arukh (Even HaEzer, 71, 4), a man cannot be obligated to provide child support if the mother claims that he is the father, without his acknowledgment. This halakhic approach, which prevailed at the time and was recognized as the official halakhic position, earned loud condemnation from women's groups. The background for this ruling was the increased number of children being born to unwed mothers, as compared to previous years.

Through dozens of literature sources, responsa, and Jewish rulings, Freimann demonstrated that in actual fact in many cases men were obligated to pay child support for a child whose single mother claimed him as the father, although he did not admit paternity. From this he concluded that:

> Legal history teaches that the legal lack of protection for a single mother and her child are not an insurmountable decree, because our independent courts in the Diaspora knew how to institute the necessary boundaries and limitations "to prevent the proliferation of *shtukim* [those whose father's identity is unknown] in Israel, who would be a burden on the community."
>
> However it is claimed that most single women in this condition today are not in need of legal assistance and the counsel of a *Sinai* [Knowledgeable] who is versed in law, but rather the medical assistance of one who is "*Okker Haroth*" [terminates pregnancy]. But this does not absolve us, the community of jurists, from seeking to rectify a flawed legal situation, one that provides an opening for those who condemn the laws of Israel.[34]

By gathering halakhic traditions from various kibbutzim, Freimann demonstrated that it was possible to find halakhic practices that provided a solution for social problems, whereas prevalent halakhic solutions no longer sufficed for modern times. In addition, like the trends that had prevailed in the field of Judaic studies since its inception and continued in the Orthodox schools of *Wissenschaft des Judentums*,[35] Freimann, too, lent his voice to the apologetics against accusers, both within and without.

### *Rulings of the Sages*

Freimann implemented his scholarly concept in his book *Law of Betrothal and Marriage after the Completion of the Talmud* (Jerusalem 1945). In the introduction to the book, he emphasizes the importance of the rulings of the sages as the main institute for innovation of halakhah in past generations. Many rulings of the sages, such as the decree of Rabbenu Gershom Meor haGolah, which aimed to solve social problems, were enacted during the period of exile by local Jewish courts.[36] Twenty years earlier, Rabbi Kook expressed his willingness to institute the necessary general rulings in the framework of the Chief Rabbinate, "so long as most of the rabbinical authorities are in agreement and are thereafter accepted by the public, they will have the power of a *din Torah* (matter of litigation)."[37] But in actual fact the only ruling that was introduced was the establishment of the Court of Appeal, which was the condition set by the British regime for recognizing the institution of the Chief Rabbinate.[38]

Approximately one year before the publication of his book, Freimann published an article entitled "New rulings of the Chief Rabbinate of Eretz Israel on Family Law."[39] In Freimann's article, which deals with the new rulings of 1944, he praises the Chief Rabbinical Council for their implementation, which has advanced the creation of a unified Torah based legal system for the general Jewish public in Eretz Israel: "The new rulings of the Chief Rabbinical Council signify a turning point in the formation of a unified legal creation for all the tribes of Israel who dwell in their land, the Holy Land. Therefore this new constitution is destined to hold an important place in the development of our rules and laws."[40]

He hoped that the Chief Rabbinical Council, which in effect constituted the supreme religious body in Eretz Israel, would institute the requisite new rulings in light of the swiftly approaching new political situation. One aim of his book was to examine this institution and draw practical conclusions for its use:

> This attempt to deal with the development of betrothals and weddings from their early Talmudic beginnings until the present day, did not stem from a desire to teach itself but rather from a desire to teach the entire method of research. This central topic in the laws of matrimony is designed to serve as the touchstone for basic questions in the legal history of our people: what are the forces that create the laws of Israel? How much legal authority do they have as regards amendment and renewal, change and annulment? And why were they enacted?
> I have chosen this topic not only for its great practical importance, but also for its dogmatic importance as regards defining the areas of legal authority for enacting legitimate amendments in Israel's constitutional law, the traditional Written Torah, precisely in the most sensitive and delicate area of all our legal system, the laws of matrimony.[41]

In his book Freimann amassed some 140 rulings on marriage, culled from various times and diverse communities "that teach us about changes and innovations that the leaders of the generations saw fit to insert into the existing legal status."[42] These changes and innovations indicate the sensitivity of these leaders to the needs of the hour and their flexibility in the face of local conditions. The main purpose of the book was to create a scholarly infrastructure for the renewal and arrangement of kiddushin (matrimonial laws) in Eretz Israel, since in the course of time "various *kibbutzim* [a cluster of communities] have moved away from one another in their customs and rulings, even as regards the laws of betrothal and marriage, upon which the unity of the nation depends."[43] It was his intention to ensure that in Eretz Israel one certified central rabbinical institution would impose its authority on all the communities through its new rulings. He proposed placing the emphasis on rulings of the Sephardic communities and Oriental Jews because they have an ongoing tradition of involvement with these laws:

> These instructions and ordinances are known to have particular importance, since most Sephardic communities and Oriental Jews have always enjoyed wide legal autonomy as regards the laws (of matrimony). Their courts have dealt unceasingly with judicial personal matters, and therefore their rulings are outstanding in their continuity of tradition and the stability of their teachings. They form the solid foundation of every sound legal deliberation.[44]

At the end of his book Freimann contends with an extremely serious problem related to the laws of matrimony, one that saw a sharp increase in his lifetime—the problem of *agunot* (lit: "anchored." The reference is to women bound in marriage to a husband who refuses to grant a divorce or is missing and not proven dead). This became a problem of national dimensions with the mass immigration from the Russian Empire to America in the 1880s.[45] The situation was later exacerbated by the two world wars:

> Our judicial independence and the power of enforcement of our courts have been abrogated in most of the Diaspora. The introduction of civil marriage and divorce in western countries and the increased flow of Jewish immigration to countries overseas has raised an extremely painful and perilous problem in marital life: that of the malicious "'anchoring" of the daughters of Israel to husbands who evade them and are estranged from them, to a degree that has been unprecedented since the time we became a nation.[46]

In a long appendix he reviews the proposals put forward in recent years as a solution to this problem, all based on legal principles: the expropriation of the wedding ceremony by the local bet din; authorization to draw up a *get* (religious divorce) during the wedding ceremony that can be implemented in the event that a woman becomes an *aguna*; and the transition to marital life with no kiddushin according to the laws that govern a concubine. Freimann rejects them all:

> Most of these suggestions have widely missed their mark: in their efforts to improve the lot of *agunot* they jeopardize the very foundations of matrimony and family upon which every Jewish home rests. "Conditional matrimony" harms the basic principles of public order and social morality. For this reason the legal systems of enlightened nations do not allow conditions to be imposed upon a marriage. Are we about to institute conditional matrimony as the norm for matrimonial relations in Israel? How stringent are the reforms when it comes to severing marital relationships? How many millions of Catholics are in marriages whose bonds will never be loosed? Yet do we intend to make divorce attendant upon every marriage, folded and tucked away in a

box from the time the couple stands under the wedding canopy? As to the last suggestion—reverting to the status of concubine—this means abrogating marriage, divorce, levirate marriage (the marriage of a man to his late brother's childless widow), and *halitza* (removal of shoe under levirate law), loosening the reins, leading to chaos, and ultimately destroying our national existence. This is not the way.[47]

In his opinion, the solution to this thorny problem can only lie in a general ruling by the Rabbinic Supreme Court in Eretz Israel, because since the destruction of European Jewry there has been no challenge to its authority. Any ruling based on the authority of this central court of law has the power to annul *kidushin*:

The remedy must come from the weak spot. The evil source of malicious "anchoring" of *agunot* stems from the abolition of our judicial independence and authority, from the collapse of our inner discipline, and from the fact that a large segment of our people has rebelled against Israeli jurisdiction. It is not in our power to restore the crown of legal autonomy to our Diaspora courts of law, but the establishment of a supreme religious institute in Eretz Israel, the place of national vitality, has reinstated a religious center with authoritative jurisdiction for the entire Jewish world. Ever since the destruction of the centers of Jewish learning in the countries of Europe, nothing has been left to us but the Torah of this land. The eyes of all Israel are turned towards this supreme religious institution as the last stronghold for safekeeping religion and tradition, all that remains of the ruins of the Diaspora. Again, we cannot expect any authoritative, legitimate action in the sphere of religion and law from any other source. We cannot apologize, saying that perhaps there is an equally great and important court of law in our generation. This status is accorded to the courts of the Chief Rabbinate of Eretz Israel. Its power and strength, along with its jurisdiction, are unprecedented in any other Jewish court of our generation. This important court of law has great power to judge and instruct, to annul marriages, and to enact rulings.[48]

Despite Freimann's intellectual daring, his grasp of the essence of the problem and his awareness of the acute need for a solution, he remained extremely aware of the sensitivity of the issue and maintained that the solution could not depend on each individual rabbi or community but must be a national rule. In this case, too, he did not pin much hope on the Chief Rabbinate.

### *Communal Enactments*

Toward the end of 1945, the year when his book appeared, he wrote his programmatic article "The Laws of Israel in Eretz Israel," which was published in *Luach Ha'aretz*. Aware that it was a time of transition from British Mandate rule to an independent Jewish government, he wished to express his views about the most suitable legal system for the Jewish state. He began with a historical overview of the legal situation in Israel during the time of the destruction of the Second Temple. He maintained that "when the state was lost to us, some aspects of public law were annulled, such as the laws of the Sanhedrin and capital offences. But the entire body of private law and some branches of public law remained in force even after the destruction and during the entire period of the Diaspora, until the legal autonomy of most Jewish communities in the Diaspora was done away with during the time of the Emancipation."[49] When legal autonomy came to an end, most of the legal aspects of halakha became *hilkhetah l'mshikha* (halakha that will be enacted in messianic times), similar to those dealing with ritual purity and impurity after the destruction of the temple. The exceptions were Jewish communities in the lands of Islam, where legal autonomy in matrimonial and family law was maintained. This limited autonomy was also passed down to the Yishuv in Eretz Israel during the time of the British Mandate, when the status and the authority of the Chief Rabbinate was established.

Nevertheless, Freimann was distressed by the fact that specifically at a time of national revival, most of the Jewish public in Eretz Israel had no desire to reinstate national law in every walk of life, preferring the legal proceedings of the mandate over rabbinic courts and Jewish magistrates. In this connection he quoted a Jewish magistrate, in 1917:

> What a historical paradox: when we lost our country we strove with all our might to hold onto our national laws and rulings. We used them to build a Chinese wall, a boundary—and in this way we managed to endure for two thousand years, to the amazement of all the nations. But now, when the dream of the nation's revival in our country is being realized, this is the first thing we have managed to do. We have abandoned the national laws and regulations that were glorious for their richness and profundity, their lofty ideals of justice and righteousness, and instead we have lovingly welcomed foreign law, one that is now foreign even to those who created it.[50]

Freimann then addressed a practical question regarding the most suitable legal system for the future state. For practical reasons he rejected the slogans of the two polar extremes then prevalent in public discourse: Torah law endorsed by the religious sector, and the separation of state and religion proposed by the liberal secularists. He argued that Jewish law had not yet been prepared for practical application at the present time. Such preparation would require legal-historic research. "It is incumbent upon the science of practical Jewish law to first ascertain the practical legal status of all the branches of law among the various Jewish *kibbutzim* until their legal independence was annulled."[51] This is like the direction he himself followed in his research on the laws of betrothal and marriage after the Talmudic period. Such research would construct "a bridge over the empty void that came into being once our law fell into disuse. That which is lacking must be restored, in the same way that our laws would have developed had they remained involved in the changing and evolving life of the nation."[52]

The next stage in processing the legal material for a new constitution requires an interpretation that accords with present day reality and new regulations in places where the judicial interpretation does not lead to the desired outcome. This stage cannot be accomplished through the yeshiva mode of study, which is ahistorical and lacks any desire for fulfillment. "It floats in a noble world of abstract study, 'making peace in the highest realms' between various theories and methods of the *Tannaim* and the *Amoraim*, the *Rishonim* and the *Akharonim*, without aiming for a practical outcome."[53] The most suitable method for this stage would be a historical-societal review of the legal material, which would result in purposeful interpretation capable of resolving the legal problems that had arisen in recent years:

> In the same way that in the past social and economic changes found expression in new legal creations such as the *prosbul, heter iska, kherem d'Rabbena Gershom*, and inheritance rights for women and daughters through community and state legislation—in contrast to the established *halakha*—so the historical-societal school of legal study will pave new roads to solve problems of our times, such as work legislation, women's emancipation, the concept of cooperation and collective economy, and so on.[54]

Freimann raised the question of who should be involved in rulings and legislation in the future state. In contrast to the discourse that developed immediately following the Balfour Declaration, the basic premise of whose religious-Zionist participants was that most of the Jewish people wanted a Torah-based legal system and recognized the authority of their religious leaders, it was now evident that most of the Jewish Yishuv in Eretz Israel did not recognize halakha as a binding authority, preferring to participate in the creation of sovereign existence according to the rules of representative democracy. Freimann did not even raise the possibility that the rabbis would exclusively lead the process of new legislature. He claimed that most of the public ordinances that were discontinued during the period of exile were terminated through the power of public authority, the authority of democracy. "The public are partners in all their affairs and every condition that they impose is firm and abiding. The public is entitled to arrange all its internal affairs, as regards regime and appointments, authority and taxes, and all other general matters, according to the majority opinion, on condition that it does not contradict what is written in the Torah."[55] In practice, the communities included the local *batei din* (Jewish courts) so they would agree with their rulings. In the past, the entire community was Torah observant, unlike today, but in the present reality of the Yishuv it would not be possible to leave legislative authority entirely in the hands of the religious public. He also brings the example of the Chief Rabbinate's 1944 ruling on family matters, which unconditionally included the community councils and local committees, regardless of their members' identity.

At the end of the article he calls upon rabbinical and *dayanim* seminaries in Eretz Israel to imbue their students with legal knowledge, ending with a moving plea to all factions of the public:

> It would serve the two sections of the Yishuv well, both the ultra-conservatives and the ultra-progressives, if they would use the transition period to delve into the entire scope of our legal problems. This group will become convinced that it is impossible "to impose" Israel's laws upon the Yishuv without thorough preparation, and there is no need to recoil from far-reaching revisions whose only purpose is to preserve and uphold, not to destroy and eradicate, as did the "reform" revisions in their time. And this group will appreciate the great value of our national legislature as a cultural asset, no less important than the Hebrew language and Hebrew education, which is not disputed in the Yishuv that is building its land and its state.
>
> Would that as the Yishuv is destined to renew its political life, the words of our Divine lawgiver will come to pass: "What great nation has laws and rules as perfect as all this teaching?"[56]

Freimann continued to deal with the legislative power of halakha in several articles, following the Anglo-American Committee of Inquiry that convened in 1946, in whose presence secular elements expressed their opposition to the imposition of Torah law in Eretz Israel since, they claimed, it is anti-democratic. In an article entitled *Samchut haChakikah beYisrael* (Legislative Power in Israel) Freimann, using Talmudic sources and responsa, based his assertion on his previous article. He maintained that alongside the legislative power of the bet din, the public has wide and binding legislative powers in its capacity as a partner with contractual freedom, on condition that it does not legislate in contradiction to what is written in the Torah:

> By virtue of the freedom of association practiced in our laws, all conditions pertaining to money are valid. In matters not relating to money it is permitted to set conditions and draw up contracts, provided that the parties do not stipulate against what is written in the Torah, for if anything is stipulated against what is written in the Torah, its terms are invalid. By virtue of the principle of freedom of association that governs the legal system of Israel, the public is also entitled to arrange matters according to its wishes and as it sees fit. Individuals such as city residents are regarded as partners in all public matters. Just as the other partners are entitled to stipulate in their partnership contract any condition they wish, so too city residents are entitled to stipulate any conditions they wish for their city's needs: Townspeople are authorized to stipulate regarding prices, measures, and the pay of laborers,

> and to enforce their decree. Townspeople are authorized to pronounce, "Anyone seen [dealing with] the authorities [*malkhut*] shall pay thus and so." And they are authorized to enforce their decree. (Tosefta Bava Metzia, XI, 23). This *halakha* determines the absolute autonomy of the city residents, the organized local public, to stipulate conditions among themselves by virtue of a mutual agreement to impose them on the public as a whole. This is the original form of a social charter.[57]

He maintained that in the Middle Ages this halakha formed the basis of legislation for Jewish communities, whose rulings were recognized as Torah law to all intents and purposes.[58] As we have seen from his early studies, Freimann claimed that this democratic principle had formed the basis of halakha ever since the acceptance of *na'ase v'nishma* (we will do and we will hear) at Mount Sinai, the covenant forged in the days of Nehemiah, continuing with the nation's acceptance of the Talmud, followed by the Shulhan Arukh as a binding halakhic codex. In effect, it is this principle that today endows the elected representative Jewish parliament with legislative authority, on condition that it does not stipulate against what is written in the Torah.

Unlike Asher Gulak and later scholars such as Menachem Elon and Shalom Albeck, Freimann claimed that communal enactments belonged in the domain of public law that was preserved after the destruction of the Temple, and not in private law.[59] He explained that our Sages needed to rely on halakhot from private law in the matter of partnerships and contracts in order to establish the authority of their regulations, according to the principle of the social contract. The source of public authority lies in the social contract which, conceptually, parallels the principle of contractual partnership in private law. According to this concept, the public can impose its authority on individuals who oppose a specific regulation. In other words, the social contract establishes the principle of public partnership in all public affairs. It has the power to appoint a legislative body to enact laws and regulations for the public benefit without the consent of each member of the public, and it is exempt from various restrictions of contractual engagements in private law, such as the need for a deed of acquisition, and the impossibility of bestowing something not yet in existence, and so on. His synthetic interpretation of diverse sources from rabbinical literature on the subject of communal enactments, and his disregard of the methods adopted by *Rishonim* who objected to the coercion of the majority over the minority who opposed the regulation, reflect his applied method, one that sometimes blurred the contradictions between various sources who had difficulty reaching an unequivocal halakhic decision.[60]

Freimann continued to study the issue of legislative authority on secondary issues stemming from the central question. In a follow-up article entitled "Public Majority and Minority: Public and State *Halakhot* in Israel" Freimann discusses the majority required by halakha to enact new public rulings.[61] He begins by saying that with regard to most of the stated opinions in the courts of law "as a general rule, the saying 'the ruling follows the majority' applies not only to the Supreme Court and all decisions in Jewish law, but to all public and state laws. Rabbi Shimon ben Gamliel and Rabbi Elazar bar Zadok say that one only sees to the needs of the public on condition that most of the public is accepting, and one does not issue public edicts unless most of the public can abide by them."[62] Any decision taken by most of the public is also binding upon the minority who oppose it, including coercive measures to enforce regulations taken by the majority.

Freimann goes on to discuss the type of majority required for public decisions: the most persons—everyone has a vote; the most property—most of the taxpayers; the most wisdom—the wisest of intellectual society. These were the three kinds of majority referred to in various places and at various times among Jewish communities. From this he infers that the type of majority required also depends on a consensus of "most individuals in the community,", since "ultimately everything depends on the basic charter and the public constitution."[63] He also came to another conclusion from the responsa of Rabbi Shlomo ben Aderet, who wrote that when it comes to communal enactments, "women are like men, for nobody would rule on their property without their consent," thus women have the right to take part in public decisions, "when it comes to public matters the rule for women is the same as that for men. This is the answer for those who would deny Jewish women their public rights."[64]

He further deduces that it is incumbent to hold a debate on the topic under discussion in the presence of all those who have a right to vote, similar to the discussion held by a panel of judges in court. The voting majority cannot exclude the others from the discussion in order to obtain a binding ruling based on the fact that they have the majority opinion:

> The rule of "most out of all" upholds the legal right of the minority to take part in all public debates and express their argument in the plenum, at the entire public debate. Perhaps they will succeed in persuading the majority to change their minds. It is forbidden to silence the opposition by holding a discussion in their absence.[65]

He bases this deduction on the criticism leveled by *Haralbach* (Rabbi Levi ibn Habib) against *Mahari* Berab (Rabbi Jacob Berab) when the Sages of Safed disputed the controversial renewal of ordination in 1538.[66] Their consent was not binding, even though they constituted the majority of Jewish Sages, because they did not consult with the Jerusalem Sages in the form of a court hearing before their decision. This deduction also anchored the rights of the minority to attend the deliberations of the legislature. He therefore concluded that:

> The law provides the Jewish public with a wide measure of autonomy to organize their own lives and to elect the form of organization and

> regime they prefer—but only on one basic condition: that they do not harm the principles of Torah and justice, for any stipulation on what is written in the Torah is void, whether specified by an individual or by the public.[67]

In effect, it was Freimann's method that secured the halakhic legitimacy of parliamentary legislation, on condition that there would be no stipulation upon what is written in the Torah. He also secured rabbinical authority to impose creative legal interpretations and amend the necessary regulations for the times, in contrast to case law. In essence, Freimann mapped out ways of adapting halakha to modern sovereign reality. His blueprint was based on three complementary foundations. First, the adoption of suitable halakhic practices from the halakhic-legal corpus of the Jewish communities in the post-Talmudic period, particularly those where legal autonomy had not been abolished in the era of emancipation. To this end, a project would be required to gather these halakhic traditions and their accessibility. Second, new regulations would be required to adapt halakha to reality, similar to those instituted in previous generations from the time of the Mishna and the Talmud to those introduced by the rabbinic courts of prominent Jewish communities in later centuries. In this context he claimed that the Chief Rabbinical Council could serve as a suitable platform. Third, *takanot hakahal* (lit. community regulations) are an ancient and legitimate halakhic institution upon which can be based the halakhic authority of a democratic Jewish parliament, on condition that it does not legislate contrary to the Torah. The historic experience of this institution also teaches the essential procedures required for the proper functioning of a legislature. Freimann's recognition of the halakhic authority of a non-rabbinic democratic House of Representatives was in line with his general concept of the democratic aspect of halakha, as expressed in the principle of national acceptance, that he emphasized from his earliest studies.

## ISAAC BREUER

Isaac Breuer (1883–1946), who was also a German Orthodox scholar and jurist, posited a completely different approach.[68] Born in Pápa, Hungary, in 1890 he immigrated to Germany with his family. His father Solomon was appointed rabbi of the separate Orthodox community in Frankfurt am Main. Between the years 1890 and1898 he studied at the Orthodox school of the community, which was established by his grandfather, Rabbi Samson Raphael Hirsch. Between 1898 and1904 he studied at his father's yeshiva in Frankfurt am Main, and from 1904 to 1909 he attended Strasburg University, Marburg University, and Berlin University and co-founded the Bund Juedischer Akademiker. In 1912, he was one of the founders of Agudas Yisroel. Unlike many of Agudath Israel, Breuer supported a unique Orthodox version of Jewish nationalism, hailing the First World War as a "Messianic War," and the Balfour Declaration as the "harbinger of the Messiah."[69]

According to Breuer, Jewish nationalism came into being after the Divine revelation at Mount Sinai, and the Torah, as the national law, is what stands at its foundation. Its principle is a historic mission to establish a Torah state—the fulfilment of the vision of law and justice—which will eventually restore Divine sovereignty to the world. National emancipation (auto-emancipation), which was made possible after the Balfour Declaration and the British Mandate, is a further stage in the fulfilment of the mission of the Torah nation, which is required to live according to the law of the Torah specifically in Eretz Israel as an autonomous people, destined to establish the Torah state which integrates law and justice and will reveal to all that Go-d is the true Sovereign. However, he believed that Zionism deviates from the essence of the Jewish people and its aim because it sees the nation as an ordinary historical nation, and ignores the fact that it is the nation of the Torah and its meta-historical nature. Religious Zionism, by joining up with Zionism, legitimizes this deviation in a similar way as communal Orthodoxy in Germany.

During the war, he served as a military censor of the German Army, and after the war he worked as a lawyer in Frankfurt am Main. In 1925, he travelled to the Land of Israel and tried to convince the mandate's authorities to give equal legal status to the Ultraorthodox community in Jerusalem. He left Germany in 1936, three years after the Nazi rise to power, and settled in Jerusalem.

In the Land of Israel he was appointed director of the Agudath Israel Yishuv Fund (Keren HaYishuv). However, after five years of differences of opinion with his colleagues he resigned and returned to the practice of law. He was a staunch supporter of Haredi settlement in Eretz Israel, the de facto spiritual head of Poalei Agudath Israel, whom he regarded as his students. In 1944, he published *Moriah*, his first book in Hebrew, wherein he presented a historiosophical view of Jewish history, determining the role of the nation in its time according to his method. He died in Jerusalem in 1946. Five years later his comprehensive work *Nahliel* on *ta'amei hamitzvoth* (the reasons for the mitzvoth) was published, in which he outlined the basis of Jewish theocracy in which his vision of a Torah state would materialize.

### *Anti-historicism*

As far back as 1910, Breuer took up the challenge posed by the modern system of jurisprudence based on equality before the law regardless of religion, nationality, or gender. He was drawn to it following the case of a Jewish couple who came before a German court seeking a divorce. The woman filed for divorce on the grounds of adultery. The court decided that, whereas according to Jewish law only the husband has the right to divorce his wife on the grounds of adultery, this blatant discrimination against the wife offends every sense of justice, rendering the halakha inappropriate for a German judge. According to German law, declared the judge, the couple must divorce. This prompted Breuer to deal with other essential differences between the laws of Israel and modern jurisprudence with regard to the concept of the inequality of slavery and discrimination against non-Jews.

In an article titled "The Philosophical Foundations of Jewish and of Modern Law," which was published in the same year, he pointed out the lack of satisfaction of many Jews from the inequality prevailing in Jewish law:

> Thus we see Jewish law surrounded by powerful partitions of an individual-sexual, social and national nature, and at the same time we see that everywhere in modern law these partitions are being overcome to an increasing extent. [ . . . ] the loftiest quality on which modern law prides itself, its eternal title to glory, consists in the removal of these partitions, a task of legislative development spanning more than a thousand years. Jewish law appears to stand in irreconcilable contradiction to this whole process of legislative development and seems able to maintain its position only alongside legal systems which have long since been covered by the dust of past eras.[70]

The solution put forward by Breuer to resolve this contradiction did not in any way resemble those proposed by Rabbi Hirschensohn and later by Freimann on similar issues.[71] Breuer did not seek to change halakha through an inner mechanism to make it compatible with modern-day reality and the sense of justice and integrity, which he greatly respected, that prevailed in the Western world. Instead, he philosophically analyzed two legal systems and their attitude toward morality. The modern legal system is based on the concept of humaneness to which Judaism subscribes, but nevertheless Judaism is committed to a higher ideal. The universal and rational idea of humaneness demands absolute equality in legal rights and does not tolerate discrimination or favoritism. In contrast, the legal system of Israel is based on the transcendent moral concept of the obligations imposed on diverse groups from their creation: the Jewish nation, males, priests, slaves, and so on, and accordingly it bestows upon them unequal rights. Yet this inequality has never arisen from a position of strength, nor does it allow for arbitrariness or abuse, as was the case with the laws of nations in the pre-modern world:[72]

> The disparity of the delegation of duties is a principle that rules Jewish law. We do not only see it effective in the relationship of man and wife, of master and slave, of Israel and the nations, we see it also effective in the way the Jewish people are divided into three: priests, Levites and laymen, in the prominence it is not the power that is delegated, the

> personal interest that is given balance, but it is rather the moral law which, in the multiplicity of the spheres of tasks, is to arrive at an ever more complete representation in mutual furtherance and completion.[73]

Breuer was opposed to the path of historicism followed by Rabbi Hirschensohn and Freimann on similar topics. Unlike them, he did not claim that inequality stemmed from accepting frameworks of the ancient world such as polygamy and slavery, and acting within them in a moral and legal manner, as far as possible. Negative frameworks disappeared from the Western world in the course of time, and Judaism was obligated to abandon them because of their inherent lack of morality. A case in point is rulings such as the herem [decree] d'Rabbenu Gershom, that abolished polygamy and the right of a husband to divorce his wife against her will. In fact, Breuer was following in the footsteps of his grandfather, Rabbi Samson Raphael Hirsch, who was opposed to historicist methods of Wissenschaft des Judentums, even in the moderate Orthodox version, and related to Torah laws and commandments as natural laws with no historical development.[74]

Hirsch was the main Orthodox spokesman against Wissenschaft des Judentums. He claimed that Wissenschaft des Judentums is a "system for the theoretical extenuation of an actual apostasy," that everything it had wrought was "more or less like throwing sand or stones at Judaism as it moves through life," and that "this science had, at least in retrospect, lent an air of scientific respectability to the vulgar ambitions of reform."[75] Hirsch's concept of Wissenschaft des Judentums proceeded from the assumption that the written and oral law were as much divine creation as is nature, and that therefore the inquiry into the laws of the Torah and their relationships must be subject to the same method of inquiry as the laws of nature. Thus, for example, just as the Law of Gravitation has no history, so, too, the laws of the Torah. According to him, this subject of research was a-historical.[76]

Breuer followed Hirsch's path. He, too, rejected applying the historicist method of halakha in any form.[77] In his autobiography he expressed his opposition to the historicization of halakha:

> In some ways we could say that the study of such law is extremely hazardous for Jewish interests if we ignore Biblical criticism. It is certainly more dangerous that the study of philosophy. The main subject of modern philosophy in no way resembles that of Judaism. But the main subject of Roman philosophy, like that of all other nations, is how individuals and nations live side by side. This is also the subject of the Torah in the form of Divine law, as well as that of the Talmud. [ . . . ] Law, like language, is subject to the general rules of national growth. We have Roman law, German law, Anglo-Saxon law, Romanian law, and so on, so why not also "Jewish" law? Are not the factual data of all laws basically the same? Why should we not include "Jewish law" in the science of comparative law? Why do we not regard "Jewish law" as

> the product of the "Jewish" people, in the same way that the laws of all nations are self-made? Indeed, whoever thinks so is completely ejected from the national-Jewish circle. He is lost to Jewish national Torah study. [ . . . ] It is only with aversion that I was able to read writings composed by Jewish jurists on the subject of "Jewish law" and I read hardly any of them to the end. To my eyes they dealt with anatomy, the anatomy of a human body whose soul has departed. Our law is the law of the Living God. The more I involve myself in the law of other nations, the more I am made aware of the wide chasm between their law and Divine law.[78]

Freimann, on the other hand, was raised in the school of Hildesheimer that dealt in the study of Wissenschaft des Judentums and regarded it as a legitimate and in fact necessary tool for a more precise and deeper understanding of the Torah. Nevertheless, this school of thought had its own concept of the nature and limitations of this field of study.

They sought to create an Orthodox alternative to the Wissenschaft des Judentums. Orthodox scholars competed with the basic values and methods of research that challenged traditional concepts of the past, such as objectivity and historicism, and developed research strategies that allowed them to hold on to their two objectives at the same time, that is, both scientific research methods and traditional values.[79]

In the second half of the 1930s, Freimann was a member in the Organization of Jewish Studies (Aluma) established in Jerusalem in 1935, by the Orthodox scholar Benjamin Menashe Levin, which was intended to be the basis of Orthodox Wissenschaft des Judentums, founded upon the religious premises outlined by Orthodox scholars throughout the years, and in the context of the national renaissance.[80]

In a critical essay written in 1947, Freimann even expressed his strong opposition to Wellhausen's documentary hypothesis. Like Allbright, he called it "an anti-Semitic libel invented by the spiritual fathers of the Nazis who claimed that the priests of Israel smuggled books of later origin into the Books of Moses."[81]

This difference between the two schools of thought also created a different type of apologia. The question of the attitude toward non-Jews in rabbinical literature was a central theme in Jewish apologetic writings in Germany during the nineteenth century. Talmudic texts that defamed gentiles and advocated a double legal and moral standard for Jews in their dealings with other Jews as compared to their dealings with non-Jews were cast in the face of those Jews who, at the time, were struggling for emancipation.

The liberals, generally, maintained that the Talmud and all the vast body of halachic literature created in its wake had become entirely irrelevant. [82] They advocated in complete religious tolerance and egalitarian relations with non-Jews. They even removed the blessing "Who has not made me a gentile" from the prayer book. The Orthodox, having been obligated to the Talmud, responded apologetically. The Hildesheimer school made efforts to find halakhic precedents, with neutral or even egalitarian attitudes to non-Jews. Abraham Berliner proposed replacing the well-known negative version of the blessing "Who has not made me a gentile," with the less-known positive "Who has made me an Israelite."[83] David Zvi Hoffmann pointed on the unusual and relatively unknown egalitarian stand taken by Rabbi Menachem Me'iri, who lived and worked in Provence in the second half of the thirteenth century.[84]

In 1919, Freimann published an article entitled "Foreign Law in Israel" wherein he depicted the attitude of Jews towards the non-Jewish residents of a Jewish state. By using biblical and halakhic sources he drew a unified picture of a halakhic policy that extended equality to non-Jews, while ignoring halakhot regarding interest and fraud, for example, where the law is not the same for Jews as for non-Jews. He pointed to the fact that Judaism is not a proselytizing religion and in fact presents difficulties to would-be converts; to the prohibition on harming or damaging the property of anyone, including non-Jews, and any form of oppression; to equal social rights and the obligation to respect the aged, including non-Jews. He referred to the fact that even in ancient times Eretz Israel attracted non-Jews because of this policy of equality, claiming that minority rights in law were abolished following the destruction of the Jewish state and the termination of Jewish Law.[85]

The apologetic stance taken by Rabbi Samson Raphael Hirsch and his followers was more limited and ahistorical.[86] As a rule they stuck to accepted texts and halakhot, interpreting them in a non-chauvinistic manner. For example, in his commentary on the prayer book, Hirsch left unchanged the blessing " . . . who has not made us heathens." "The same applied to . . . who has not made us women." However, he provided a non-chauvinistic commentary on these blessings:

> This is not a prayer of thanks that Go-d did not make us heathens, slaves or women. Rather, it calls upon us to contemplate the task which God has imposed upon us by making us free Jewish men, and to pledge ourselves to do justice to this mission. These three aspects of our own status impose upon us duties much more comprehensive than those required of the rest of mankind.[87]

Breuer himself, as we have seen, followed a similar path. In this article he rated the blessings "Blessed be Go-d, who has not made me a Gentile, . . . not made me a slave, . . . not made me a woman,"[88] as central motifs of Jewish law:

> In these sentences from the daily liturgy we find expressed with surprising clarity the completely unique character of Jewish law and is partitions. In these sentences we find these partitions related to God himself, the eternal relevance for all persons subject to Jewish law. *To eradicate these sentences from the liturgy would be tantamount to rendering*

> *invalid the complete structure of Jewish law.* It is precisely because the contents of these sentences are perhaps "unpalatable" for many that they bear the greatest importance in our day. To eradicate them, yet to consider the partitions expressed in them as binding, constitutes an act of dishonorable cowardice.[89]

## *Meta Law*

Breuer's objection to historicism in the research of the oral law was consistent with his view about the essential difference between the Torah and the law of the nations,[90] a difference, which is reflected in his attitude toward making significant changes in reality. In an article titled "The Great Turning," which was published in 1944, he clarified his view:

> Revolution is a political concept common among the other nations of the world. Among them law is the fruit of reality, and if it is in harmony with reality, then it is a just law. When the existing order changes, the law has to be changed; if we do not change it, then a contradiction arises between law and the existing order. Should this contradiction become intensified, and if there are no men of wisdom who understand the times and are able to rectify matters before it is too late, then a revolution breaks out and effects a change in the law by force, strength, and power. As the law of the people of Israel, the Torah is eternal. A revolution against the Torah is violence and revolt, and remains forever violence and revolt, which thousands of years cannot cure and turn into law and justice. It was for this reason that the author of the *Hatam Sofer*, of blessed memory, said: "According to the Torah, whatever is novel is forbidden". [ . . . ] except that which is new in the Torah itself.[91]

As an example for legitimate revolution, Breuer brought the case of his grandfather, Rabbi Samson Raphael Hirsch, who brought the new order "under the sway of the eternal Torah."

In 1938, following the hearings of the Peel Commission (1937) on the establishment of a Jewish state in part of the Land of Israel, Breuer wrote a constitutional program for the Jewish state, which is consistent with his view.[92] The Oral Law, as well as the Bible, were dictated to the people heteronomously. They are not a product of the people's spirit and historical development. The first three sections of the proposal are:

1. The Torah is the law of the Jewish people.
2. If the Israeli public gains autonomy, the Torah will be incumbent upon the public as the law of the Jewish people, within boundaries specified according to the Torah.
3. The binding force of the Torah, as the law of the Jewish people, does not depend upon its acceptance or non-acceptance by the people.[93]

He even extracted a clause from the regulations of his congregation in Frankfurt am Main that read: "every Jew must be circumcised according to the law of the Torah."[94] In contrast to Rabbi Kook, Rabbi Hirschensohn, and Freimann, Breuer completely rejected every democratic aspect of halakha. His proposal contained hardly any attempts to contend with the modern and sovereign challenges facing halakha, not even by creating new systems capable of doing so. According to his proposal, the Chief Rabbinate would not have the authority to introduce new rulings according to the new needs dictated by time and status. Its most far-reaching purpose would be "to immediately begin processing workers' laws according to the Torah,"[95] out of concern for social justice and peace. Although, like Freimann, he pointed to the need for a modern codex of work laws, unlike him Breuer did not mention the need for "women's emancipation." Some eight years later, in his autobiography, Breuer even maintains that the agreed-upon representatives of the Torah must be "precisely versed in these manifestations of economic life and draw them close to the laws and judgments of the Torah, in order to prove the eternal relevance of these laws and judgments" because "the manifestations of modern economic life are entirely different from the time of Abaye and Rava, Rabbi Yosef Karo, and Rabbi Sabbatai HaCohen."[96] In other words, suiting the Torah to the political constitution can only be done through a process of applying the principles of existing halakhot to modern systems that were formerly not in existence, by "clearly formulating the concepts, with reference to the reality of our times, by defining them from a meta-lawful point of view compared to other nations, and wherever possible, developing them in practice."[97] Beyond this, nothing should be changed, nor should we consider the concepts of justice and integrity of international law.

Amichai Radzyner and Shuki Friedmann maintain that from the outset Breuer couched his constitutional proposal in extreme terms from which it would be possible to withdraw, thus achieving gains for preserving the communal interests of the Haredi public. His proposal should therefore be regarded chiefly as a plan for a "defensive" constitution, rather than a "formulated" constitution.[98] In my opinion, Breuer fully believed in his proposal, although he was aware of the unlikelihood of its acceptance by the majority of the Yishuv, as he wrote to Jacob Rosenheim in a memorandum. He believed in presenting the ideal vision while fighting for the fulfillment of its basic aspects for the existence of the Orthodox community. He wrote to Rosenheim that a state which rejects this constitution is not legitimate from a halakhic perspective.[99] Unlike most of his colleagues in Agudath Israel he was, even at an early stage, enterprising and visionary in all that pertained to the Yishuv in Eretz Israel and its future statehood. His writings from that time and up until the end of World War II are imbued with this belief, and his intention to realize his uncompromising vision of a "Torah state."[100]

Indeed, after coming to Eretz Israel Breuer came to the conclusion that the religious reality in the Yishuv would not change in the foreseeable future. Agudath Israel had missed the opportunity provided by the Balfour Declaration to become the dominant force in Eretz Israel and effect the shape of the new state. Now that the balance of power had shifted within the Yishuv, the vision of a Torah state would not come to fruition any time soon.[101] As far as Breuer was concerned, withdrawal from the state was absolutely not an option, and the situation did not resemble that of Germany seventy years early. Withdrawing from the Jewish state is not the same as separating from the Jewish community in Germany:

> Faced with the imminent prospect of the formation of a Jewish state, we must beware not to indulge in the luxury of restrained theorizing in discussing the ideology and constitution of a Jewish state. Instead, on the basis of concrete reality, we must seek clarification on these points: what should be the structure of the Jewish state; what can be accomplished; what must be accomplished; what may be left to future efforts. There can be no doubt that the Jewish state will fall short of our Torah-ideals. While it is possible to counteract an assimilationist community with the creation of a second, independent community, we must realize that we cannot oppose an equally defective state by the formation of a second, independent, and "ideal" state.[102]

All that was left to the supporters of Agudat Israel was to influence Jewish society in the state, when it came into being, in order to accept the vision and make sure that every Jew could live there according to his religious faith, without secular coercion, and in fact to ensure broad communal autonomy for the Torah observant public. Such autonomy would allow for the need to attain compromises with the secular majority regarding the character of the state and legitimize a state that does not accord with the Torah vision. This issue formed the basis of the status quo agreement reached with Agudat Israel and the leadership of the national institutions on the eve of the establishment of the state.[103]

And yet, in his last book *Nahliel*, which he wrote in the final year of his life as the platform for the ideal Torah state to which we should aspire and educate, Breuer describes the characteristics of his visionary state, its institutions, and law and how it essentially differs from the modern state:

> A sovereign state whose laws come to it from outside, apart from it, from Mount Sinai, from the Creator: how difficult it is to explain the characteristics of such a state to the nations of the world! How difficult it is to explain it to the straying people of our nation! They cannot understand something unique in history, and therefore they are always seeking other historic phenomena similar to that of Judaism. Exert yourself and you shall find—priesthood, the clerical regime, the Catholic church.[104] Once you have found this bed, make haste to take the visionary state, chop it up, castrate it, and destroy it, until its dimen-

> sions perfectly match those of the bed you have made. But know that that which you lay upon the bed is nothing but—a bruised corpse.[105]

Once again, he elucidates that the scientific method of legal and religious study is completely irrelevant. It is essential to understand the laws of Israel, and although he appreciates the legal knowledge he acquired in German universities, and he esteems and respects the conceptual clarity and functionality of Roman law and the sense of justice of modern law, nevertheless: "It is crucial that according to the Jewish Torah law is metaphysical, whereas according to the nations the law is a matter of physics, of statehood, of state priests or secular institutions, of political benefit, and even—in normal times—of individual morality."[106]

In Breuer's visionary Torah state, not only is there no place for reforms or new halakhic rulings devised to suit halakha to the modern reality, even old rulings that circumvented Torah prohibitions will be annulled. In this way the original halakhic status, which is a faithful expression of God's will, will be restored. The prozbul and *heter iska* will be invalidated and the economy of the Torah state will return to its earliest principles, where labor is productive and money is futile, since it has only contractual substance and no concreteness:

> What are we? Where is our state, the Torah state which alone can regulate our national economy according to the laws of Torah, according to the laws of the futility of money, until there is no need to shirk those laws that show us the glory and elegance of the Torah? What remains of its glory and elegance? A *shtar iska* (bill of transaction)! Alas we have sinned. We have no Torah state nor do we have a Torah economy! May the Almighty have mercy on us and once again take us out of Egypt to give us the land of Canaan, to be our God. [ . . . ] There is no mighty fanfare in a *prosbul*. It is a weak voice. May the Almighty grant us His commandments and His blessing.[107]

Breuer's outlook was more radical than that of Rabbi Abraham Yeshayahu Karelitz (*Hazon Ish* 1878–1953), the religious leader of the Lithuanian haredim in the Land of Israel, who was also adamantly opposed to the institution of new rulings in his time, but he was not restricted to the rulings of previous generations. His objections stemmed mainly from his attitude toward his own generation, which he regarded as spiritually orphaned, without the authority to institute new rulings. The Hazon Ish expressed his opposition to two matters in which the rabbis advocated new rulings: the establishment of a fast day to mark the Holocaust and a ruling regarding inheritance which bestowed the same rights on daughters as on sons.[108] In his words, "How dare we, a generation that would do well to remain silent, think of such a thing, to set things down for generations to come."[109] He went on to say, "For we are an orphaned generation, we are not worthy to institute rulings, which only Torah greatness can aspire to. [ . . . ] How dare we be so stiff-necked as to say that we are wise, that we have the power to forfeit money and lay down rulings for future generations."[110]

Similarly, regarding social frameworks such as slavery that have departed from the world and are universally condemned, there is room in Breuer's Torah state to resurrect the ancient laws of Israel:

> The Torah has entrusted the slave relationship between one man and another in the hands of the Jewish people, out of a belief that the Jewish people, who are taught and sanctified by its commandments, will not exploit this relationship, that is liable to destroy the image of all humanity unless the Creator always stands between the master and his slave.[111]

Discrimination against minorities also remains in place, as in ancient times. Their status is that of a *ger toshav* (a non-Jew living in the land of Israel who accepts the Noahide laws) and they cannot be appointed to positions of authority, "and there is no such thing as 'tolerance' or 'intolerance,' or excessive nationalism, or the deification of race. None of these concepts are appropriate for this state, which is in its entirety holy unto God."[112]

Unlike Freimann, who sought to collate all the rulings of the communities up to recent times, in order to derive halakha pertaining to all modern aspects of society, economics, and politics, Breuer based his halakhic dispensation of everything relating to modern society and economy mainly on the *Mishne Torah* of Maimonides. This was practically the only halakhic source on which he based his final book, *Nahliel*, regarding his utopian state. The anthology proposed by Freimann also constitutes a part of the offensive Wissenschaft des Judentums and historicization of halakha, and therefore it has no place in Breuer's method.

While Freimann and Breuer dealt with the same issues, they did not react to one another's opinions. Freimann's ideas were publicized on several academic and Torah-research platforms, whereas Breuer published his theories as political and Torah-philosophy proposals.

In effect, Freimann and Breuer presented two diametrically opposed ways for Orthodox thinkers to grapple with the question of halakha and the challenge of sovereignty. Freimann sought to apply Torah law to the state, and to this end he utilized methods derived from critical study. He prepared the ground for the changes and adjustments required so that halakha would properly suit a sovereign, modern reality, most of whose citizens do not recognize its authority, seeking instead to establish the laws of the state by themselves. He wanted to reinstate the institution of regulations in the framework of the Chief Rabbinate, in order to adjust halakha to the new reality, paving the way for a representative parliamentary institution as a legitimate legislative institution in all matters that do not go against the Torah.

Breuer, on the other hand, held fast to an inflexible utopian halakhic outlook fiercely opposed to any historicization of halakha. For him, the early Orthodox instinct to reject reform of any kind was elevated to an even higher metaphysical level than it was for his grandfather, Rabbi Samson Raphael Hirsch. Any possibility of renewing halakha was tightly sealed. Realizing that the balance of power in the Yishuv made it impossible for the haredim to impose their halakhic worldview on the secular community, he focused on enabling religious Jews to live in a Jewish state according to halakha, free of secular coercion, by means of broad community autonomy.[113]

According to the research of Alexander Kaye, Freimann represents a pluralistic attitude to law. He maintains the idea that Jewish sovereignty may have within it a plurality of legal regimes and a plurality of legitimate sources of legal authority. This position had the advantage that it was able to preserve a distinction between current halakha and the state, thereby avoiding the imposition of current halakha on people who did not recognize its authority and preventing the imposition of radical modifications on halakha in order to engineer its accommodation with the requirements of modern law. Breuer represents the legal philosophy of legal centralism, which maintained that all legal authority in the state must derive from a single source of authority—the current halakha.[114]

Despite the fact that these two men shared a vision of statehood based on Torah law, the policies they envisaged were poles apart. Ranged between them were many Orthodox thinkers with varying opinions regarding the degree of halakhic flexibility for our time, the correlation between the ideal and the reality when it came to integrating halakha into the laws of the state, and what was required to change this correlation. Prominent among them was Rabbi Isaac Halevy Herzog, who was chief rabbi at the time. He delved intensively into the issue of halakha and sovereign reality, attempting to anchor his halakhic decisions in a manner that would be acceptable to all parties, as far as possible.[115] His approach to the study of Jewish law stood somewhere between the positions of Freimann and Breuer.[116]

## NOTES

1. Y. Y. Yehoshafat, "Hit'hadshut ha-Mishpat (Legal renewal)," *Ha-Mishpat ha-'Ivri* 2 (1927): 2.

2. Asher Gulak, "Le-Sidur Hayenu ha-Mishpatiyim ba-Arets (On Organizing our Legal Life in Palestine)," *Ha-Toren*, 33-34 (1930/1), repr. in Jacob Bazak, ed., *Ha-Mishpat ha-'Ivri u-Medinat Yisra'el: Leket Ma'amarim* (Jerusalem: Mossad Harav Kook, 1969), 28.

3. Assaf Likhovski, "The Invention of 'Hebrew law' in Mandatory Palestine," *American Journal of Comparative Law* 46,2 (1998): 339–373; Joseph David, "The 'Jewish Law' Vision: Background, Trends and Aspirations," in Ravitzky, *Religion and State*, 77–113.

4. Daykan, *Toldot*, 25; Abraham Isaac Kook, *Iggrot haReaya*, II (Jerusalem: Mossad Harav Kook, 1961), 9–0, 211–12.On this term, see: Amihai Radzyner, "'Hefqer Bet-Din

Hefqer' (the Court has the Power to Expropriate) in Talmudic Sources," *Sidra: A Journal for the Study of Rabbinic Literature* 16 (2000): 11–133.

5. Maimonides, *Hilchot Sanhedrin*, 24: 6; *Shulchan Aruch*, Hoshen Mishpat, 2.

6. Ha-Ma'arekhet, "Te'udatenu (Our Goal)," *Ha-Mishpat ha-Ivri: Riv'on Mada'i* 1 (1918): 6.

7. Amihai Radzyner, "'Jewish Law' between 'National' and 'Religious': The Dilemma of the Religious-National Movement," *Bar-Ilan Law Studies*, 26 (2010): 148–50.

8. Ibid., 91–178.

9. "Takanot Hevrat 'ha-Mishpat ha-'Ivri' be-Erets Yisra'el (Regulations of the "Hebrew Law Society" in Palestine)," *Ha-Mishpat ha-'Ivri* 1 (1926): 206.

10. Y. Junovits, "Al ha-Sifriyah ha-Mishpatit (On the Legal Library)," in Simcha Assaf, *Ha-Onshin Ahare Hatimat ha-Talmud* (Jerusalem: HaSifria HaMishpatit, 1921/2), 5–6.

11. Dickstein, "Review: Kitve M. Z. Rapaport al ha-Mishpat ha-'Ivri," *He-Avar* 1 (1918): 199.

12. Dickstein, "She'elat ha-'Ona 'ah be-Mishpat ha-Shalom ha-'Ivri (The Question of Fraud in the Hebrew Courts of Arbitration)," *Ha-Mishpat ha-'Ivri* 1 (1925/6): 150.

13. Ibid.

14. Ibid., 151.

15. Likhovski, "The Invention," 367.

16. G. Frumkin, "Disabilities of Women under Jewish Law—Can they be Remedied?" *Journal of Comparative Legislation and International Law* 3rd Ser. Vol. 12 (November 1930): 277.

17. "Al HaVe'idah HaMishpatit HaIvrit HaOlamit (On the Universal Hebrew Judicial Conference)," *Ha'aretz*, March 23, 1934.

18. Radzyner, "Jewish Law," 162–76.

19. "Da'at HaRav Kook Shlita al ha-Ve'idah ha-Mishpatit (The opinion of Rabbi Kook on the juridical conference)," *HaTor* 14 (April 1934): 11.

20. *HaTor* 8 (May 1928): 1.

21. Simcha Assaf, *Bate ha-Din ve-Sidrehem Ahare Hatimat ha-Talmud* (Jerusalem 1923/4), 6–9.

22. Simcha Assaf, *Ha-Onshin Ahare Hatimat ha- Talmud* (Jerusalem: HaSifria HaMishpatit, 1921/2), 12.

23. Ibid., 12–15.

24. Radzyner, "Jewish Law," 133–44.

25. On this, see: Amihai Radzyner, "The Origins of Procedural Regulations for Rabbinical Courts: 'Takkanot Ha-Diyun' 1943," *Dine Israel* 25 (2008): 185–260.

26. I. E. Herzog, *Tehuqah leYisrael Al-Pi haTorah*, vol. 3, (Jerusalem: Yad Harav Herzog, 1989), 109–58.

27. A letter from A. C. Freimann to Gershom Scholem, Adar I 5687, The National Library of Israel Archives (NLI), Gershom Scholem Collection, ARC. 4* 1599.

28. Ibid.

29. A. C. Freimann, "Die Ascheriden (The Descendants of Asheri)," *Jahrbuch der Juedisch- Literarischen Gesellschaft* 13 (1920): 198–99.

30. This method was like Simchah Assaf's method. On this, see: Radzyner, "Jewish Law," 136–42.

31. Ibid., 140.

32. Assaf Yedidya, "Benjamin Menashe Levin and Orthodox *Wissenschaft des Judentums*," *Cathedra*, 130 (2008): 103–28.

33. A. C. Freimann, *Seder Kiddushin ve-Nissu'in Aharei Hatimat ha-Talmud: Mehkar Histori-Dogmati be-Dinei Yisra'el* (Jerusalem: Mossad Harav Kook, 1945), 6.

34. Idem, "Mezonot Shel Yeled she-Nolad she-lo be-Nissu'in al pi Dinei Yisra'el (Maintenance of a Child Born out of Wedlock, According to Jewish Law)," *Ha-Praklit* 2 (1945): 173.

35. Asaf Yedidya, "The Nazi Attacks on the Talmud and the Apologetic Responses of the Jews in Germany and Austria in the 1930s," *Search and Research* 25 (2016): 45–54.

36. For historical and legal review of the Sages' Regulations, see Elon, *Jewish Law*, 643–65, 780–879.
37. Rabbi Avraham Isaac HaCohen Kook addresses the Conference of the Chief Rabbinate in Eretz Israel. In Morgenstern, *Ha-Rabbanut ha-Rashit*, 180.
38. Radzyner, "Rabbi Uziel," 132–37.
39. A. C. Freimann, "Ha-Takanot Ha-Hadashot Shel Ha-Rabbanut ha-Rashit le-Erez Yisra'el be-Dinei Ishut (The New Enactments of the Chief Rabbinate of Israel on Family Law)," *Sinai*, 14 (1944): 254.
40. Ibid., 263.
41. Freimann, *Seder*, 5.
42. Ibid.
43. Ibid.
44. Ibid., 6. On continuity and changes in the Jewish communities in the Islamic countries, see: Zvi Zohar, *The Luminous Face of the East: Studies in the Legal and Religious Thought of Sephardic Rabbis of the Middle East* (Tel Aviv: Hakibbutz Hameuchad-Sifriat Poalim Publishing Group, 2001), 77–195, 183–298; Yosef Tobi, "The Organization of the Jewish Communities in the East in the 19-20th Centuries, " in *Kehal Yisrael: Jewish Self-Rule Through the Ages*, Vol. 3, ed. Israel Bartal (Jerusalem: Shazar Centre, 2004), 191–209.
45. On this problem, see: Aviad HaCohen, *The Tears of the Oppressed: an Examination of the Agunah problem: Background and Halachic Sources* (New York: KTAV Publishing House, 2004); Michael J. Broyde, *Marriage, Divorce and the Abandoned Wife in the Jewish Law* (New York: KTAV Publishing House, 2000); David J.Bleich, "Survey of Recent Halachik Periodical Literature: A 19th Century 'Agunah' Problem and a 20th Century Application," *Tradition*, 38, 2 (2004): 15–48.
46. Freimann, *Seder*, 385.
47. Ibid., 396–97.
48. Ibid., 397. On Rabbi Uziel's approach to the authority of High Rabbinical Court, see: Radzyner, "Rabbi Uziel," 161–64.
49. A. C. Freimann, "Dinei Yisra'el be-Erez Yisra'el" (Jewish Law in the Land of Israel)," *Lu'ah ha-Arez* (1946): 110.
50. Ibid., 118.
51. Ibid., 120.
52. Ibid., 121.
53. Ibid., 122.
54. Ibid., 121–22.
55. Ibid., p. 122. On *Takanot Hakahal*, see: B. Lipkin, "Shittot ha-Rishonim be-Takkanot ha-Kahal (The Approach of the *Rishonim* to Communal Enactments," *Ha-Torah ve-ha-Medinah* 2 (1950): 41–54; Louis Finkelstein, *Jewish Self Government in the Middle Ages* (New York: The Jewish Theological Seminary of America, 1964); Ephraim Kanarfogel, "Unanimity, majority, and communal government in Ashkenaz during the high Middle Ages: a reassessment," *Proceedings—American Academy for Jewish Research*, 58 (1992): 79–106 ;Elon, *Jewish Law*, 678–779; Idem, "On Power and Authority: The Halakhic Stance of the Traditional Community and Its Contemporary Implications." In Elazar, *Kinship & Consent*, 293–326; Y. S. Kaplan, "The Public Welfare," *Dine Israel*, 17 (1993–4): 27–91; Idem, "The Status and Authority of Communal Leaders in the Middle Ages," *Dine Israel*, 18 (1995–6): 255–319.
56. Freimann, "Dinei Yisra'el," 125.
57. A. C. Freimann, "Darkhei ha-Hakikah be-Yisra'el (The Methodology of Jewish Legislation)," *Yavneh* 1 (1946): 43.
58. Actually, Rabbi Chaim Hirschenson had already evaluated the importance of *Takanot Hakahal* to the democratic character of halakha, although he did not centralize them, as well as Freimann. Hirschenson, *Malki Bakodesh*, vol. 3, 68–76.
59. Elon, *Jewish Law*, 681–85; A. Gulak, *Yesodei ha-Mishpat ha-'Ivri* (Jerusalem 1923), 50–52; S. Albeck, *The Law of Property and Contract in the Talmud* (Tel Aviv: Dvir, 1976), 504–16. Elon maintained that communal enactments were only interpreted by our

Sages as public law from the tenth century. Elon, "On Power and Authority," 11–12. Freimann also disregards the fact that several Rishonim disputed the two terms that appear in Tannaic literature regarding communal enactments: "*kofin*," suited to public law and "*rasha'in*," suited to private law. Kaplan, "To'elet Hatzibur," 41–47.

60. Freimann did not foresee the discrepancy between the limited authority of the public (which functioned with limited autonomy within the larger state) and the wider authority of a sovereign state. But in referring to the Social Contract principle, he assisted in establishing the legal principle which is valid in both cases. On this, see: Benjamin Porat, "Five Jewish Terms of Israeli Democracy," in idem, ed., *Reflections on Jewish Democracy* (Jerusalem: Israel Democracy Institute, 2009), 19–20.

61. On different aspects of majority and minority in communal decisions in the Middle Ages, see: Y. S. Kaplan, "Majority and Minority in the Decisions of the Jewish Community in the Middle Ages," *Annual of the Institute for Research in Jewish Law* 20 (1996–7): 213–80.

62. A. C. Freimann, "Rov u-Mi'ut ba-Zibbur (Majority and Minority in the Community)," *Yavneh* 2 (Tishri 1948): 1.

63. Ibid., 5.

64. Ibid., 4. On this debate, see: Shilo, *Girls of Liberty*.

65. Freimann, "Rov u-Mi'ut ba-Zibbur," 5.

66. Jacob Katz, "The Controversy on the Semikha (Ordination) between Rabbi Jacob Bei-Rav and the Ralbah," *Zion*, 16, 3–4 (1951): 28–45; Meir Benayahu, "The Revival of Ordination in Safed," in *Yitzhak F. Baer Jubilee Volume*, eds. S. W. Baron and others (Jerusalem: The Historical Society of Israel, 1960), 248–69; Shlomo Zalman Havlin. "The Ralbah," *Jeschurun*, 11 (2002): 884–900; 14 (2004): 997–1011.

67. Freimann, "Rov u-Mi'ut ba-Zibbur," 6.

68. See: Isaac Breuer, *Mein Weg* (Jerusalem: Mossad Yitzhaq Breuer, 1988); idem, *Concepts of Judaism: Isaac Breuer*, ed. Jacob S. Levinger (Jerusalem: Israel Universities Press, 1974); Matthias Morgenstern, *From Frankfurt to Jerusalem: Isaac Breuer and the History of the Secession Dispute in Modern Jewish Orthodoxy* (Leiden: Brill, 2002); Alan L. Mittleman, *Between Kant and Kabbalah: An Introduction to Isaac Breuer's Philosophy of Judaism* (Albany:

69. Isaac Breuer, *Messiasspuren* (Frankfurt am Main: R. L. Hammon, 1918); idem, *Mein Weg*, 106–09.

70. Isaac Breuer, "The Philosophical Foundations of Jewish and of Modern Law," in idem, *Concepts of Judaism*, 61.

71. On the approach of Rabbi Hirschensohn to the correct halakhic attitude toward women and minorities, see: Hirschensohn, *Malki BaKodesh*, vol. 2, 192; idem, *Eileh Divrei HaBrit*, vol. 1, 5–6; Zohar, *Jewish Commitment World*, 192–93.

72. On this distinction, see more: Amos Israel-Vleeschhouwer, "A Jewish Ultra Orthodox Critique of Nationalism Individualism and Rights-Based Regimes: The Alternative Model and Thought of Yitzhak Breuer," *HaMishpat: Law Review* 15, 2 (2010): 636–41.

73. Breuer, *Concepts of Judaism*, 75–76.

74. On continuity and change in Breuer's ideology as compared to that of S. R. Hirsch, see: Benjamin Brown, "Breuer, Hirsch and Jewish Nationalism: Change and Continuity—Principle versus Supra-Principle," *Journal of Jewish Studies*, 64 (2013): 383–402.

75. S. R. Hirsch, "Wie gewinnen wir das Leben für unsere Wissenschaft?" *Jeschurun* 8 (1861), 88. (trans. in: Breuer *Modernity*,178).

76. Breuer, *Modernity*, 179.

77. On Breuer's opposition to historicism, see: David N. Myers, *Resisting History: Historicism and Its Discontents in German-Jewish Thought* (Princeton: Princeton University Press, 2003), 130–56.

78. Breuer, *Mein Weg*, 66–68.

79. A. Yedidya, "Orthodox Reactions to *Wissenschaft des Judentums*," *Modern Judaism* 30 (2010): 69–94.

80. Yedidya, "Benjamin Menashe Levin," 150.
81. A. C. Freimann, "Critique of E. M. Epstein, Marriage Laws in the Bible and the Talmud," *Kiryat Sefer* 23 (1947): 109.
82. Meyer, *Response to Modernity*, 91.
83. Abraham Berliner, *Randbemerkungen zum tagelichen Gebetbuch* (Berlin: M. Poppelauer, 1909), 14–16.
84. David Zvi Hoffmann, *Der Schulchan-Aruch und die Rabbinen über das erhältnis der juden zu Adersgläubigen* (Berlin 1885), 4–7. On *HaMe'iri's* stand see chapter 3.
85. A. C. Freimann, "Die Behandlung der Volksfremden bei den Juden," *Mitteilungsblatt des Juedischen Volksrats* 8 (1919): 102–03.
86. Hirsch's apologetics focused on promoting a moral attitude to non-Jews, by selectively quoting supporting texts and presenting the principal position of loyal Jewish behavior in the exile, under the "*midrash* of the three oaths."
87. S. R. Hirsch, *The Hirsch Siddur: The Order of Prayers for the whole Year* (Jerusalem: Feldheim Publishers, 1978), 13.
88. Ibid.
89. Breuer, *Concepts of Judaism*, 61–62.
90. Meir Seidler, "Isaac Breuer's Concept of law," *Jewish Law Association Studies*, 8 (2000): 167–71.
91. Isaac Breuer, "The Great Turning," in: idem, *Concepts of Judaism*, 310–11.
92. Elon, *Jewish Law*, 1613.
93. I. Breuer, "Tokhnit la-Hukkah ba-Medinah ha-Yehudit (A Constitutional Program for the Jewish State)," *Yavneh* 3 (Nissan 1949): 33–40.
94. Ibid.
95. Ibid.
96. Breuer, *Mein Weg*, 254.
97. Ibid., 117.
98. Shuki Friedman and Amichai Radzyner, *The Religious Community and the Constitution: What Can History Teach Us?* (Jerusalem: Israel Democracy Institute, 2006), 29–30.
99. Quoted in: Isaac Levin, ed., *Material for the Preparation of a Constitution for the Jewish State on a Religious Basis* (New York: Research Institute for Post-War Problems of Religious Jewry, 1948), 5.
100. Isaac Breuer, *Weltwende* (Jerusalem: Mossad Yitzhaq Breuer, 1979). This book contains two long articles, written in 1938 and 1942.
101. Yossef Fund, *Separation or Participation: Agudat Israel Confronting Zionism and the State of Israel* (Jerusalem: Magnes Press, 1999), 39–41.
102. Isaac Breuer, "Jewish State and Torah-Front," in *Fundamentals of Judaism*, ed. Jacob Breuer (New York: Kessinger Publishing, LLC, 1969), 264.
103. On this, see: Menachem Friedman, "The structural foundation for religio-political accommodation in Israel: fallacy and reality," in *Israel— the First Decade of Independence*, eds. S. Ilan Troen and Noah Lucas (Albany: State University of New York Press, 1995), 51–81; Charles Liebman and Eliezer Don-Yehiya, *Religion and Politics in Israel* (Bloomington: Indiana University Press, 1984), Ch. 3.
104. Historical examples of religious regimes.
105. Isaac Breuer, *Nahaliel* (Jerusalem: Mossad Yitzhaq Breuer, 1951), 311.
106. Ibid., 314.
107. Ibid., 328–30.
108. Benjamin Brown, *The Hazon Ish: Halakhist, Believer and Leader of the Haredi Revolution* (Jerusalem: Magnes press, 2011), 668–77; Idem, "'Let Us Not Be Presumptuous': The Hazon Ish's Opposition to Commemoration of the Holocaust," in *When Disaster Comes from Afar: Leading Personalities in the Land of Israel Confront Nazism and the Holocaust, 1933–1948*, ed. Dina Porat (Jerusalem: Yad Ben-Zvi Press, 2009), 210–34.
109. Abraham Yeshayahu Karelitz, *Kovetz Iggrot* (Jerusalem: HaMassorah, 1955), 113.
110. Ibid., 112.

111. Breuer, *Nahaliel*, 353. See also Hirsch's idealization of the institution of the Hebrew slave in "the Torah State." S. R. Hirsch, *The Pentateuch—with Translation and Commentary* (New York: Judaica Press, 1962), Leviticus 25, 41.

112. Breuer, *Nahaliel*, 375.

113. Indeed Freimann, too, has claimed in his last article that the principal of defending the minorities' rights as per their religious courts system, which supervise family laws and personal status, requires the continued existence of rabbinical courts with parallel authority to those of the minorities, otherwise "it would be absurd if the Jewish State supports Moslem and Christian religious courts but cancels the Jewish ones—something which is analogous to Jewish religious persecution in the Jewish State." A. C. Freimann, "Batei ha-Din ha-Rabbani'im ba-Medina ha-Yehudit (The Rabbinical Courts in the Jewish State)," *Yavneh* 3 (Nissan 1949): 124–25.

114. Kaye, "The Legal Philosophies."

115. Herzog, *Tehuqah leYisrael*, 1–3.

116. Kaye, ibid., 106–88.

# FIVE

# The Rabbinical Debate on the Eve of the Establishment of the State of Israel and in its Early Years (1947–1953)

## THE CHIEF RABBINATE OF ISRAEL: HALAKHA IN THE GRIP OF DEMOCRACY

On November 29, 1947, the UN General Assembly accepted Resolution 181. It stated that a Jewish state and an Arab state would be created in the territory of the Land of Israel. Among other things, the resolution required that each state accept a democratic constitution, according to a detailed outline, by October 1, 1948. The constitution would include, inter alia:

> A guarantee that all persons will have equal and nondiscriminatory rights in civil, political, economic and religious matters and will enjoy human rights and fundamental freedoms, including freedom of religion, language, speech and publication, education, assembly and association; [ . . . ]
>
> No discrimination of any kind shall be made between the inhabitants on the grounds of race, religion, language or sex.[1]

Approximately one week later, the provisional government imposed on jurist Dr. Leo Cohen, secretary of the Political Department of the Jewish Agency Executive, the task of drawing up the draft of the constitution.[2] The Council of the Chief Rabbinate, for its part, asked Ashkenazi chief Rabbi Yitzhak Isaac Halevy Herzog (1888–1959) to prepare a draft of the constitution that would reflect the halakhic position on various subjects.[3]

Yitzhak Halevy Herzog was born in Łomża, Poland. His family moved to the United Kingdom in 1898 and settled in Leeds. His father, who was a rabbi in Leeds, was his primary Talmud teacher. He studied at the Sorbonne and then at the University of London, where he received his doctorate. His thesis, which made him famous in the Jewish world, concerned his claim of re-discovering *tekhelet*, the type of blue dye once used for making tzitzit. Herzog served as rabbi of Belfast from 1916–1919 and was appointed rabbi of Dublin in 1919. He was the first chief rabbi of Ireland (1921–1936). From 1936 until his death in 1959, he held the position of Ashkenazi chief rabbi of the British Mandate of Palestine and of Israel after its independence in May 1948.[4]

Rabbi Herzog undertook the task he had been entrusted with. The document he drew up endeavored to reconcile halakha with the democratic constitution specified by the UN resolution, as far as possible. In an article published in *Yavneh* in 1948 he explained the rationale underlying his proposal:

> Religious Jewry in this country and in the Diaspora must aspire to a constitution that includes the basic provision that the legal system of the Land of Israel is based on the fundamental principles of the Torah. However, in order for such a provision to be acceptable to a large part of the population of the Land of Israel (who are far from knowledgeable about the Torah and, to our sorrow, so remote from our sacred tradition, that they believe that the Torah and democracy are inconsistent), it is essential at this time to work out a proposal for a legal system that will take into account the democratic nature of the state. This is also essential because the State will be established under a resolution of the United Nations, which calls for a state founded on democratic principles, and because a considerable and important minority of the citizens of the State will be non-Jews, so that although the State will be a Jewish state it will include, in no small measure, non-Jews as well as Jews.[5]

He understood that without some compromise of this sort between halakha and basic democratic values, there was no possibility that the Jewish population of Eretz Israel would have a constitution that was faithful to halakha, and the result would be a constitution diametrically opposed to Torah. Such an outcome would cause irreversible damage, deepening the animosity between the religious and secular segments of the population to a rift that could never be mended. Although he conceded that the chances that his proposal would be accepted were slim, he nevertheless made every effort to complete it. In 1948, he wrote as follows to religious jurist Dr. Mordecai Eliash:

> Following the decision of the Council of the Chief Rabbinate, I took upon myself the task of preparing a proposal for a constitution based on Torah, and a legal proposal with ordinances and supplements that accord with the democratic character of the state, within a Torah framework. Both proposals will be submitted to the Audit Committee appointed by the Rabbinical Council, in consultation with Torah sages

> who are not members of the Council or even of the Knesset, along with legal experts, among whom you yourself will hold the prominent position you deserve. There is a rumor that, due to pressure brought to bear by many lawyers and outspoken secular members of the public, the chances of these proposals being accepted are insultingly small at the moment. They are even proposing to institute secular marriages and divorces and to take away our legal authority, including the personal law granted by the gentile government. I have it from a reliable source that the optimal Jewish Agency proposal offers a compromise whereby every individual can marry and divorce either according to Jewish law or according to the law of the government, which is not Jewish law. Even this compromise proposal, if it should come to pass, God forbid, will ultimately split the nation in such a way that religious Judaism will be forced, wrathfully and against its will, to erect a dividing wall separating us from the rest of the nation, refusing to marry our daughters to them or taking their daughters as wives. May the Merciful One preserve us from such a situation![6]

In the first chapter of his proposal Rabbi Herzog discusses the nature of the appropriate regime according to halakha. He negates the possibility of appointing a king, or proposing priestly rule at this time, bringing rabbinical sources to bolster his argument. He suggests that members of the Sanhedrin were elected through a kind of democratic election. He also refers to the institution of the "seven dignitaries," a form of democratically elected local leadership that adopted the opinion of the rabbinical authorities, headed by Rabbi Meir of Rothenburg, that "every taxpayer, whether he be rich or poor, has the right to elect the seven dignitaries." [7] He concludes his historical halakhic review with the words: "The Israeli state in its traditional framework is not entirely theocratic, nor is it entirely democratic, but rather nomocratic. It has the power to expand and adapt, especially in monetary affairs, but in matters of criminal law, too, the Jewish constitution has a great deal of flexibility." [8]

## THE STATUS OF NON-JEWISH MINORITIES

The main issue that Rabbi Herzog had to contend with was the status of non-Jewish minorities in the sovereign Jewish state.[9] The UN resolution explicitly forbade any form of religious or political discrimination. However, halakhically some laws discriminate between Jews and non-Jews. First and foremost, halakha states that a gentile resident cannot be accepted in a Jewish state, if the laws of the Jubilee do not apply. Secondly, there is an injunction forbidding the sale of land in Eretz Israel to non-Jews. Thirdly, one is forbidden to observe idolatrous rituals in Eretz Israel, an edict which apparently infringes upon the religious freedom of Catholic Christians. And finally, it is forbidden to appoint a non-Jew to a public position, in keeping with the verse: "You may not place over yourself a foreigner who is not your brother."[10] Neither can a gentile judge be appointed, in keeping with the injunction not to be judged according to gentile values.

Unlike Rabbi Margolies, Rabbi Herzog did not follow a legal track that paralleled the halakhic track of the "laws of the monarchy." Similar proposals were raised on the eve of the establishment of the state by two young rabbis, Shlomo Goren[11] and Moshe Zvi Neria, but they were rejected by Rabbi Herzog.[12] He explicitly rejected the method of the Ran (Rabbenu Nissim of Gerona):

> With respect to my efforts to solve the problem of bringing Torah law into correspondence with a democratic Jewish state, I anticipate puzzlement: Why all this effort? One of the later medieval authorities, Rabbenu Nissim [Gerondi] of blessed memory, has already provided the solution. In his *Derashot,* sermon XI, Ran presumes that there are two kinds of law in Israel, the law of Torah and the law of the state, or royal law [in a monarchy]. According to the laws of the Torah, a criminal would rarely be punished and a murderer would easily go free. There exist similar difficulties with regard to monetary laws because of the laws of testimony. [So] royal law serves to complete Torah law.[13] [ . . . ] I maintain my position that it is inconceivable that the laws of the Torah should allow for two parallel authorities—like the courts of law and the courts of equity, the latter stemming from the authority of royal law that operated in the past in England. According to [Torah law], there is no basis for this assumption of double or parallel jurisdiction of two authorities.[14]

Alexander Kaye claimed that Herzog departed from the Ran's legal pluralism and sharply opposed the notion that the Jewish constitution might accommodate multiple legal systems. The Jewish state, he argued, had to be a centralized, all-encompassing regime with a single legal hierarchy that incorporated all valid law in the state. He was aware to the European intellectual discourse, which celebrated centralism and positivism and looked down upon religious law and the pluralistic legal models of colonial societies. Furthermore, he knew that halakha would only have a chance of being made into the law of a new Jewish state if it was viewed as the equal of modern European law. He therefore took great pains to describe Jewish law in positivist terms, rejecting the legal pluralism of many of his religious Zionist colleagues and taking every opportunity to demonstrate parallels between the ancient Jewish constitution, as he portrayed it, and the constitutions of modern Europe.[15]

Rabbi Herzog sought to solve the question of the non-Jewish minority through traditional halakha. He did so by making a fundamental distinction between full sovereign reality, where these laws applied, and partial sovereign reality, halakhically defined as where "the hand of Israel does not decide"[16] and it is therefore not possible to implement these laws. He maintained that since the establishment of the State of Israel came about through a United Nations resolution, we are in a kind of partnership with non-Jews in this regard, and therefore we are not free to enact laws that discriminate against non-Jews:

> The commandments under discussion are public commandments. They are not addressed to particular individuals but to the governing body, [that is,] to a Jewish government, whatever its formal [regime], that is powerful enough to discharge them. These commandments were originally addressed to the Jewish people conquering the land, who became sovereign over it independently of the [other] nations [goyim]. These are the Torah's background assumptions with regard to these commandments, as is self-evident. In the absence of this background and given the realistic circumstances whereby this state is given [to us], under this condition [of minority rights and freedom of worship], these commandments do not apply. Such is the case in exile, or even in the Land of Israel "when the gentile's power is predominant."[17]

From Rabbi Herzog's remarks concerning partial sovereignty, cooperation with the local Arabs, and the need for the model of seven dignitaries, Chaim Burgansky concludes that Rabbi Herzog related to the State of Israel as if it were a large overseas community, making it possible for him to deviate from the laws of a Torah state.[18] In my opinion, this is not necessarily the case because Rabbi Herzog, like other rabbis, based his practical decision on a large number of halakhic sources without considering the structural differences between them.

Moreover, Rabbi Herzog sought to justify a comparison between the status of non-Jews in the Jewish state and that of Jews, basing himself on halakhic minority views in order to strengthen the Yishuv in Eretz Israel, and he was in the correct position to do so. "Seeing that this attitude of discrimination may endanger the achievement of the Jewish state or cause havoc thereafter, Go-d forbid, we must rely on the lenient opinion."[19] This was in keeping with the path outlined by Rabbi Kook in his ruling on *Heter Mechira* in a *Shmitta* year, as we have seen. It was based on the opinion of Rabbi Abraham ben David, and Rabbi Yosef Karo's commentary on Maimonides *Kesef Mishne* (hilchot avoda zara, chapter 10:6), which states that although a gentile is not accepted if the laws of the jubilee year do not apply, nevertheless he is not forbidden to settle in the land, so long as he is not an idolater. He bases himself on the responsa of Rabbi Kook (Mishpat Kohen, laws of Shmita and *yovel,* clause 63) that the injunction "you should not have pity" does not apply to Muslim Arabs, who are collectively regarded as non-idolaters, although they are not *gerim toshavim* in the full halachic sense. He also brings the opinion of Rabbi Zeev Wolf Halevy Baskowitz (*Seder hamishna al Harambam, Hilchot yesodei Hatorah,1*) who says that since the sons of Noah were not forewarned not to worship idols along with the worship of one Go-d, they cannot be regarded as idolaters and there is no obligation to eradicate idolatry. And finally, he brings the opinion of Rabbi Chaim Benveniste (1603–1673) in his commentary on *Shulhan Arukh—Kenesset HaGedolah* (Choshen Mishpat, clause 7), according to which the restriction on appointing non-Jews to positions of authority does not apply in public matters. He added that it also does not apply in cases of appointments for a limited time, which are not inherited.[20]

The Rishon Letzion, Rabbi Ben-Zion Chai Uziel, relied on Rabbi Herzog's halakhic ruling on the status of minorities and accepted the principle he laid down, whereby Jewish sovereignty is not complete but involves association with non-Jews. Therefore, there cannot be discrimination between the partners, even if they are non-Jews. He also maintained that the appointment of non-Jews does not apply in the case of receiving the public, adding that "public policy for obtaining testimony is useful for preparing evidence from non-Jews on monetary and penal laws."[21]

He added, "If in all of the enlightened world a law has been accepted that a testimony will be believed without differentiation on the grounds of religion or race, how will we make such a difference?"[22] and even emphasized that the egalitarian attitude is "not only due to the conditions of statehood imposed on us by the United Nations, but due to our recognition and conscience, because it is the heritage of our fathers, and because the Torah commands us: love, respect, equality, and national and religious freedom for every nation and every person who dwells in our land in peace and loyalty."[23]

Rabbi Reuben Katz, rabbi of Petach Tikva and a member of the Chief Rabbinical Council, took a different view when it came to the public appointment of non-Jews. He claimed that according to halakha the restriction on appointing non-Jews to positions of authority applies only when the authority applies to Jews themselves and not to non-Jews. Therefore, it is possible to appoint Jews to positions of authority over their brethren. And if the principle here is that the appointment of non-Jews is intended for their community, then they can also be appointed to positions of authority over Jews, by inclusion.[24]

In order to circumvent the injunction "not to have mercy," Rabbi Katz took a different line. He based it on the story of the gifts of real estate exchanged by King Solomon and Hiram, King of Tyre. "For purposes of forging an alliance it is permissible to cede property in Eretz Israel if, in exchange, one receives property abroad. In such a case, the injunction 'not to have mercy' does not apply."[25] He regards this mutuality as a legal option for the Arab state to sell land to the Jews who live there:

> However, if we assume that the Arab state passes a law such as the discriminatory law of the British White Paper, which stipulates that it is forbidden for Jews to sell lands in their state, it will be necessary to enact a similar law within the borders of the Jewish state. This will ensure that the foundations of democracy are not harmed, since the

right to purchase land in both the Jewish state and the Arab state is contingent upon ethnic quality, both for obligations and for rights.[26]

## A DAUGHTER'S INHERITANCE

Rabbi Herzog also grappled with the question of daughter and widow inheritance. According to the Torah, a daughter cannot inherit from her father if she has brothers, and a woman cannot inherit from her husband. In the course of time, significant amendments were introduced beginning with the ketubah (marriage contract), through the sons' ketubah (ketubat benin dikrin)[27] and the enactment of "One-Tenth of the Estate"[28] and up to the deed for a son's half share (shetar hazi zakhar),[29] but daughters and widows were still discriminated against, compared to males.[30]

Following changes that were instituted the nineteenth century regarding inheritance laws in Western countries, along with women's struggle for equality, many women in the Jewish Yishuv in Eretz Israel demanded that their share of inheritance be equal to that of their brothers. During the mandate period the rabbinical court had the authority to arbitrate in matters of inheritance according to Torah law, but only if both parties agreed. In the event that one party refused to be involved in litigation in the rabbinical court, the case would be heard in the civil court, where, under mandatory law, the daughters' share of the inheritance equaled that of the sons. However, in the event that the litigating parties asked for judgment to be passed according to mandatory law instead of Jewish law, the rabbinical court complied, on the grounds that since the British government had the power to enforce the mandatory laws of inheritance on whomsoever they pleased, the rule that "the law of the land is the binding law" applied.[31]

Rabbi Herzog realized that public consent would not be forthcoming if any attempt was made to reverse the situation with regard to women's portion of inheritance. The majority of the public would not agree to any discrimination against women in this regard. If the rabbis insisted on arbitrating according to Jewish law, it would have two negative results. First of all, the abrogation of halakha and the introduction of an alien codex of law:

> The danger for our holy Torah and our holy religion is that the State, yielding to the overwhelming majority, will accept an alien codex of law. This will destroy us from within and it will be an affront to the Torah, it will be a great blasphemy, and it is our duty to prevent such a catastrophe. Clearly, a major factor here is gender discrimination with regard to inheritance.[32]

Secondly, the authority of the rabbinical courts would be weakened. During the mandate these courts were partially authorized to arbitrate on personal issues and matters of inheritance, as we have seen. Rabbi Herzog hoped that once the State was established, their powers would be expanded so they would be at least equal to the Muslim courts:

> For some months now the Chief Rabbinate of Eretz Israel has vehemently demanded that the government abolish the restrictions on rabbinical courts of law that have been with us since the Mandate government, on the subject of the diminishment of Personal Status. But despite all our efforts and despite the firm position taken by Rabbi Maimon, the Minister of Religion, we have not yet succeeded in motivating the government to equalize our authority with that of the Muslim courts. The main reason for this is the abovementioned discrimination.[33]

Therefore, in 1949 he wrote a pamphlet entitled "Proposed Regulations Regarding Inheritance" that dealt extensively with the need and possibility of introducing a religious ruling that would make women equal to men regarding inheritance. Since he was aware that he would be criticized for his proposal, he attempted to appease Israel's government and the secular public. Therefore, he explained his proposed regulation as an inherent need of religious Judaism:

> We are not attempting to make a deal with the government—saying we will amend the laws of inheritance if you give us the wider authority we are asking for. Not so! It is because we are aware of the reality, and we know that instituting these amendments will on the one hand stop the growing demand to adopt an alien codex, God forbid, and on the other hand it has an innate benefit in itself.[34]

In effect, Rabbi Herzog was proposing that in the absence of an explicit will, daughters could inherit equally with sons and a widow could inherit one-third of her husband's estate. The rulings would be instituted by the Chief Rabbinical Council, which had the "same standing as the Great Bet Din" and they would be ratified by the Knesset "whose power was that of the seven dignitaries."[35] Since they were financial rulings, they would be enacted by virtue of the Talmudic edict that "the Bet Din has the right to forfeit one's property" which was indubitably the right of the Chief Rabbinical Council. In order to reinforce this ruling, the following clause should be inserted into the ketubah: "The division of any inheritance must be in accordance with the rulings."[36]

At the same time the Rishon Letzion, Rabbi Ben-Zion Chai Uziel, was dealing with the same issue. He wrote his own proposal, which was subsequently published in *Talpiot*, a religious journal. He also noted the imperative need for a religious ruling to enable daughters and widows to inherit: "In our generation we are called upon by a large segment of the people who dwell in Israel, to follow the paths of our revered sages and enact the rulings on inheritance that have become a pressing need."[37] However, his proposed rulings did not resemble those of Rabbi Herzog. Instead he emphasized the aspect of choice: "These rulings are like the *prozbul* ruling issued by Hillel, which is a right but not an obligation. This will provide satisfaction to every man and woman who so desires, while those who wish to specifically follow the Torah ruling will retain the full right to do so."[38] In fact the proposal, intended to preserve the status quo that had prevailed during the Mandate, could not continue from a halakhic point of view. The right of equality bestowed by mandatory law because "the law of the land is the binding law" was irrelevant in a sovereign Jewish reality where any ruling that went against Jewish law was inappropriate. The existence of such a law would be sacrilege. Rabbi Uziel even maintained that the concept of "the law of the land is the binding law" should not be applied in matters of inheritance. Therefore, he proposed an amendment whereby every couple would agree, at the time of their marriage, that every daughter born to them would inherit equally with their sons, according to the law of wills and testaments:

> Every Jewish man and woman who want their daughters to receive an equal portion of their estate with their sons are entitled to make this conditional at the time of their wedding before a Bet Din. This will have the validity of a Torah law that gives every Jewish man and woman the right to divide their property by will, either in health or sickness.[39]

This stipulation would be written on a special form, signed by witnesses, and attached to the ketubah.[40] Unlike Rabbi Herzog's proposal, where daughters inherited equally with sons by default, and anyone who wanted his children to inherit according to Torah law would have to write a will to this effect, in Rabbi Uziel's version the Torah ruling was the default, and anyone seeking to provide equally for his sons and daughters would have to clearly indicate it during the wedding, although it would be available and offered to every couple by the Bet Din.

Both proposals were submitted to the members of the Chief Rabbinical Council, additional rabbis, and public figures. The majority did not agree to the proposal and it was not put to the vote. The chief opponent of the proposed rulings was Rabbi Yeshaya Karelitz (the Chazon Ish), who, as a general rule, vehemently objected to any new rulings in his time, as we have seen. His objections stemmed mainly from the attitude that his generation was at a spiritually low ebb and had no authority to enact new rulings.[41]

## LEO COHEN'S DRAFT OF CONSTITUTION

In the summer of 1948, Dr. Cohen's draft constitution, devoid of halakhic content, was ultimately submitted to Rabbis Herzog and Uziel, as well as other leading rabbis.[42] Rabbi Herzog issued his opinion in detail. It was made up of comments on the various formulations along with his protest that it would probably clash with halakha. He was troubled, for example, that the draft did not include a clause prohibiting the inclusion of laws that lacked Torah and mitzvoth observance:

> There is no restriction here regarding laws and the passing of laws. According to this anyone who so wishes can introduce a law in our parliament that bans *shechita* (ritual slaughter), or circumcision, Go-d forbid. Although there is no danger that such a law will be passed, the very fact of the debate and the argument, as well as the very attempt to introduce it, is frightening and terrifying, alarming and destructive! The same goes for our brethren in the Diaspora.[43]

He proposed inserting the following: "No law shall be enacted that goes against Torah law, according to the opinion of Torah authorities who are recognized in the State of Israel, in other words, the Chief Rabbinate."[44] In this context Rabbi Herzog also objected to the fact that the location of the Supreme Rabbinical Court of Appeals and Israel's Chief Rabbinate was absent from the draft constitution. The proposal merely included the lower rabbinical court, which was only authorized to deal with matters of personal status. Thus, from the outset Torah law was at a disadvantage in relation to the civil courts of law.

Rabbi Herzog further maintained that "it is imperative at the very least to introduce a clause into the constitution stating that Jewish weddings and divorces must be conducted according to Jewish law,"[45] and equally essential to specify in the constitution that naturalization does not automatically imply conversion to Judaism. Conversion must be the unlimited jurisdiction of the rabbinical courts. He also asserted that a Jew is defined as one born to a mother who is held to be Jewish "so long as he has not changed to another faith and religion."[46] This accords with the halakhic ruling of Rabbis Shmuel Mohilever, Mordechai Gimpel Jaffe, and Yosef Zechariah Stern, that in the case of a childless widow whom an apostate refuses to release from a levirate marriage so that she is free to marry, "the apostate—he who has accepted another faith [ . . . ] is not a full Jew."[47] Similarly, he declared, the government must authorize the rabbinical courts as civil courts, not only for arbitration: "In any event the constitution must recognize the right of Torah courts of law to exist, in the governmental sense, not only for matters of personal status but also in civil law, so that any Jew who is sued has the option of saying, 'I will appeal to a Torah court of law.'"[48]

Finally, Rabbi Herzog sought "to officially acknowledge in the constitution the religion of the great majority in the State of Israel,"[49] that is to say, Judaism. He argued that it in no way harms the democratic nature of the state, citing as proof the constitution of Ireland, where the Catholic Church is recognized as the official church of the Irish people, because it is the church of most of its citizens.

Rabbi Uziel also responded to Dr. Cohen's draft constitution, making several comments. He objected to the wording of the oath taken for public appointments because of the halakhic prohibition against swearing in vain, in other words, where it is not required by law. Like Rabbi Herzog, he, too, maintained that an explicit clause must be inserted in the constitution giving exclusive authority to the rabbinic court in matters of conversion, "So that this essential matter should not be neglected, for then it will cause many problems."[50] For the most part, the other rabbis who reviewed the draft constitution repeated the comments made by Rabbis Herzog and Uziel, but they also added remarks of their own. For example, a few rabbis wanted to make it clear that freedom of religion and conscience did not include idol worship in the conventional sense. Rabbi Meir Bar-Ilan, not content with specific comments, noted that in general it is not enough that the constitution does not contradict the Torah. It must essentially include the laws of Israel.[51]

He strongly opposed the idea of two parallel court systems with concurrent jurisdiction—one system for the religious and the other for the secular, as he noted in his memorandum:

> There is great danger in the sort of tacit agreement that appears to exist in our religious circles, to the effect that if the State of Israel has a dual system of both religious "rabbinical" courts and secular courts, with the parties having the option to choose which court will try their cases, and if they [the religious courts] are accorded official recognition, this will be all that is required and nothing more will be needed. This policy, which is based on a purely parochial concern to remain separate and apart and is content to "relegate the Torah to a corner," was our basis for the last two generations and could have calamitous consequences for the Jewish state for generations to come.
>
> The only course open to every true Jew is to exert every effort to see to it that there is but one law throughout our country, not only for ourselves but for all the people, including non-Jews. As in all other countries, the law should be based on territorial authority and not personal affiliation, except, of course, in cases involving matters of religion. And this one law must be based on the Torah of Israel in all its ramifications, not on some other law.[52]

He believed, as he had written thirty years earlier, that there was no choice but to base the Israeli legal system on Jewish law. He expressed his regret for the grossly negligent failure of rabbis and religious leaders to prepare Jewish law for incorporation into the legal system of the Jewish state. Actually, part of this failure was due to his passive approach, precisely because immediately after the Balfour Declaration he was the first to recognize the challenge. Now, he stressed the need to immediately begin the task of making the entire corpus of Jewish law a suitable foundation for the legal system of the State of Israel, by enacting appropriate regulations and formulating the law in a manner consonant with contemporary legal circumstances. He suggested basing the law on the many suitable precedents from the huge body of responsa literature from various regions and from the period when Jews were autonomous. He pressed for an urgent search for a solution to the problems impeding the acceptance of Jewish law as the law of the state, such as, for example, problems relating to the disqualification of witnesses and judges, and the law of inheritance:

> If we are not flexible enough to find a practicable and acceptable solution, our rigidity will ultimately lead to disrespect [for Jewish law]. In that event, the law of government will certainly not be our own, and societal life in our state will not reflect our spirit or outlook. The pattern that emerges will reflect and influence all of life—all our public and private actions, even those pertaining to religious matters—for when one foundation stone is removed, the whole superstructure crumbles.[53]

In the summer of 1948, only weeks after the declaration of independence, Bar-Ilan convened a "legislative committee" of the Mizrachi World Movement, of which he was president, which he was to supervise jointly with Rabbi Herzog. The goal of the committee was to prepare samples of a book of laws regarding contemporary issues, in both civil and criminal matters, as part of a Torah-based constitution, for the State of Israel. According to Bar-Ilan, this book of laws should be in modern form, comprehensible to every judge and lawyer, including the non-religious. The committee produced pamphlets on the jurisdiction of rabbinical courts, murder, theft, robbery, extortion, incarceration, contracts, business law, laws of partnerships, tort, labor law, inheritance law, and laws pertaining to the national mint. Not all of these were edited, but some had been approved by Bar-Ilan and Rabbi Herzog.[54] Actually, only two books of Jewish law were published by the committee's members, one dealing with the law of sales, the other with the authority of the courts and government, and the laws of murder.[55]

In the end, there never was a constitution.[56] Israel's first legislation, the Law and Administration Ordinance, was accepted by the Provisional State Council on May 19, 1948. It was intended to establish governmental continuity and actually contributed to maintaining the status quo in matters of religion and state that had prevailed during the mandate period.[57]

Actually, the status quo concept first appeared in a letter sent on June 19, 1947, by David Ben-Gurion, Yehuda Leib Fishman, and Isaac Greenbaum, on behalf of the Jewish Agency Executive, to the World Agudath Israel Organization, as part of their effort to present the UN with a united Jewish front supporting the Zionist position. The purpose of the letter was to convince ultra-Orthodox Jews that they could live in the Jewish state and observe their own customs. Therefore, they should not object to its establishment. The letter guaranteed the following:

a. The Sabbath: It is clear that the legal day of rest in the Jewish state will be Saturday [ . . . ]

b. Kashruth: One should use all means required to ensure that every state kitchen intended for Jews will have kosher food.
c. Marital Affairs: [ . . . ] All bodies represented by the Jewish Agency Executive will do all that can be done to satisfy the needs of the religiously observant in this matter and to prevent a rift in the Jewish people.
d. Education: Full autonomy will be guaranteed to every stream in education; the government will take no steps that adversely affect the religious awareness and religious conscience of any part of Israel.[58]

Actually, this letter was inconclusive.

The Law and Administration Ordinance preserved the existing authority of the rabbinical courts as regards personal status, and even determined that "Sabbath and Jewish holidays [ . . . ] are fixed days of rest in the State of Israel." [59] The clause referring to Sabbath and Jewish holidays was largely symbolic. It did not deal with the public sphere at all, only addressing the socialist aspect of the official days of rest. Zerach Warhaftig attempted to amend clause 46 of the 1922 King's Order-in-Council, which stated that in every case where there is no explicit mandatory law, the judge must seek a solution in English law by revoking the similarity to English law and replacing it with a similar Jewish law, but his initiative was not accepted.[60] A request submitted by the chief rabbis to expand the jurisdiction of the rabbinical courts and give them equal powers to those of the Muslim courts during the mandate was also rejected. The principle of freedom of conscience and absence of religious coercion, that had already appeared in the status quo letter to World Agudath Israel, ultimately caused most of the members of the Provisional Council of the State to oppose any legal expansion on religious matters in the first legislation of the State of Israel. Religious leaders depended on the temporary nature of the legislation, hoping that in future it would be possible to combine Torah and State law. As we have seen, this was the thinking behind Rabbi Herzog's proposal to amend the laws governing the inheritance of daughters and widows, although they realized that their chances were slim.

## AMERICAN RABBIS: DEMOCRATIC HALAKHA

During that time American Zionist rabbis were also grappling with the burning halakhic issues on the agenda as they sought solutions for the problems inherent in the new sovereign reality. The basic premise that united them was their complete identification with the principles of procedural and substantive democracy. They saw it as the most appropriate vision of the spirit of Judaism, similar to the opinion expressed by Rabbi Haim Hirschsohn some three decades earlier.

Rabbi Dr. Samuel Kalman Mirsky (1899–1967) was born in Russia in 1899, and at the age of five emigrated with his family to Eretz Israel. After attending yeshivot connected with the Old Yishuv in Jerusalem and the Beit Midrash Le-Morim (Hebrew Teachers Seminary) founded by David Yellin, he received rabbinical ordination and a teacher's certificate. In 1924, he obtained a law degree from the Council of Legal Studies established by the Mandatory government and joined the Hevrat Ha-Mishpat Ha-'Ivri (Jewish Law Society). In 1926, he moved to the United States and settled in New York, where he completed his academic studies for a PhD degree at Columbia University. He served as a rabbi in Brooklyn and taught at the Teachers' Institute of Yeshiva College. He was also one of the leaders of the Mizrachi movement in the United States.[61]

Already in 1939, deeply moved by the celebrations of the 150th anniversary of the Constitution, Mirsky wrote in the pages of *Ha-Do'ar*, that democracy is not only a procedure but a spirit, inseparable from the Torah. Democratic equality "is about equanimity, tolerance, and the creation of social and political organs in which the voices of all countrymen will be equally heard."[62] Just as the Torah teaches us to trust, in an ultimate sense, none but God, so, too, democracy teaches the illegitimacy of human tyranny, and that the state exists to serve human dignity. Go-d's universal fatherhood is the ultimate source of fraternity. The social contract is no more a fiction than is the covenant at Mount Sinai. The foundation of Jewish religion and the foundation of democracy are one and the same.

On the eve of the establishment of the state Mirsky published an article entitled "The Law of the Jewish State" in *Talpiot*, the journal he edited on halakhic issues and the challenge of sovereignty. Drawing a parallel between US democracy and Jewish principles, he came to the conclusion that the social contract at the heart of the US Constitution originated with the earliest beginnings of Jewish tradition.

> The concept of the contract as the ethical and legal basis of state government that is firmly imposed on the public, permeates the nature of Jewish law and religion. Even the Holy One, Blessed be He, does not castigate those who contravene His commandments unless they have first entered into a covenant with Him. They are not bound by His edicts and obligations unless they first agreed to accept His suzerainty for themselves and their descendants (Mechilta Yitro). The same covenant that was entered into at Sinai was repeated at Arvot Moab and in Shechem [Nablus] and other places, in order to confirm and strengthen it. In the days of Ezra, too, they wrote and signed a contract and undertook to observe the commandments.[63]

The principle of government by the people, expressed by the fact that new legislation must reflect the will of the public, is also taken from Jewish tradition:

> Government by the people goes hand in hand with the rule that edicts cannot be issued, nor can rules or customs be imposed on the public, unless most of the public can conform to them. [ . . . ] One recent example from the American constitution, the law of Prohibition, which was revoked because it was not widely obeyed, suffices to show its similarity to the true way of the Jewish law.[64]

He regards this as proof that US democracy should serve as a model for the nascent Jewish political regime. In particular, Mirsky focused on the subject of state-enforced religious coercion, which was halakhically binding but went against the principle of freedom of conscience, which is a fundamental principle of democracy. Mirsky maintained that halakhically all the punishments listed in the Torah: death and lashes for willful wrongdoing and the offering of sacrifice for unintentional transgression, do not apply today. The punishment of death and sacrifices were applicable during the time of the temple, while whipping was contingent upon nearby *dayanim*. Punishments not listed in the Torah but by the Sages were dictated by the current situation and not intended as permanent rulings. They were in fact sanctioned by the community and carried out in accordance with the political leadership of the time. He quoted several halachic responsa from the Rishonim as evidence, including Rabbi Asher ben Yechiel, Rabbi Shlomo ben Aderet, and community edicts:

> Some communities explicitly asserted that these punishments are within the purview of representatives of the community, leaving the religious figures to deal only with money matters. In the ledgers of the Lithuanian community from 1639, clause 304, we read: "The leaders of the community will deal with quarrels and arguments, fines and punishments, whereas the community dayanim will deal with monetary matters; the leaders are not to involve themselves in monetary matters, nor are the dayanim are to involve themselves in matters that do not concern them." This regulation is the main determinant of the separation between religion and state, not in layman's terms derived from the language of the gentiles, but in the words of sages, in light of Jewish experience that has been studied over generations. Religion cannot prevail over the state except in the mind of one who is involved in the opinion of gentiles, one who is far removed from the Torah.[65]

From a halakhic point of view this insight endorses the separation of religion and state, which Mirsky feels should be adopted. If there is no penalty, there is no religious coercion, and each person is free to follow the dictates of his conscience. In actual fact, this was clear to anyone who was familiar with the nature of the Jewish Yishuv in Eretz Israel during the mandate period and was dealing with halakhic issues and the challenge of sovereignty on the grounds of feasibility, in view of the internal balance of power in the Jewish Yishuv. But Mirsky wanted to establish it as a moral principle from a halakhic point of view.

In his article on punishments after the Talmud was sealed, Rabbi Herzog emphasized that corporal punishment would not be permitted in the Jewish state, because "It is clear that the state will not recognize such corporal punishments. [ . . . ] This will remain the case even if ordination is restored." [66] Rabbi Herzog further asserted that the legal division between the community leaders and the rabbis customary in former times, came at a time when rabbis ceased to deal with penal law because "the rabbis did not want to take upon themselves the crown of ordination to deal with punishments" or else because "the rabbis felt that due to their extremely compassionate nature they are unable to be criminal judges" [67] and therefore this division was not worthy of sovereignty under Torah leadership.

Rabbi Dr. Shimon Federbusch (1892–1969) of New York also dealt with the democratic principles of Judaism and the question of religious coercion,[68] in his comprehensive book *The Kingdom of Law in Israel,*[69] whose early chapters were written on the eve of the establishment of the state. Federbusch was born in Galicia and received a traditional Torah education. He attended the Viennese Rabbinical Seminary and the local university. In his thirties he held the position of rabbi of Helsinki until 1940 when he emigrated to the United States and was appointed president of Hapoel Hamizrachi. Like Mirsky, Federbusch believed that the social contract was rooted in the Torah: "This view is based on the covenant between Israel and Go-d. The fact that it preceded the Giving of the Torah teaches that there is no ethical virtue in forcing the people to accept a political ruling without their consent. Even the law of the Torah state was contingent on the prior consent of the entire nation." [70]

He, too, insisted that the process of lawmaking must reflect the will of the people, and therefore "no edict can be imposed upon the people against their will, nor can a law be valid if the people refuse to accept it." [71] He brought proof from a number of Talmudic sources that halakhic legislation is democratic, contrary to the prevailing impression in Haskala literature that halakha has stagnated and the rule imposed by adjudicators is arbitrary:

> From this we learn some democratic fundamentals of Talmudic legislation: that Talmudic legislation depends on the opinion of the majority of the people, not just their representatives; secondly, that even after the law has been ratified the people or their representatives have the right to revoke them, if due to altered circumstances the law is no longer acceptable; thirdly, it is forbidden to impose a law on the public against their will; and fourthly, if a law has become obsolete to the extent that the people no longer obey it, the law becomes invalid.[72]

Like Mirsky, Federbusch was opposed to all forms of religious coercion on the grounds that in our day the prescribed Torah punishments for religious offences (death or lashes ordained by the Bet Din) no longer apply.[73] Dissatisfied with this formal argument, he followed the path of Moses Mendelssohn, not only in matters of expropriating the power of religious coercion but also in defining religious commandments as moral directives whose purpose is to educate.[74] "The religious commandments have moral, spiritual, and educational value."[75] He emphasizes that this approach does not stem from coercion by the religious sector, who are a minority in the new Jewish state, but because "these would even be the pleasing nature and peaceful ways of the Torah if there was a religious majority in the state and the government."[76]

Another American rabbi who addressed this issue was Rav Tzair (Chaim Tchernowitz). In an article entitled "Questions of Religion and State in Israel,"[77] published several months after the establishment of the state in *Betzaron*, the journal he edited, he stated that he was opposed to imposing religious observance on the state. One reason for his objection to religious coercion was the lack of ***halakhic*** uniformity between various communities and congregations. In his opinion this prevented standardized legislation that could be penalized:

> Several questions have arisen about religion itself regarding what should be included and what should be removed. What religious affiliation should be accepted; which *halakhot* should be enforced and which should be optional; what to accept and what to remove; Torah injunctions or Talmudic injunctions, the rulings of Maimonides or those of Rabbi Abraham ben David (Rabad), the opinion of the Vilna Gaon (HaGra) or that of the Baal Shem Tov, of Mizrachi or Agudath Israel? At present there is no single ruling. One person accepts the ruling of Maimonides, another follows the Rabad, or the *Shulkhan Arukh*, or Rabbi Moses Isserles (the Rama). Everyone rules as he sees fit. But a political state has no uncertainty, there is only the path followed by the state, and there is no law without punishment for offenders. If, for example, the *Shulkhan Arukh* is authorized by the state, judges and police must be appointed to ensure that it is meticulously observed, and as we know there are many details that most people cannot comply with.[78]

Nevertheless, he was not prepared to accept the US model of separating religion and state but sought instead to hold fast to the principles of democracy and halakha as much as possible. One solution to this problem, similar to the one he proposed for the problem of enforcing religious observance in general, was to distinguish between religious rules that must appear as laws, and the details and powers of coercion that emanate from them, that could be observed by each community in its own way. Here is his proposal for Sabbath observance:

> Similarly, the constitution can adopt a general law regarding the observance of Sabbath and Jewish holidays. But the state does not determine the particulars, leaving the details of forbidden tasks to the communities who will have recognized autonomy over public life. In this way each community will be free to define the nature of Sabbath observance

> in its own purview. Naturally some communities will go according to the *Shulkhan Arukh* while others will be more lenient in some respects, undertaking to observe the bare minimum of forbidden tasks. Once they have accepted the strictures on working on Sabbath the police will be obligated to protect them, to the degree that they have accepted them. I imagine that the constitution will determine the law in the following terms: a) Sabbath is a day of rest in Israel and its contravention will be punished accordingly; b) the definition of forbidden work and the degree to which offenders will be punished will be determined by each community according to the laws published for this purpose.[79]

In general, he proposes starting with the strenuous task of drawing up a new Hebrew constitution that will integrate the laws of halakha with the demands of time and place, in all aspects of life, to "arrange it in such a way that it will preserve the special historical nature of the Jewish people according to which it lives and develops, incorporating a regime compatible with its spirit and psyche, one that will not deviate from the straight path delineated by history and will not obscure its unique national features from one generation to the next."[80]

He maintained that most state laws that had been observed by the ancient kingdoms of Israel were forgotten because they were orally transmitted, whereas laws of the state that were steeped in Talmudic literature do not reflect historical reality, and therefore they should not be followed literally:

> Thus if we establish the state that is now being renewed based on the laws of the former state, we will lose our way. Many of them are inapplicable to our lives and we cannot employ them—laws of the kings, rules of war, strangers and residents, some international laws, and so on. Even the most religious will acknowledge this. Nor do we have historical documents attesting as to whether what is listed in Biblical and Talmudic literature accurately reflected life in those days. In other words, they may be *hilkhta limeshicha* (only applicable in the time of the Messiah). According to the Bible itself the Jewish people did not observe the injunction "you shall not leave a soul alive," and according to the Talmud they did not observe the Jubilee year during the time of the Second Temple (Maimonides, Shmitta VeYovel, 10:3). Similarly, there is no historical proof that the laws ordained by the Sanhedrin and the laws of capital offence as described in the Talmud were actually enforced. They themselves said: There never was and never will be a rebellious son (*ben sorrer umoreh*) (Sanhedrin 71). And probably most of them were only ordained in the context of demanding and receiving wages.[81]

He brought several examples of how, in his opinion, the spirit of halakha could be integrated with the reality of modern times. For instance, he argued that those who are halachically exempt from going out to war (one who is betrothed but not married, one who has built a house but not dwelt in it, and one who has planted a vineyard but not harvested) correspond to those who are exempt from defense by US law—in other words, they keep the economy functioning as normally as possible. The exemption on the fearful and fainthearted corresponds to the exemption of conscientious objectors. In this he somewhat approached the position of secular Zionist thinkers such as Herzl, Jabotinsky, and Bialik, who wanted to combine Torah principles with modern societal institutions without resorting to halakhic details.

A similar concept was proposed by Dr. Moses Silberg (1900–1975), an eminent jurist and Talmudic scholar, and later a member of the Supreme Court of Israel. In an article published on the eve of the establishment of the State of Israel, he claimed that the law of the Jewish state must be Jewish law:

> in the sense that it must be based on the ideas of Jewish law, the national law that has accompanied us for two thousand years [ . . . ] based on the ideas of Jewish law, but not identical with it; I do not suggest that the *Shulhan Arukh* be proclaimed in toto as the law of the land. Even if we had the possibility of doing so, we would not possess the moral right, in view of the non-Jewish population of the state of Israel. [ . . . ] This is a task for many years, perhaps for a whole generation, but the result would be a modern law that would at one and the same time retrieve the basic principles of traditional law, and constitute a historical continuity of the ancient legal tradition.[82]

Although Silberg's proposal, which came close to that of national poet Haim Nachman Bialik, was in the spirit of the Hebrew Law Society, it was not supported by the political forces that could have promoted it.

Rav Tzair also believed this would be a constitutional body of many years standing. He imposed this complex legislative role on a judicial institution, like the federal Supreme Court of the United States, comprised of scholars and jurists, charged with drafting and approving laws in accordance with modern legal principles, in the spirit of Israel's religious ordinances. He no longer referred to the idea, put forward nearly thirty years ago, of restoring the Sanhedrin, preferring to establish a modern legal institution tasked with legislative audit:

> The task of classifying and processing the *halakhic* material to adapt it to our lives is a work for generations. The undertaking is immense and must be approached gradually and carefully. [ . . . ] The work must be undertaken by experts in the history of *halakha* who are also proficient in modern law. They must observe the precept "he ate the inside and tossed away the peel."[83] As a rule the primordial material of *halakha* cannot be used, but its kernel, its essence and its inner spirit must be retained and processed in accordance with the national psyche and the spirit of Jewish law. We should not take inclusively laws and rules of other nations and force them upon the Jewish nation, who will be unable to digest them. . . . Which tools should be used to transfer the

> ancient laws from theocracy to the authority of state government, and how should they be adapted? I believe the institution of the Supreme Court is the best means of processing historical *halakhic* material and adapting it in a practical manner. The Supreme Court, especially as it has developed in America, is the third decisive power between the legislature and the government that puts laws into practice. It is the weight that tips the balance between the ancient past and the present. [ . . . ] Thus, by adapting laws according to our requirements, bearing in mind the spirit of ancient Jewish law, a bridge will be formed between the past and the present. The body of law will be suited to the demands of the time, and the historical spirit of law will be preserved. What is more, this will build a bridge between religious law and state law, and together they will go hand in hand.[84]

As a matter of fact, in the summer of 1948 the Supreme Court of the State of Israel was established on the model of the mandate supreme court.[85] Its secular composition largely reflected the fact that most of the Provisional Council were opposed to mixing religion and law. Rabbi Simcha Assaf was the only judge who was also a scholar well-versed in Jewish law. The chief rabbis, regarding its establishment as an irreversible step in the separation of Torah law and state law, boycotted the opening ceremony that took place on September 15, 1948. Rabbi Herzog, in a letter to Moshe Kleinman, had previously expressed his resentment at the "outrageous harm that has been done to our holy Torah, specifically during the time of the establishment of the State of Israel":

> Woe to us that the Torah has been affronted! The words of the prophet have been fulfilled: "They have made kings, but not with My sanction; they have officers, but not of My choice." They have appointed court of law, lower courts and higher courts, and a supreme court, intended as the great court of law of Eretz Israel, without even consulting with the Torah! Were it only a temporary appointment it would not be so bad, but since they have ratified the appointment of that supreme court (where apart from one man, they are all laymen when it comes to proficiency and understanding of Torah law)—for their entire lives, and naturally I wish them all long lives, they have committed something that will, Go-d forbid, bring about irreversible damage, uprooting Torah law at the very time when we were hoping, as we repeat in our daily prayers, to "restore our judges as in former times." How can it be that from now on, in the usual way of government, the noble lady will inherit from the slave, in other words Torah law, as interpreted by the Torah Sages, with proper regulations made possible by the Torah itself, will once again be the law of the State of Israel, when it has already been determined by the genius judges, most of whom are not versed in our Torah, at least in its legal aspects. It is alien to them (apart from one who is an important, learned man, although he himself would not say that he is knowledgeable in this field).[86]

Later, Rabbi Herzog was even more skeptical that Torah law could be combined with state law. Early in 1950, he rebuffed the initiative proposed by Rabbi Yehuda Leib Maimon, the Minister of Religion, to revive the Sanhedrin.[87] His arguments included the claim that in the present situation the institution of the Sanhedrin would have no real impact on life in Israel. On the contrary, it would only emphasize the ineffectiveness of Torah law on the laws of the state:

> As regards Torah law, it is obvious that so long as the current situation endures, where most of those in the Knesset and in the government are not Jews of our own kind, even seventy one of the greatest rabbis cannot help, even all the rabbis together. Furthermore, such a body would not be recognized by distinguished rabbis overseas. To this end we need to train dayanim and publish literature on Torah law that will reveal the light inherent in the legal Torah profession. [ . . . ] But the decree of a Sanhedrin would not be of any real use in this direction. It would only emphasize our inability. A hint should suffice to the wise.[88]

As a result, halakhic debates became more academic, and religious politicians entered the halakhic legal arena with religious legislative proposals.

The United Nations Partition Resolution of November 29 called for the establishment of a Jewish state in Eretz Israel alongside an Arab state. This obligated the religious leadership to provide concrete solutions for halakhic issues and constitute a challenge to sovereignty. The chief rabbis of Eretz Israel regarded themselves as authorized to deal with these issues by virtue of their position. As far as possible they sought to avoid contradictions between halakha and the emerging practices in the new state. Two specific questions dealt with at the time were the question of the status of non-Jewish minorities in the state and the question of the status of women, particularly their right to inherit. Whereas for the first question, the senior rabbis agreed that non-Jewish minorities should not be discriminated against despite halakhic sources that teach otherwise, with regard to the second question, the chief rabbis failed to convince their colleagues of the need to introduce new regulations making women equal to men in matters of inheritance. The first question was perceived as an international question in which the political leadership of the Jewish state had no space to maneuver, and therefore there was nothing left to do but make an effort to accept the given reality, whereas the second question was seen as an internal national matter in which there was no need to make concessions.

Furthermore, since the first question had been irrelevant throughout the long years of exile, the rejection of halakhic sources from ancient times by means of halakhic sophistry was not perceived as an abrogation of an entrenched ruling, whereas the law according to which a daughter does not inherit with the sons had been upheld in one form or another even during the period of exile, and a ruling to cancel it was perceived by some rabbis as religious reform.

The cultural reality generated in Eretz Israel during the British Mandate led the chief rabbis to understand that the vision of a Torah state cannot be realized in the short term, and therefore all their efforts were directed toward ensuring the status quo in such a way that the order of the regime and the laws of the state would not be contrary to the Torah. This effort failed, as did their struggle to upgrade the status of the rabbinical courts. From now on, the arena was transferred to academic halakhic study and the political work of religious legislation.

## NOTES

1. A/RES/181(II) of November 29, 1947, United Nations. 1947.
2. On this, see: Amihai Radzyner, "A Constitution for Israel: The Design of the Leo Kohn Proposal, 1948," *Israel Studies* 15, 1 (2010): 1–24.
3. On Herzog's draft, see: Kaye, "The Legal Philosophies," 144–88. On how the religious circles reacted to the idea of an Israeli constitution in the Land of Israel, in the late mandate period and the early Israeli period, see: Friedman and Radzyner, *The Religious Community*.
4. On him, see: Itamar Warhaftig, "Rabbi Herzog's approach to modernity," in *Engaging Modernity: Rabbinical Leaders and the Challenge of the Twentieth Century*, ed. Moshe Z. Sokol (Northvale, N.J.:
5. I. E. Herzog, "Ha-Tehiqah ve-ha-Mishpat ba-Medinah ha-Yehudit (Legislation and Law in the Jewish State)," *Yavneh*, 3 (1948): 9–10.
6. A letter of Rabbi Herzog to Mordechai Eliash, 29 Shvat 5708, The Israel State Archives (ISA)—Privatecollections-RabbiHerzog-0006qjb.
7. Herzog, *Tehuqah leYisrael*, 10.
8. Ibid., 11.
9. Josef Achituv, "Halakhic Vacillations of Chief Rabbi Isaac Halevi Herzog during the Early Years of the State of Israel," in *The Challenge of Independence: Ideological and Cultural Aspects of Israel's First Decade*, ed. Mordechai Bar-On (Jerusalem: Yad Ben-Zvi Press, 1999), 205–10.
10. Deut. 17: 16.
11. On Goren's legal plurlism, see: Kaye, "The Legal Philosophies," 91–98.
12. Herzog, *Tehuqah leYisrael*, 146–204.
13. On the Ran's method, see: Suzanne Last Stone, "Religion and State: Models of Separation from within Jewish Law," *International Journal of Constitutional Law* 6, nos 3&4 (2008): 631–61; idem, "Law Without Nation? The Ongoing Jewish Discussion" in *Law Without Nations*, eds. Austin Sarat, Lawrence Douglas, and Martha Merrill Umphrey (Stanford, Calif.: Stanford University Press, 2011), 101–37; Warren Zev Harvey, "Liberal Democratic Themes In Nissim of Girona," in *Studies in Medieval Jewish History and Literature*, vol. III, eds. Isadore Twerski and Jay M. Harris (Cambridge, MA.: Harvard University Press, 2000), 197–211; Gerald J. Blidstein, "On Lay Legislation in Halakhah: The King as Instance," in *Rabbinic and Lay Communal Authority*, ed. Suzanne Last Stone (New York: KTAV Publishing House, 2006), 1–18.
14. I. E. Herzog, "The Law in the Jewish State," *HaTorah VehaMedinah* 7–8 (1955–6): 13. Quoted in: Michael Walzer et al., eds., *The Jewish Political Tradition*, vol. I—Authority (New Haven and London: Yale University Press, 2000), 474–75.
15. Kaye, "The Legal Philosophies," 186–88.
16. Maimonides, Hilchot Avodah Zarah, 10, 6.

17. Herzog, *Tehuqah leYisrael*, 19. Quoted in: Michael Walzer et al., eds., *The Jewish Political Tradition*, vol. II—Membership (New Haven and London: Yale University Press, 2003), 529–30.
18. Chaim Burgansky, "Community and Kingdom: The Halakhic Approach of R. Isaac Halevi Herzog and R. Shaul Yisraeli towards the State of Israel," in Ravitzky, *Religion and State*, 278–82.
19. Herzog, *Tehuqah leYisrael*, 16.
20. Ibid., 23.
21. Ibid., 249.
22. Uziel, *Mishpatei Uziel*, vol. 4, HM section 17; see also Zvi Zohar, "Ahrayut Hakneset Leitzuv Hahalacha-Iyun Bema'amaro shel Harav Uziel Behagdarat Pesuley Edut," in *Rav Tarbutiyut Bemedinah Demokratit Veyehudit: Sefer Hazikaron LeAriel Rozen-Tzvi Z'L*, eds. Menahem Mautiner et al. (Tel Aviv: Ramot, 1998), 301–39.
23. Ben-Zion Uziel, "HaTorah ve-HaMedinah," *Sinai* 22 (1948): 119. See also: Moshe Hellinger, "Religion and State in Sephardi Religion-Zionist Thought: R. Meir Hai Uziel and R. Hayyim David Halevi," in Ravitzky, *Religion and State*, 224–28.
24. Herzog, *Tehuqah leYisrael*, 272.
25. Ibid., 274.
26. Ibid.
27. The male children inherited the ketubah even if their mother died before the death of their father; if there were children by other wives, the amounts of the ketubah were first subtracted from the inheritance and distributed among the respective heirs on the mother's side, the residue of the property being then divided equally among all the sons.
28. Under this enactment, a daughter has the right to receive, in addition to her support, a one-tenth share of her father's estate.
29. A deed given by a father to his daughter when she weds, ensuring that she will inherit one-half of what a son inherits.
30. Elon, *Jewish Law*, 559–61, 575–81, 655–56, 835–46.
31. Itamar Warhaftig, "Introduction," in Herzog, *Tehuqah leYisrael*, vol. 2, VII–VXI.
32. Herzog, *Tehuqah leYisrael*, vol. 2, 4.
33. Ibid., 4–5.
34. Ibid., 5.
35. Ibid., 63–64.
36. Ibid., 177.
37. Ben-Zion Uziel, "Mishpat Yerushat HaBat [Law of Inheritance of Daughters]," *Talpioth*, 5 (1952): 452.
38. Ibid., 453.
39. Ibid., 6 (1953): 64.
40. Actually, Rabbi Samuel Kalman Mirsky of New York, already suggested a similar proposal in 1948. Samuel Kalman Mirsky, "Mishpat HaMedinah HaIvrit (The Law of the Hebrew State)," *Talpiot* 3–4 (1948): 345.
41. On this, see: Brown, *The Hazon Ish*, 668–77
42. On the rabbis' responses to this proposal, see: Friedman and Radzyner, *The Religious Community*, 68–78.
43. Herzog, *Tehuqah leYisrael*, vol. 3, 18.
44. Ibid., 28.
45. Ibid., 21–22.
46. Ibid., 26.
47. Ibid.
48. Ibid., 23.
49. Ibid., 29.
50. Ibid., 35.
51. On Bar-Ilan's legal centralism, see: Kaye, "The Legal Philosophies," 190–98.
52. Meir Bar-Ilan (Berlin). "Hok u-mishpat bi-Medinateinu [Status and Law in our State]," *Yavneh*, 3 (1948): 29 (quoted in: Elon, *Jewish Law*, 1616).

53. Ibid., 32 (quoted in: Elon, *Jewish Law*, 1617).
54. Kaye, "The Legal Philosophies," 199–205.
55. Yaakov Meshulam Ginsburg, Mishpatim Le-Yisra'el: ha-hoq ha-pelili ve-dinei ha-onshin bizman hazeh le-fi mishpat ha-torah, ha-talmud u-meforshim (Jerusalem: Mechon Harry Fischel le-derishat ha-talmud, 1956); Binyamin Rabinowitz Teomim, Hilkhot mekhira (Jerusalem: Mechon Harry Fischel le-derishat ha-talmud, 1957).
56. On the constitutional debate in Israel, see: S. Z. Abramov, *The Perpetual Dilemma: Jewish Religion in the Jewish State* (New York: Associated University Presses, 1979), 135–46.
57. Ron Harris, "Absent-minded Misses and Historical Opportunities: Jewish Law, Israeli Law and the Establishment of the State of Israel," in, *On Both Sides of the Bridge: Religion and State in the Early Years of Israel*, eds. Mordechai Bar-On and Zvi Zameret (Jerusalem: Yad Ben-Zvi Press, 2002), 21–55; Amichai Radzyner, "Forgotten Basic Elements in 'The Law and Administration Ordinance' and the Covert Struggle over Religion and State in Israel," *Cathedra*, 136 (2010): 121–50.
58. "Status-Que Agreement," in *Israel in the Middle East: Documents and Readings on Society, Politics, and Foreign Relations, Pre 1948 to the Present*, eds. Itamar Rabinovich and Jehuda Reinharz (Waltham, MA: Brandeis University Press, 2008), 59.
59. Zerach Warhaftig, *Constitution for Israel—Religion and State* (Jerusalem: Messilot, 1988), 40–44.
60. Ibid., 45–46.
61. S. K.Mirsky, "Megilat Hayyay," in *Samuel K. Mirsky Memorial Volume: Studies in Jewish Law, Philosophy and Literature*, eds. Gershon Appel, Morris Epstein, and Hayim Leaf (New York and Jerusalem: Yeshiva University and Sura Research Institute, 1970), Hebrew section, 279–91. I would like to thank Professor Yehuda Mirsky for sending me his lecture on his grandfather S. K. Mirsky.
62. "Ha-Yesod Ha-Democrati be-Dat Yisrael (The Democratic Element in Judaism)," *Ha-Doar*, 25 Nisan, 5699, 391–92.
63. Ibid., 352.
64. Ibid., 355.
65. Ibid., 372.
66. Herzog, *Tehuqah leYisrael*, vol. 1, 51–52.
67. Ibid., 55.
68. On Federbusch's legal pluralism, see: Kaye, "The Legal Philosophies," 80–83.
69. On this book, see: Cohen, *The Talit*, 73–80.
70. Simon Federbush, *Mishpat ha-Melukhah be-Yisrael* (Jerusalem: Mossad Harav Kook, 1952), 34.
71. Ibid.
72. Ibid., 35.
73. Ibid., 28.
74. "The state has physical power and uses it when necessary; the power of religion is love and beneficence ." Moses Mendelssohn, Jerusalem , 45.
75. Federbush, *Mishpat ha-Melukhah*, 28.
76. Ibid.
77. Chaim Tchernowitz, "Questions of Religion and State in Israel," *Betzaron* 9 (1948), 293–304.
78. Ibid., 297–98.
79. Ibid., 300.
80. Ibid., 293.
81. Chaim Tchernowitz, *Chevley Geulah* (New York: Shoulson Press, 1949), 358–59.
82. Abramov, *The Perpetual Dilemma*, 133–34.
83. bChag. 9b.
84. Tchernowitz, *Chevley Geulah*, 365–68.
85. Ron Harris, *The Israeli Law—The Formative Years; 1948–1977* (Tel Aviv: Hakibbutz Hameuchad-Sifriat Poalim Publishing Group, 2014), 72–82; P. Lahav, "The For-

mative Years of Israel's Supreme Court: 1948–1955," *Tel Aviv University Law Review*, 14 (1989): 479–501.

86. A letter from Rabbi Herzog to Moshe Kleinman, 6 Av 5708, in: Herzog, *Tehuqah leYisrael*, vol. 1, 238.

87. On this attempt, see: Cohen, *The Talit*, 56–71.

88. A letter of Rabbi Herzog to Rabbi Yehuda Leib Maimon, 19 Tevet 5710, ISA-Privatecollections-RabbiHerzog-0006qjb.

# SIX

# The Younger Generation of Zionist Rabbis Faces the Challenge of Sovereignty (1948–1962)

## HALAKHIC VALIDATION: THE THEORETICAL HALAKHIC DEBATE ON DIVERSE ASPECTS OF STATE INSTITUTIONS

The initiatives proposed by Chief Rabbis Hertzog and Uziel did not bear fruit. Both the government and the Knesset disregarded their opinions in all matters pertaining to the structure of the government in general and the rabbinical courts in particular. Moreover, most of the members of the Chief Rabbinical Council obstructed their proposals to introduce new regulations for the laws of inheritance. Instead, halakhic engagement with the challenge of sovereignty came from another direction. Immediately after the establishment of the state, religious-Zionist rabbis who were aligned with HaPoel HaMizrahi began to systematically address the halakhic issues that had surfaced in light of imminent Jewish sovereignty.

The deliberations were undertaken within the framework of the Board of Rabbis of HaPoel HaMizrahi, founded in August 1948, a rabbinical body that united the religious-Zionist rabbis. Its main activities included annual conferences; establishing steering committees for specific issues; regular publication of Torah anthologies reflecting the approach of the Chief Rabbinate; and concern for the rights of rabbis. From the outset the Board of Rabbis was intended as a rabbinical advisory body for party representatives in government establishments and not as a body that rules on issues such as the Council of Torah Sages of Agudath Israel.[1]

One of the board's committees was the halakha committee. Its purpose was to propose halakhic solutions for new questions that arose with the establishment of the State of Israel. In the opinion of many HaPoel HaMizrahi rabbis, the Chief Rabbinate was dragging its feet and not tackling these questions adequately. Members of the organization sought to fill the vacuum and take the lead regarding state laws, or at least to raise the halakhic issues in such a way that the Chief Rabbinate would be compelled to address them. The Board of Rabbis published *HaTorah VehaMedina* (The Torah and the State), a yearbook dealing with these matters. Thirteen such yearbooks were issued between 1949 and 1962.

The topics discussed in these compilations fall into six categories:

1. Legal and juridical matters, including monarchy in Israel and Israeli government, parliament, courts, and punishment.
2. Economic matters, including taxes and fines.
3. The land of Israel, including Shmita.
4. Laws pertaining to the military and war.
5. Laws of marital relations.
6. Religious topics, such as conversion, circumcision, and the Sabbath.[2]

The yearbook was edited by Russian-born Rabbi Shaul Yisraeli, who immigrated to Eretz Israel in 1934 to attend the Merkaz HaRav yeshiva founded by Rabbi Abraham Isaac Kook. In 1938, Rabbi Yisraeli was appointed rabbi of Kfar HaRoeh, a HaPoel HaMizrahi religious settlement, and two years later he headed the Bnei Akiva yeshiva founded in Kfar HaRoeh by Rabbi Moshe Zvi Neria. In 1948, he helped found the HaPoel HaMizrahi Rabbinical Council. In this capacity he pioneered the halakhic approach to modern agriculture and laws specific to the Land of Israel.

In his introduction to the first yearbook, Rabbi Yisraeli lamented the fact that in previous years the rabbis had not addressed halakhic issues relating to the challenges of sovereignty. In fact, they had been caught unprepared by the United Nations General Assembly partition plan. Nevertheless, he believed it would still be possible to influence the constitution of the state if they hastened to clarify these issues and regarded them as imperative. This work should be carried out in such a way that would dispel the fear harbored by many that halakha is not entirely compatible with the reality of modern sovereignty: "Clarification is required in order for the awareness to penetrate that the laws of the Torah are not irrelevant, that God's commandments are true and eternal. Judaism awaits this clarification. The scholars of this generation must respond to this demand. The sooner the better."[3]

Five years later he expressed his opinion in more specific terms, in essence calling for an empathetic halakhic approach to the state, so that the voice of the rabbis would be heard and would carry practical weight:

> Torah and the state are linked in our hands. Not only do we regard this integration as possible, we feel it is essential, not only as *halakha* for

> messianic days, but as a line of action for us, for our time. Therefore we must not attack the state for Torah's sake. On the contrary, we must strengthen and support it, encourage and direct it. Because, to the degree that we approach the state with the Torah in our hands, the state will draw closer to the Torah, its way of life and its *mitzvoth*.[4]

Rabbi Yisraeli had taken this line ever since he began dealing with the laws of the state in the first edition of the yearbook. In an article entitled "The Authority of the President and Elected Government Institutions in Israel" that appeared in this edition he maintained that prophecy and the Sanhedrin's approval were not necessary for the appointment of a king, as Maimonides wrote (*Hilchot Melachim* 1,3). On the contrary, this only became necessary in the event that the people were not involved in choosing the king. "But if the people themselves agree to appoint him by election or by any other means, there is no need for a prophet or the Sanhedrin, because the nomination certainly applies and is valid. If the people agree to this authority, what more do we need?"[5]

In other words, state authority is bestowed first and foremost by the people. He based his claim on the words of Rabbi Kook in his book *Mishpat Cohen* (responsum 144), that when there is no king, authority reverts to the nation as a whole.[6] But Rabbi Yisraeli went far beyond Rabbi Kook, presenting sovereignty as a principle from the outset and not after the fact.[7] The nation is the sovereign and it has the right to delegate authority to the king. In the same way that it can appoint a king, the nation can appoint group leadership that holds the powers of government. Therefore, the elected leadership in the State of Israel enjoys the authority of kingship, as was customary in Israel in ancient times:

> From now on, all government appointments decided through elections by the majority of the people will have authority and validity. It is my humble opinion that in the same way that one man can be appointed as a leader and a judge, so too can a council be appointed who hold the same authority together. Therefore it appears that a governmental council chosen by proper elections will have the same authority in all matters pertaining to the management of the nation as was once held by the king of Israel.[8]

Governmental authority is not limited to certain spheres. The nation can extend them to include areas and institutions not explicitly mentioned in the Torah. "If everything depends on the nation's acceptance, the powers of the president and the government will also depend on the decision of the people, or their specifically chosen representatives. Everything the people decide regarding the powers of the government and the president will prevail, whether it be a monetary or a civil matter. It will have the validity and authority of Torah law."[9]

Other articles appearing in *HaTorah VehaMedina* yearbooks over the years established the authority of government institutions of the State of

Israel from a halakhic point of view, whether according to state authority, popular authority (the seven dignitaries), or the halakhic principle of *dina de-malkhuta dina* ("the law of the land is the law"),[10] which originally referred to non-Jewish government abroad. Thus, for example, Rabbi Ovadyah Haddayah (1889–1969), who was a member of the Supreme Rabbinical Court in Jerusalem, wrote that the authority of government institutions in Israel depended upon these three principles:

> Therefore we must say in the case at hand, of a house of representatives, that if all these conditions are met, it is certainly equivalent to the "good men of the town." They too were initially chosen by the *kahal* since they were elected by all the citizens for the express purpose of laying down laws and statutes and imposing taxes, as in any other country. The condition that none should benefit at the expense of others is also met. Since . . . the taxes are [imposed] upon all residents [equally], each according to his income and profits, no one benefits at the expense of another. But it seems that the condition that this legislation should meet the approval of the "town's rabbi" is missing in this case, for he was not consulted. Since, however, the town's rabbi is also among the voters, it is as if he had already initially concurred with whatever they do for the good of the town, so long at is does not contravene Torah law. Even regarding the principle *dina de-malkhuta dina,*[11] it is explicitly stated that it only applies when it does not contravene Torah law. It applies only with regard to issues of *mamona* [which *dina de-malkhuta dina* resembles] the rule that the court has the power to expropriate—provided again that it does not involve benefiting some at the expense of others. Furthermore I say, in line with the explanation provided above, that our house of representatives has a status equal to that of a king, and nowhere is it required that a Jewish king must consult the town's rabbi.[12]

Other writers whose articles appeared in *HaTorah VehaMedina* also followed the line taken by Rabbi Yisraeli to bring halakha closer to the existing state apparatus. For example, Rabbi Yaakov Meshulam Ginsburg followed this guideline with regard to criminal law. At around that time Rabbi Ginsburg published a halakhic codex on criminal law entitled *Mishpatim LeYisrael,* under the auspices of the Torah Institute headed by Rabbi Herzog. In accordance with the legal practice of Western countries, self-incrimination is regarded as the best evidence. This seems to go counter to halakha, where a principle of criminal law is *ein adam sam atzmo rasha* (one cannot incriminate himself).[13] In his article "Self-incrimination According to Torah Law," Ginsburg, basing his argument on responsa of the Rashba (Rabbi Shlomo ben Aderet), reasoned that in our time, where there are no *rabbanim s'muchim* (rabbis who have been ordained in an unbroken line from the Sanhedrin), and in many cases we cannot adjudicate according to Torah law, an accused person can also be convicted by his own confession for *tikkun olam*. The Rashba wrote:

> For if you were to restrict everything to the laws stipulated in the Torah and punish only in accordance with the Torah's penal [code] in cases of assault and the like, the world would be destroyed [*ha-olam harev*], because we would require two witnesses and [prior] warning. The Rabbis have already said that 'Jerusalem was destroyed only because they restricted their judgments to Torah law' (BT Bava Metzia 30b).[14]

Ginsburg accordingly deduced that:

> If at such a time it is said that a man should not be punished on the basis of his own admission, these are the young men and the like, who are bereft of any religious, moral, Jewish and human feeling. If they are freed and absolved of all punishment, who can foresee the outcome? The same applies to all others who are convicted of criminal acts. We need to punish all offenders now, even on their own admission. Since the *halakha* states: "A law court issues penalties that are not from the Torah," when the times require it, in order to restrict and limit wrongdoers, and as expressed by Maimonides (*hilchot rotzeach 8"2, 5"5*): "To frighten and threaten other evildoers, that it should not be a stumbling-block for them."
>
> For this reason I have written in my book (*Mishpatim LeYisrael p. 91*) "In every criminal offence, even the testimony of relatives and of those who are disqualified, even the testimony of a single witness or the admission of the accused himself, is enough for a verdict of severe punishment." I think everything I have written on this matter is sufficient to prove that this part of the section dealing with a confession by the accused, is based on the words of the Rishonim, who in practice taught this.[15]

A similar approach can be found in an article by Rabbi Katriel Fishel Tchorch entitled "Ma'arechet HaMissim LeOr HaTorah" (the tax system in light of the Torah), in which he wanted "to show that the Torah's view confirms the right of the state to obligate its citizens to pay sundry taxes in accordance with its needs."[16]

Rabbi Katriel Fishel Tchorsh was born in Poland in 1896. He founded and headed the Board of Rabbis until his death in 1979. In this article he reviewed the halakhic precedents for taxation and concluded that halakha recognizes two kinds of taxation: per person and per wealth. In other words, the basic tax is determined for each person in order to provide common basic needs such as water and security. The progressive tax is determined according to one's financial status in order to provide for public needs and welfare for the poor. He goes on to review the state's tax system, and concludes that these two forms of taxation co-exist to a degree:

> From this I deduce that the totality of our taxes, both governmental and municipal, merge into two kinds of tax, per person and per wealth, and this is appropriate, since expenses are also made up of these two. Indeed the main foundation on which taxes are usually built is per prop-

> erty, according to the progressive method, in other words—each according to his financial ability and status. This is truly appropriate according to Torah Law, as defined by the Maharam, Rabbi Baruch of Rothenburg, in his response (article 104) and emphasized even more in the book *Masa Haim* by Hagaon Haim Palagi [third edition, 4:12), as follows: "It is a rule of the Law of Moses, the custom of Rishonim in the town and agreed upon by all the rabbis." And in another place, "Since the obligation is imposed by our holy Torah on people of means." However, there are some kinds of tax which apply to persons and deviate from the wealth framework, whose purpose is to finance poor people. According to the rule cited above in the name of the Tosefoth in Baba Batra, that whenever there is danger to life we go according to persons, this has to be taken into account. In any case we must take a temperate line: half according to wealth and half according to persons, as the Rishonim and the Aharonim decided. Thus, if we take the entire tax system as one unit, taking into account the various types of payments as they were fixed, we will see that there is indeed a kind of merger that is appropriate according to the Torah, and according to common usage and *halakha*.[17]

Articles on other subjects also appeared in *HaTorah Veha'Medina* yearbook, including the question of routine security measures. The most complex halakhic problem in this field was police work on the Sabbath. Ongoing police work, which included frequent vehicle patrols and arriving on the scene after being summoned by citizens, involved desecration of the Sabbath by bearing weapons, traveling in vehicles, and going beyond prescribed limits. In other countries this issue hardly concerned the Jewish community because nearly all policemen were not Jewish. However, the Israel Police was established as the police force of the Jewish state and most of its members were Jews.

Rabbi Herzog addressed this issue after despairing of any likelihood that the Israeli Police would be receptive to the halakhic precepts of the Chief Rabbinate. He dealt with questions theoretically related to police work on the Sabbath, basing himself on existing halakhic rulings on the subject of saving lives on the Sabbath. He did not expand on permissions derived from the reality of saving lives, or on the halakhic definition of this concept, and his theoretical conclusions did not in fact permit the normal functioning of the police on the Sabbath. He assumed that in any event the Israeli Police would not heed his halakhic instructions.[18] Among other things, he ruled that:

> It is permitted to use a vehicle to arrive at a location where a quarrel has broken out and there is a possibility that a homicide will take place. It is also permitted to use a vehicle in order to frustrate a robbery, when information has been received that unknown persons have been found in suspicious circumstances. [But] this permission is valid only for the purpose of reaching the place of the criminal act; thereafter it is not

> permitted to return from that place by car until the end of the Sabbath.[19]

Rabbi Yisraeli disputed the premises and conclusions reached by Rabbi Herzog. In his article "HaBitachon HaPnimi BaMedinah BeSabbath" (Internal Security in the Country on Sabbath) that appeared in the yearbook, from the outset he formulated the work of the police on the Sabbath in halakhic terms.[20] To this end he proved creative in establishing new rules. He based himself on a halakhic ruling by Maimonides (*hilchot Sabbath,* chapter 2) whereby one who goes out to save a life on the Sabbath is permitted to return to the place whence he came. "And when they save their brethren they are permitted to return with their weapons to their place on Sabbath in order that they may not be thwarted in the future,"[21] although most commentators disagreed with his words or consigned them to one particular case. Accordingly, he permitted police called to the scene of a crime to return on the Sabbath even if the condition of saving life (*pikuach nefesh)* no longer applied. Furthermore, he extended the definition of saving life to a more general description that included the likelihood of someone getting hurt if a police patrol had not been carried out on the Sabbath. His innovation was that a police patrol, which is part of a chain reaction in the event of pikuach nefesh, falls under the category of "tools for pikuach nefesh" and as such it is permitted on the Sabbath:

> We learn a rule, that when we are not yet faced with a situation of *pikuach nefesh,* either immediately or later, but it is clear to us that it will occur at some point in time, then we regard it as if it were already facing us. Because the injunction that "you shall live by them" applies not only with regard to saving life in this moment but also to saving life that must be lived at some other time, even though we do not know when and how. So too the commandment of "in its time" is incumbent upon us at this moment and also on what the future may bring.[22] If so, whatever we can do in order to carry out what is imposed on us by these commandments in the future are all devices which, if they are permitted on the eve of the Sabbath, are permitted on the Sabbath as well, like the commandment itself. From here we learn a great *halakha* that the saving of life in the future, is as if it is happening now.[23]

Another innovation by Rabbi Yisraeli related to property damage and bodily harm from the point of view of pikuach nefesh, which made it possible to conduct police patrols and arrest wrongdoers on the Sabbath. He arrived at this conclusion through a wide-ranging interpretation of the method of the Gaonim:

> It is appropriate to introduce another halakhic explanation here, one that can serve as a corollary, if not a basis that is important in itself. This is the method of Rav Hai Gaon and Harav Ba'al Halakhot [Gedolot] and HaRach [Rabenu Hananel] on the matter of [permission to

> extinguish] a glowing ember on Sabbath in public (Sabbath 42, 7"1). They explained it as based on Shmuel who permitted it because of metal despite the prohibition being mandated by the Torah (melakha d'oraita) [ . . . ], because otherwise it would cause damage to many. Maimonides and the Rashba wonder how it could be possible to permit a (forbidden) melakha d'oraita for fear of causing damage, and they both wrote as follows:
> "As it is its way to cause damage and many are damaged by it, Shmuel considered it a danger to life, as it is not possible for the many to be careful of it [ . . . ]" It is not inconceivable that the entire world recognizes the principle that damage to many is considered the same as *pikuach nefesh* of one individual. Hence conducting a patrol in order to prevent quarrels and fights among the public or to catch thieves etc, even if the saving of lost lives is somewhat far-fetched, the saving of money and prevention of bodily harm is very possible, and this is no worse than a glowing ember and even preferable to it, because in this case the damage is not limited to one place, but harms the public as a whole. Certainly in the matter under discussion there is an element of saving the public from harm, which, according to the Gaonim, is a consideration equivalent to *pikuach nefesh,* and as we have written it stands to reason that the other Rishonim also acknowledged the principle of the law in the matter in question.[24]

Thus, he ensured that police work on Sabbath was halakhically permissible from the outset, both in order to prove that halakha does not constitute an obstacle to the functioning of the modern Jewish state, and to enable religious Jews to enlist in the police force.

It must be borne in mind that the halakhic discussion conducted on the pages of *HaTorah VehaMedina* was theoretical, since no government institution ever sought to clarify the halakhic position, nor did they regard themselves to be bound by it. This naturally influenced the character of the discussion, whether consciously or unconsciously. Any misgivings about initiating halakhic rulings were dispelled, since the discussion was not on a practical level, nor was there any likelihood of halakhic censure, which requires exactitude and optimal external and self-examination.

## RELIGIOUS LEGISLATION

Some ten years after the state was established, the hopes of the optimists who anticipated that the country would be run in accordance with halakha, or at least not in opposition to it, were dashed. Conflicts between religion and state such as the dispute regarding "who is a Jew" for purposes of the Law of Return and the Citizenship Law,[25] had the religious parties calling for religious legislation. The fact that they constituted part of the coalition gave them some clout in the legislative sphere. Religious legislation did not profess to fully reflect the halakhic position, but rather, through political compromise, to achieve a situation whereby its religious character would be preserved to some extent while halakha would be breached to the least degree possible.[26]

The overriding concern of the religious parties related to the Sabbath. In the State of Israel's laws this subject is extremely unclear. The status quo letter sent by the Zionist leadership to the heads of Agudath Israel in 1947 includes an extremely broad definition: "It is clear that the legal day of rest in the Jewish state will be Saturday." Wide-ranging declarations regarding the importance of the Sabbath were made on quite a few occasions, but they were not legally binding. Even the Ordinance of Rest Days of 1948, which decreed that the Sabbath and Jewish festivals would be fixed days of rest in the State of Israel and was incorporated in the constitution of the Law and Administration, was not accompanied by punitive authority. Since, to the secular way of thinking, the Sabbath is a socialist value, a day of respite from work, places of entertainment should remain open and public transport should be available to make it possible to visit them. The religious way of thinking aspired to a general, national Sabbath law that would forbid all forms of labor on this day. In the absence of any means of reaching an agreement, the practical decision was passed to the local councils, resulting in vast differences in Sabbath observance in each city as regards entertainment and public transport. However, the Knesset did rule on the issue of work on Saturday. In 1951, the Hours of Work and Rest Ordinance was passed, defining Saturday as the exclusive day of rest for Jews and forbidding the public sector to employ Jewish workers on the Sabbath. The law did not apply to independent employers, nor did it include any prohibition on conducting trade on the Sabbath. Furthermore, it did not relate to the nature of public places on the Sabbath, referring solely to the rights of workers.

The religious parties did not regard it as sufficiently binding. They did not want a socialist law dealing with workers' rights, but a Sabbath law to prevent public desecration of the Sabbath. Once again, they tried to legislate the Sabbath laws as they had originally envisioned them. In 1955, HaPoel HaMizrachi even inserted a commitment to this effect in a coalition clause. But marked differences were apparent in the religious community. The Religious Zionist camp maintained the position that if disagreements with the largely secular public were unavoidable, they should strive to minimize differences of opinion wherever possible and even agree to legislation which, while possibly harming halakha, nevertheless provided a partial basis for the religious position. Agudath Israel, representing the Haredi sector, maintained that they should not sign on a partial agreement, only one that is consistent with halakhic observance of the Sabbath. One topic of dispute was the city of Haifa, with its large Arab population and distinctly secular majority, which, in accordance with the status quo, had been operating public transportation on the Sabbath even during the mandate period. The Haredim were strongly opposed to any agreement permitting the desecration of the Sabbath in any Israeli city, while the Religious Zionists believed it should be agreed to if it meant that the legislation would apply everywhere else in the country. The chief rabbis were not prepared to express a halakhic opinion on the partial law.[27]

When Rabbi Yisraeli was required to intervene in the dispute he took a halakhic position. In his article entitled "Partly Religious Legislation" he clearly laid out the halakhic dilemma, but in practical terms he gave up on fully realizing the dream at this stage:

> The situation of Torah observance in the public domain has unfortunately not improved in recent years. On the contrary, in some places the state of affairs has deteriorated. Elections to the Knesset and municipal institutions occasionally result in an overwhelming majority of representatives of secular parties, and the small number who represent the religious public does not enable us to alter the legislation in order to impose Torah rule in the state. The little we can achieve, both in the Knesset, the government and in the municipal institutions, is obtained through coalition partnerships with the representatives of other parties. If we cooperate with them, which necessarily requires that we waive full Torah demands, they will consent to pass laws with a degree of constraint against irresponsibility. This raises a question of *halakha* and religious outlook: what are the limits of concession that the religious representatives can agree to in order to achieve the little it is possible to achieve? Are they permitted, or even obligated, to support the passing of a regulation or a law that leaves a gap [in the wall] near the one standing? Or would it be better that such a law not be passed at all, so as not to give the impression that the Pharisees permitted this thing.[28]

First, he dealt with the practical benefit of the law to reduce desecration of the Sabbath in general and particularly in public, saving many from the sin of desecrating the Sabbath. Then he addressed the problematic aspects of the law from the halakhic point of view. One argument was that permitting public transport to operate legally on the Sabbath constitutes aiding and abetting a transgression. Rabbi Yisraeli countered this by saying that helping with a transgression constitutes an act without which the wrongdoer could not perpetrate his offense, but that "here we are not helping them with anything relating to desecration of the Sabbath in Haifa, we are just not hindering them from continuing with their acts."[29] Another objection was that by voting in favor of a law that partially desecrates the Sabbath, the religious delegates themselves were in effect "desecrating Go-d's name." Rabbi Yisraeli proved from several halakhic sources that such desecration only occurs in cases of encouraging and identifying the transgression, whereas "as stated above, when the law is brought to the Knesset for a vote the religious Knesset members will certainly not be encouraging transgressors. On the contrary they will do so reluctantly, with expressions of pain because it is not in their power to pass an amended law true to our hearts. In no way does this constitute the desecration of Go-d's name which is sometimes bound up with the law of one who helps [a forbidden act], as we have seen."[30] He concludes that "accepting the Sabbath legislation even in its truncated form will be a great achievement for religious Jews in the land, and can serve, Go-d willing, as the cornerstone for the rule of Torah in public life in the state of Israel."[31] In the end, this partial Sabbath legislation was not accepted, and general religious legislation virtually ceased.

## HALAKHA THAT REGULATES AND HALAKHA THAT CHALLENGES: RENEWING HALAKHOT OF BATTLE AND THE ARMY

One independent establishment of sovereignty that merited extensive halakhic attention from the earliest years of the state was the army. A number of halakhic treatises were published about the form a Jewish army should take in accordance with Torah law. This literature already showed the beginnings of a change toward adopting an offensive ethos instead of the defensive ethos born in the Diaspora, one that found expression in the definition of the role of the military and its place in advancing the process of divine redemption.[32] Yet this literature, that summarized and regulated those sections of the Torah and literature of the Sages relating to militarism, was theoretical and even utopian, and did not correspond with the reality of the IDF in those days.[33] Ancient military laws were laid down against a totally different background from that of a modern army in a modern state. In ancient times a dimension of holiness was associated with Israel's army, as evidenced by the fact that the Ark of the Covenant accompanied Israel's battles. It was from this reality that various halakhot were derived regarding the holiness and purity of the military camp, the priest anointed for war who performed a form of religious rite for those setting out for battle, and more. Furthermore, the laws of battle, weapons, and the international legal aspects of modern warfare are completely different today. The option of legally taking a woman forcibly from a defeated nation and marrying her [*eshet y'fat to'ar*], for example, which in ancient times could be regarded as a form of moral progress from the norm, is unacceptable in international legal reality today. By contrast, responsa from recent centuries have largely dealt with questions regarding individual Jewish soldiers serving in non-Jewish armies, and for the most part they were irrelevant in delineating the shape of a Jewish army that conducts itself from the outset according to halakha and whose geographic arena of action is Eretz Israel.[34]

However, there are some laws relating to various military issues which, even if certain items are no longer relevant, apply in principle in all matters relating to armies and warfare. The distinction made by the Sages between a religiously mandated war (*milchemet mitzvah*) and a religiously permissible war (*milchemet reshut*), which are based on King David's wars, forms the basis for all army *halakhot*. According to most commentators and adjudicators, *milchemet mitzvah* refers to war for the purpose of taking Eretz Israel from an alien regime, or a war of liberation and defense against attacking enemies. *Milchemet reshut* refers to a war for the purpose of expanding the borders of the Jewish state beyond those of the Promised Land indicated in the Torah. Halakhic literature includes the important consequences of defining a specific battle as milchemet mitzvah or milchemet reshut. For example, milchemet mitzvah does not require the consent of the Great Assembly (*HaSanhedrin Hagdola*). The leader of the people can make this decision on his own. However, this is not the case for milchemet reshut.

The list of those who are exempt from going out to battle enumerated in Deuteronomy (20: 5-8) and *tractate Sota* of the Mishnah: one who is betrothed to a woman but has not yet married her; one who has built a new home but has not yet dedicated it; and one who has planted a vineyard but has not yet harvested it, as well as a newlywed during the first year of marriage, gave rise to a discussion on full or partial exemptions in similar situations. This comes in addition to the more general deliberations on the question of recruiting women and yeshiva students,[35] the actual sources for which are relatively late. The Babylonian Talmud attributes the custom of issuing those departing for battle with a *get milchama*—a written deed of divorce for their wives, to prevent a situation of *aginut* (where a woman is "chained" to her marriage even though her husband does not return), raising the possibility of adopting this custom for the Israel Defense Force. Finally, there is the issue of fighting on the Sabbath, which engaged Torah scholars throughout the ages, including during the diaspora. Rabbinical halakhic literature regarding the army during the first years of statehood related equally to both biblical and sources[36] and therefore could not serve as a contemporary *Shulkhan Arukh* for army regulations. Another publication dating from that time that attempted to adjust halakha to modern military reality is Rabbi Shimon Federbush's *Mishpat HaMelukha be-Yisrael.* Rabbi Federbush was fully cognizant of this problem, and the latter part of his book deals with army regulations. From the outset he points to the vast difference in the concept of warfare then and today:

> The basic changes that occurred in appreciating war and peace clearly show how far human morality has developed. War, which the ancient world regarded as the pinnacle of majesty and grandeur, became through Israel's Torah and the nations whom it influenced, the height of evil and cruelty. Very few moral concepts have passed through such a transition from one extreme to the other.[37]

According to Federbush, the Torah objected to the concept of war as waged in the ancient world, and therefore its principles, which form the foundation of mitzvoth relating to the army, are also relevant today. In his discussion of various army-related halakhot, Federbush derives the principles of the Jewish army from the Torah and the literature of the Sages and applies it to our times. For example, like Rav Tsair, he maintains that the exemption given to one who is "afraid and disheartened," which applies in milchement reshut, is analogous to conscientious objectors. "It is permissible to apply the virtue expressed in this ancient statute of recruitment that even at a time of emergency concerns itself with the moral feelings of the individual."[38] He brings another example from a ruling by Maimonides, according to which in times of war the government has the right to confiscate property and mobilize skilled workers for the army effort, under terms that will fully compensate the owners and the workers. This is in contrast to the right to impose a war tax on the population, which is general and equal for all citizens, whereas requisition only takes the property of one person and does not harm another.[39]

Another example is his discussion of the nature of preventive war, which refers to "war against non-Jewish enemies so they will not rise against you" (BT, Sota, 44a): Is this milchemet reshut or milchemet mitzvah? In the Babylonian Talmud, Rabbi Yehuda and Rabbi Yochanan dispute the definition of such a war. Federbush is inclined to accept the halakhic opinion that it is milchemet reshut, and therefore the state or military authorities cannot make the decision but require authorization from the supreme court:

> The decision on this complicated matter of ruling whether the neighbor intends to wage war or not, cannot be left in the hands of the political or military authority. Every nation that provokes war seeks self-justification for the sake of outward appearances, claiming that the other nation intends to attack them and therefore they must launch a preemptive strike. It is therefore essential to submit this matter to the judges for a thorough and unbiased investigation, to determine whether there really are enough signs of warlike intentions, or whether this is a pretext on the part of the politicians and army generals to wage a war of occupation against an innocent nation.[40]

Furthermore, Federbush infers the moral approach that must be taken toward enemy citizens and prisoners of war from several rulings relating to war. From the biblical prohibition against destroying trees during a siege and its derivatives in the literature of the Sages, he derives the prohibition against harming uninvolved citizens:

> From here it follows that it is also forbidden to launch a blockade against a country or a city for the purpose of starving its inhabitants. It is also forbidden to engage in germ warfare. [ . . . ] It is forbidden to destroy any structure that was erected for the purpose of agriculture

> repair and improvement, and there is no doubt that this includes the prohibition against destroying any industry and factory that serves to supply the essential needs of the population.[41]

From the section relating to women taken in captivity he derives the moral conduct that must be displayed toward prisoners of war. But even Federbush, who sought to adapt the halakhot of ancient warfare to modern reality, did not recognize Israel's military reality, nor did he truly engage with it.

Following David ben Gurion's realization that in a national army religious Jews can and should serve in all units without conflicts of conscience, halakha found its place in the General Staff command, and the remit of the military rabbinate was "to determine laws and rulings on matters of religion for the army; to teach laws and rulings on matters of religion in the army; to supervise the execution of these rulings."[42] This understanding was due to the first military rabbi of the IDF—Shlomo Goren.

Rabbi Shlomo Goren (1917–1994) was born in Poland and immigrated to the Land of Israel with his family in 1925. He attended Yeshivat Hebron in Jerusalem before he was thirteen, and he was acquainted with Rabbi Abraham Isaac Kook, the first Ashkenazi chief rabbi of the British Mandatory Land of Israel. Rabbi Goren also studied at the Hebrew University. He founded the rabbinate of the Israel Defense Forces immediately after the establishment of the State of Israel and served as its head for more than two decades. Subsequently, he served as chief rabbi of Tel Aviv and then as chief rabbi of the State of Israel.

Rabbi Goren opposed the establishment of separate military units for religious soldiers demanded by the religious ministers and parliament members of the first Knesset, in accordance with the stand taken by Israel's chief rabbinate. He insisted that religious soldiers be integrated into all army units in order to ensure that they would receive equal treatment, and also so that, based on this principle, he could claim a religious way of life for the entire army. Ben Gurion accepted his position and the army was required to adopt halakhic standards regarding kashruth, the Sabbath, burial, and more.[43] The halakhic activities of the military rabbinate fell into two categories. First, every soldier who so wished was given the opportunity to continue observing mitzvoth in the military framework. The army undertook to maintain kosher kitchens, to refrain from any activity that was not necessary for security on the Sabbath and festivals, to give religious soldiers time to pray, and to conduct burials according to halakha for soldiers who fell in the line of duty. The second category dealt with general halakhot relating to how the army functions in times of war, based on biblical sources and literature of the Sages. In the opinion of Aharon Kampinsky, the status and functioning of the military rabbinate under the leadership of Rabbi Goren "constitutes a form of 'minimalist model' of the concept of a Torah state. Through the regulation of religious matters the army is obligated to function as a 'Jewish army'. [ . . . ] This model is extremely relevant to the utopian reality in which the Torah state exists, thus the regulation of religion in the IDF is unique in comparison to other issues regarding religion and state, where the operative reality from a *halakhic* point of view is far from utopian."[44]

Rabbi Goren formulated the laws of the army that are still practiced today, disregarding the halakhic literature published in the early years following the establishment of the state. In other words, faced with biblical and halakhic precedents from ancient times on the one hand, and the broad security needs of the young state on the other, Rabbi Goren was required to correlate them as far as possible.

He barely dealt with ancient laws that do not touch on the reality of a modern army with all that it entails. His focus was those halakhot that are relevant for our times. Rabbi Goren sought to bridge the gap between ancient sources and contemporary reality, as he noted in the preface to his book *Meshiv Milhama*:

> From the time of Bar Kochba [ . . . ] there were no laws of the military, of war, and of national security that had a real connection with the lives of the people. For nearly 2000 years, these issues appeared as "laws for the messiah." Even Maimonides' *Laws of [Kings and] War[s]* are not capable of guiding the establishment of military procedure for the modem day State of Israel, since they are also directed to messianic times. [ . . . ] I am happy to point out that these rulings [ . . . ] have become established standards not only for the religious soldier, but for the Israel Defense Forces as a whole. Orders given by the upper command and the Chief of Staff in matters of religion that have been publicized in our time have been based on *halakhic* foundations that are established in this book, which is destined to be the military *Shulhan Arukh.*[45]

He was guided by the perception that general laws must be updated from halakhic literature through the ages, rather than far-fetched, partial halakhic solutions:

> These problems have not been solved, nor will they be solved, through dispensations, but rather through comprehensive *halakhic* study of all the Torah's studies and its encryptions, through in-depth analysis and comprehensive investigation carried out responsibly, and through a sovereign approach to the subjects under discussion. This is the only and most reliable guarantee for attaining solutions and authorizing *halakhic* achievements in daily life.[46]

One of the main topics he dealt with was military action on the Sabbath. In his discussion of this topic Rabbi Goren deviated from the traditional halakhic method, instead devoting a long review to external historical sources: the books of the Maccabees, the writings of Josephus Flavius and others describing ancient battles that had been waged on the Sabbath.

After comprehensively reviewing all the relevant sources—biblical, historical, and halakhic—he concluded that military action on the Sabbath depends upon two kinds of halakhic dispensation. Defensive action is permitted in the case of *pikuach nefesh*. This was nothing new, but Rabbi Goren's innovation revolved around offensive action. He maintained that offensive action, even in a milhemet reshut, was permissible because of the rule of *ad rideta* (lit. "until it has been reduced." This refers to the permission to continue waging war against a city ad rideta). This rule is preferable to pikuach nefesh because it permits offensive military action on a wide scale, rather than rejecting specific prohibitions whose observance would constitute a security risk, on the grounds that "the Sabbath can be deferred to save lives" and not permitted on a broad scale:

> From all of this an important principle is apparent, that permission to fight on the Sabbath is not based on the grounds that the Sabbath can be deferred to save lives, as we are accustomed to thinking, but rather on a special license intended exclusively for combat. This is based on the interpretation of Shammai the Elder in the Babylonian Talmud, in the Yerushalmi Talmud, in the Tosefta and in Sifri, regarding the phrase *ad rideta*—even on the Sabbath. The permission to save lives on the Sabbath is derived from the biblical injunction *vehai bahem*—"you shall live by them." Our sages understood this to mean that we should not die by them, as clarified in [BT] *Masechet Yoma* 85b and in *Sanhedrin* 74a. Since there is always a problem of saving lives in combat, why do we need another interpretation for permission to fight on the Sabbath other than *ad rideta*, which we also derive from *vehai bahem*. Indubitably the special permission comes to teach us that according to Shammai the Elder combat defers Sabbath in that it is a *mitzvah* in itself, not only in a *milhemet mitzvah* where there is a possibility of *pikuach nefesh* that necessitates engaging in hostilities, but *milhemet reshut*, too, defers Sabbath, even if there is absolutely no *pikuach nefesh*. Because, were it not for this we would not need the injunction *ad rideta*, but rather we could depend on the ruling that saving lives defers Sabbath.[47]

Based on this view he formulated the "Orders and Instructions in Religious Matters" of IDF, concerning the Sabbath and holidays, which distinguishes between offensive and defensive activities:

a. Sabbaths, holy days and official state holidays as determined by the Knesset shall be complete days of rest for all ranks, and in all installations of the Israel Defense Army.
b. On these days all operations shall be discontinued, except such as are essential for the security of the state, of the army and of its installations, i.e.,

1. works which constitute a military operation or any part thereof or are auxiliary thereto.

2. works which are urgently required for the defense and security of the state, which, if not carried out, would endanger the security of the state and the essential functions of the army and its installations, or would harm the war effort, the army or its installations.[48]

Another subject that occupied Rabbi Goren during the inception of the Military Rabbinate was the "war *get* (divorce)."

The goal of a war get is to avoid a situation of aginut. The concept of a war get was formulated to address the absence of a husband who disappeared after participating in a battle. This is a get given to the woman before the war and activated in practice if the husband does not return from the battlefield. Thus, the woman does not remain an agunah and is permitted to marry another man. The main source for the war get is the Babylonian Talmud where it is written that "every man who goes out to a war of the House of David writes a writ of divorce for his wife".[49]

The nature of this writ of divorce is not fully understood. According to its plain meaning, it refers to a regular divorce. During the First and Second World Wars a number of rabbis employed various kinds of war gets which would only take effect in the event that the husband did not return from the battlefield.[50]

In the Netherlands, during the deportations of World War II, three halakhic solutions regarding divorce were based on the "war get" in order to solve the problem of agunot: divorce after time (which terminates the marriage only after a specified date, until which it can be cancelled); conditional divorce (which terminates the marriage only under certain conditions—for example, if the husband does not return home within a designated number of months/years), granted in the case of a husband sent to an unknown place; and writing and granting a divorce in place of the husband, when it was known that he was taken to the Westerbork concentration camp, leaving his wife behind.

The Chief Rabbinate of Israel sought to adopt this practice for the IDF in order to prevent the problem of agunot, which might arise during wartime. But Rabbi Goren was opposed to it for several reasons, the main one being that he feared that the soldiers' morale would be damaged if they were concerned about the uncertain status of their legal standing vis-à-vis their partners. The main source for the discussion of morale is Deuteronomy 20:8: "What man is there that is fearful and faint-hearted? Let him go and return unto his house, lest his brethren's heart melt as his heart." Rabbi Goren argued that making soldiers sign permission for a war get, which in a sense is a document "predicting" their deaths in battle, would severely damage their morale, and therefore they should not be made to sign the document.

Rabbi Goren also dealt with questions of military morality in an attempt to draw conclusions from biblical precedents and general principles of the Sages. From the incident of Shimon and Levi, who killed all the inhabitants of the city of Shchem through cunning to avenge the rape of their sister Dina at the hands of Shchem ben Hamor, and against the wishes of their father Jacob, he concluded that it is forbidden to harm an uninvolved enemy population. Rabbi Goren did not negate the words of Maimonides, who maintained that the inhabitants of Shchem deserved to die because they did not judge Shchem for his crime and therefore they contravened one of the seven Noahide laws. But he claimed that Shimon and Levi were not punished because from the outset it was forbidden to behave in this manner, as Nachmanides had written in his commentary on the Torah.[51]

Further to his opinion that it is forbidden to harm an uninvolved enemy population, he maintained that the regional commander is responsible for the welfare of all the inhabitants of the region, and he cannot shirk this responsibility:

> [With regard to] the measure of legal or ethical responsibility that falls on officers assigned to take charge of the welfare and security of Jewish or non-Jewish individuals, groups, or squads. . . .: To what degree does the *Torah* view those appointed, to be indirectly responsible for crimes and transgressions committed against the population for which they are accountable?[52]

He also deduces this from the episode of the decapitated heifer in the book of Deuteronomy (21:7-8). The Sages explain that the reason why the elders of the town nearest the place where the corpse was discovered decapitate the heifer and declare that their hands did not spill this blood, although nobody truly suspects them, is that, as leaders, they are morally responsible for the man who came from their town: "Rather, [they declare that] he did not come to our area and we allowed him to depart without food, and we did not see him and allow him to go without escort."[53]

Similarly, the regional commander is morally responsible for each and every inhabitant of the region.

Unlike Rabbi Goren, who sought to teach martial morality from the traditional sources and thus to bridge the gap between consolidated halakha which did not deal with these questions and sovereign reality, Rabbi Shaul Yisraeli took a different approach. He formulated it after the retaliatory action in Kibiyah in October 1953 during which several dozen inhabitants of the village were killed, among them women and children. This aroused public outcry in Israel, and consequently, calls were heard to adopt Jewish war ethics. Rabbi Yisraeli claimed that we must not follow unique Jewish laws of war because from a halakhic point of view the laws of war must be subject to international law.[54] If the combat operation goes against international law it is forbidden, even though it is consistent with ethical sources. If it is consistent with international law it is permitted, despite the fact that it is inconsistent with ethical sources.

Otherwise, the state of Israel would be forced to fight according to rules and restrictions that are not acceptable to other nations, and this would tie its hands and it would risk defeat, and its end would be impossible to foretell. This is no idealistic concept but practical wisdom.[55] He derived this principle from the halakhic ruling of *dina demalkhutah dina* (the law of the state is the law), which in his opinion also encompassed international law, not only local national systems:

> The foundation of *dina demalkhutah dina* relates not only to what transpires within a state, but also to international matters as is the accepted custom. [ . . . ] One of the manifestations of *dina demalkhutah dina* is war and military conquest. Just as there is *dina demalkhutah* within a country, so too there is accepted international practice. Therefore, military conquest must be conducted according to this practice, for only then is it valid by virtue of *dina demalkhutah dina.*[56]

Rabbi Yisraeli expanded the halakhic ruling of dina demalkhutah dina to include all dealings between Jews and non-Jews, making no distinction between an individual Jew living in a foreign country or the overall conduct of the state of Israel under international law, of which warfare is a key aspect. From the traditional sources it is only possible to deduce laws touching on the new sovereign reality as they pertain to the functioning of the state and its institutions in the local arena.[57] He even went so far as to argue that the very legitimacy of milhemet reshut in Israel is taken from international law, and if international law regarded war as completely illegitimate then milhemet reshut would be absolutely prohibited:

> And from now on it is said that *dina demalkhutah* between one country and another is also with the consent of the member countries, and despite the fact that it concerns capital offences, their consent is beneficial. This is the basis of all the legality of war. It is indeed the case that if all the nations agree to ban war, in such a way that it will no longer be the custom among nations, neither war nor conquest will be legal, and a nation that goes to war will be charged with murder and bloodshed. However, so long as the custom of war is acceptable among nations, war is also not forbidden by Jewish law, and for this reason it is also permissible for Israel to engage in *milhemet reshut.*[58]

Rabbi Yisraeli did not renew Jewish laws of war based on the traditional sources, as did Rabbi Goren, nor did he claim that halakha is unconcerned with this sphere. Halakha simply lays down a general principle that subjugates the norms in this matter to an outside source—international law—like the civic conduct of a Jewish individual in a foreign country. Thus, halakha endorses the reality which exists in any event, rather than challenging it, as did Rabbi Federbush.

Rabbi Yisraeli's halakhic position complemented Rabbi Goren's undertaking of making the army a state organ faithful to halakha without intervening in the security policies of the political leadership. The laws of the Sabbath, the festivals, and kashruth were observed in the army framework; religious soldiers could preserve their religious lifestyle without religious-conscientious coercion on the part of their commanders, and furthermore, the morality of battle was subject to the principles of international law and did not constitute an additional burden for the political leadership.

The harnessing of a new generation of Zionist rabbis to the challenge of sovereignty by fundamentally exploring halakhic questions that arose in light of the new situation, coupled with the reality itself, forged a basic halakhic infrastructure to systematize the Jewish state in accordance with Torah law, although the leaders of the state and most of its lawmakers saw no need to change their lifestyle to conform to this challenge. Nevertheless, the army, as an autonomous establishment under the command of military regulations that apply to the army as a whole and to each individual soldier, is organized and run in a manner that conforms with halakha.

However, when a halakhic approach was required for the question of war ethics, which have clear international aspects and political constraints, no continuous halakhic tradition with a clear position could be found. The rabbis were ultimately forced to resort to unconventional avenues of arbitration to confirm Israel's commitment to international laws of war. This entailed either referring to the Bible or expanding the halakhic ruling that regulates the life of a Jewish individual in a non-Jewish state to one that guides the conduct of the Jewish state in the international arena.

## NOTES

1. A. Cohen & A. Kampinsky, "Religious Leadership in Israel's Religious Zionism: The Case of The Board of Rabbis," *Jewish Political Studies Review*, 18, 3–4 (2006): 119–39.
2. Ibid., 134.
3. Shaul Yisraeli, "Im HaKovetz," *HaTorah veHamedinah* 1 (1949): 12–13.
4. Idem, "Introduction," *HaTorah veHamedinah*, 5–6 (1954): 6.
5. Idem, "Samchut HaNassi UMossdot Mimshal Nivcharim BeYisrael," *HaTorah veHamedinah*, 1 (1949): 64.
6. On this, see chapter 3.
7. Chaim Burgansky, "Community and Kingdom: The Halakhic Approach of R. Isaac Halevi Herzog and R. Shaul Yisraeli towards the State of Israel," in: Ravitzky, *Religion and State*, 275–77.
8. Yisraeli, "Samchut HaNassi," 77.
9. Idem, "Tokef Mishpatey HaMeluchah BeYameynu," *HaTorah VehaMedinah* 2 (1950): 76.
10. On this legal principle, see: Shmuel Shilo, *Dina De-Malkhuta Dina* (Jerusalem: The Institute for Research in Jewish Law at the Hebrew University of Jerusalem, 1974); Elon, *Jewish Law*, vol. I, 64–74.
11. According to Haddayah, "no distinction should be made between a gentile king and a Jewish king" and "there are no grounds for a distinction between a crowned

king and a minister or governor who has no crown: *dina de-malkhuta dina* applies to all."

12. Ovadyah Haddayah, "Does *dina de-malkhuta dina* apply to the State of Israel?" *HaTorah VehaMedinah* 9 (1958): 44. Quoted in: Walzer, *The Jewish Political Tradition*, vol. I, 478–79.

13. Burgansky, "Community and Kingdom," 278–82.

14. Solomon b. Adret (Rashba), *Responsa*, vol. 3, 393. Quoted in: Walzer, *The Jewish Political Tradition*, vol. I, 402–03.

15. Yaakov M. Ginsburg, "Ha'ashamah Atzmit lefi Mishpat HaTorah," *HaTorah veHamedinah* 9–10 (1958–1959): 90.

16. Katriel Fishel Tchorsh, "Ma'arechet HaMissim LeOr HaTorah," *HaTorah VehaMedinah*, 5–6 (1953–1954): 233.

17. Ibid., 262–63.

18. I. E. Herzog, "Al Darchei Shmirat HaBitachon HaPnimi BaMedinah BeSabbath veYom Tov," *HaTorah VehaMedinah*, 5–6 (1953–1954): 25.

19. Herzog, Al Darchei, 32. Quoted in: Abramov, *The Perpetual Dilemma*, 205.

20. Shaul Yisraeli, "HaBitachon HaPnimi BaMedinah BeSabbath," *HaTorah VehaMedinah* 5–6 (1953–1954): 343–44.

21. Maimonides, *Hilchot Sabbath*, 2: 23.

22. The commandment to sanctify the moon at its appointed time, for which the Sages permitted the witnesses to return to their homes on the Sabbath, in order that in the future other witnesses would not be negligent in arriving on the Sabbath.

23. Yisraeli, "HaBitachon HaPnimi," 343–44.

24. Ibid., 345–46.

25. On this, see: Abramov, *The Perpetual Dilemma*, 270–320; Arye Edrei, "Identity, politics, and 'Halakha' in modern Israel," *Journal of Modern Jewish Studies*, 14,1 (2015): 109–25; Eliezer Don-Yehiya, "Religion, National Identity, and Politics: The Crisis over 'Who is a Jew' 1958," in Bar-On and Zameret, *On both Sides of the Bridge*, 88–143.

26. On the Pig Raising Prohibition Law (1962), see: Daphne Barak-Erez, *Outlawed Pigs: Law, Religion and Culture in Israel* (Madison: University of Wisconsin Press, 2007).

27. Aviad Hacohen, "'The State of Israel—This is a Holy Place!': Forming a 'Jewish Public Domain' in the State of Israel," in: Bar-On and Zameret, *On both Sides of the Bridge*, 156–66.

28. Shaul Yisraeli, "Hilchot Koalitzia," *HaTorah VehaMedinah* 11-13 ( 1960-2): 75.

29. Ibid., 101.

30. Ibid.

31. Ibid., 102.

32. Amir Mashiach, "Offensive Ethos of Orthodox Jewish Rulers: Primarily Thoughts," *Daat: A Journal of Jewish Philosophy & Kabbalah*, 76 (2014): 246–51.

33. On this, see: Yosef Ahituv, "From Bible to Sword: The Torah Image of the Israel Defense Forces during Israel's Early Years," in: Bar-On and Zameret, *On both Sides of the Bridge*, 414–434.

34. In this context a relevant question arose with regard to the recruiting of Jews who are cohanim (priests) in the British Army during the Second World War. Rabbi Joseph Hertz, the chief rabbi of Britain, permitted it, basing himself on the participation of the Hasmoneans, who were cohanim, in battle. However, Isaac Hertzog, who was the rabbi in Belfast at the time, claimed that it was forbidden, in light of the words of Maimonides (*Hilchot Shmitta veYovel*, 13: 12) referring to the sons of the tribe of Levi: "They do not go to war like the rest of Israel." When the IDF was established, Rabbi Uziel ruled that it is incumbent on cohanim to enlist in the army like everyone else.

35. Mikhael Benadmon, *Religion and Creativity in Religious Zionist Thought: Moshe Unna and the Religious Kibbutz Revolution* (Ramat Gan: Bar-Ilan University Press, 2013), 71–75.

36. For example, see Rabbi Eliezer Waldenberg's *Hilchot Medina*, vol. 2, which includes archaic subjects such as purifying the camp and women taken in captivity, along with topical subjects such as recruiting women and battle divorces.

37. Federbush, *Mishpat ha-Melukhah be-Yisrael*, 186.
38. Ibid., 196.
39. Ibid., 200.
40. Ibid., 203–04.
41. Ibid., 209.
42. Aharon Kampinsky, *The Development of the Military Rabbinate in Israel* (Jerusalem: Carmel Press, 2015), 29.
43. Ibid., 31–43.
44. Ibid., 80.
45. Shlomo Goren, *Meshiv Milhama: She'elot U-teshuvot Be-inyene Tsava Milhamah U-vitahon*, vol. 1 (Jerusalem 1983), 10–12. Quoted in: Arye Edrei, "Divine spirit and physical power: Rabbi Shlomo Goren and the military ethic of the Israel Defense Forces," *Theoretical Inquiries in Law*, 7,1 (2006): 273–75.
46. Shlomo Goren, *Mishnat HaGoren* (Tel Aviv: Miskal, 2016), 39.
47. Shlomo Goren, "Lechimah beSabbath leOr haMekorot," in *Sinai: Jubilee Volume*, ed. Y. L. Maimon (Jerusalem 1958), 178–79.
48. IDF code, Orders and Instructions in Religious Matters, article 8. Quoted in: Abramov, *The Perpetual Dilemma*, 265–66.
49. *bKetub*. 9b.
50. Aaron Kampinsky, "The Rise and Fall of the 'War *Get*' in the Early Days of the IDF," *Jewish Law Association Studies*, 18 (2008): 103–22.
51. Edrei, Divine spirit, 284–85.
52. Goren, *Meshiv Milhama*, 29. Quoted in Edrei, Divine spirit, 285–86.
53. *mSotah* 9: 6.
54. On Rabbi Goren's attitude toward international law, see: Ilan Fuchs and Aviad Yehiel Hollander, "National Movements and international Law: Rabbi Shlomo Goren's Understanding of International Law," *Journal of Law and Religion* 29, 2 (2014): 1–16.
55. Arye Edrei, "Law, Interpretation, and Ideology: the Renewal of the Jewish Laws of War in the State of Israel," *Cardozo Law Review* 28,1 (2006): 211–17.
56. Shaul Yisraeli, "*Takrit Kibiyeh le-Or ha-Halakha*," *HaTorah VehaMedinah* 5-6 (1954): 102–03. Quoted in: Edrei, "Law," 214.
57. Edrei, "Law," ibid.
58. Yisraeli, "Takrit Kibiyeh," 110.

# SEVEN

# Religious Academics and the Challenge of Sovereignty (1948–1967)

After Israel declared its independence, more voices joined the discourse on halakha and the challenge of sovereignty: they belonged to a group of religious academics with ties to the Hebrew University in Jerusalem. Although the group was not consolidated and its members did not agree about optimal solutions, they saw themselves working with the rabbis, taking the helm as the intellectual-spiritual leaders of the religious national public, and they all agreed on the need to contend with the challenge of sovereignty through scientific knowledge of all kinds, not only halakhic literature. They publicized their thoughts and suggestions in *Yavne,* the religious academic journal edited by Pinhas Wollman and published by the Association of Religious Students at Hebrew University. Although most of them criticized the rabbis for not responding to the new challenges by issuing lenient rulings, there was also criticism from the opposite quarter, in that the rabbis preferred flimsy halakhic solutions to the original halakha.

## "PERMISSIVE STATE OR TORAH STATE"—CRITICIZING THE NEED TO MAKE HALAKHA MORE FLEXIBLE IN ORDER TO ADAPT IT TO REALITY

This was the line taken by Yehuda Elizur (Hershkovitz) (1911–1997), the Hungarian born Torah scholar, brother-in-law and student of Professor Shmuel Klein, a founder of the faculty of Jewish Studies at the Hebrew University. In his article *Medinat Heterim o Medinat HaTorah* (Permissive State or Torah State), published in *Yavne* in 1948, Elizur criticized the tendency to cope with sovereignty by finding farfetched dispensations for various halakhot, which, in his opinion, was driving the longed-for state further away. He claimed that "their goal is not to build a state based on the laws and regulations of the Torah, but to permit accepted legal practice through all kinds of tricks, and to reconcile the Torah with a modern state, with all its rules and manners."[1] While he acknowledged that in the initial stages of the state it would indeed be necessary to follow this path, he maintained that permanent adoption of these solutions would not bring the vision closer to reality but on the contrary, would drive it further away:

> The laws of the Jewish state will not be Torah laws but European laws, patched and prepared under pressure, which perhaps will not gainsay Torah laws. In the same way the *Shmitta* permit does not imply the fulfillment of the mitzvah of *Shmitta* and the establishment of an economic system as ordained by the Torah, but indirectly saves our foreign economic and social order from conflicting with the Torah laws and prevents us from transgressing in the seventh year.[2]

He claimed that in this case the Torah would not direct everyday life in the new state and the Rabbis would have to give halakhic sanction to conduct incompatible with the spirit of Judaism and halakhically approve every whim of a political leader. "It is for this that kings and ministers fought against prophets and wages for many generations, but they did not prevail, because this is not the path of Torah truth and it was not for this that it was given to us."[3]

He suggested that each sphere should be tackled by experts who desired a Torah state. They would consult on how to shape each topic with Torah guidance, without causing economic or other damage. For example, the ways of observing *Shmitta* in our day "must be formulated by financial experts, first class economists who must be proficient in *hilkhot shevi'it* and who desire a Torah system above all things."[4] In the same way, experts would deliberate on essential services that must continue to function on the Sabbath, and would formulate them accordingly.

A similar suggestion had been made a decade earlier, after the hearings of the Peel Commission (1937), by Rabbi Isaac Unna (1872–1948), the rabbi of Manheim and a graduate of the Rabbinical Seminary in Berlin, who immigrated to the Land of Israel in 1935. In 1946, he wrote an article that included the following:

> Years ago I made the suggestion that in conjunction with the Chief Rabbinate permanent committees should be set up to regularly deal with new problems. I shall mention some fields for which these committees should be appointed: first, for questions of work on Sabbath in agriculture, industry, and public utilities; second, for questions connected with precepts concerning Palestine in particular; third, for questions of civil law, criminal law, commercial law, and marriage law. These committees should be composed of rabbis and laymen and each

> committee should not comprise more than five members. They should study the problems at regular meetings and pronounce their decisions. The Chief Rabbinate could convene a conference of eminent scholars to confirm the decisions reached by the committees. The committees themselves—as is the custom with scientific academies—should issue regular reports which could serve as a basis for decisions in everyday life.[5]

Unna's proposal, which was addressed to the chief rabbis of Eretz Israel, was not published at the time, and did not provoke any reactions.

Elizur was not satisfied with a one-time proposal, seeking rather to anchor the interaction between men of Torah and men of science in a process of rabbinical training. To rectify the situation in which rabbis are not proficient in finance, agriculture, industry, medicine, transportation, and so on, and in fact are not trained to have expertise in any of these fields, while those who are proficient are not interested in Torah guidance, Elizur proposed combining rabbinical expertise with systematic professional specialization. The rabbis would then have expertise in various practical areas and would be able to find the way to fulfill Torah commandments in any sphere without impeding its function:

> If we truly and sincerely desire a Torah state, the first practical step is to establish a *bet midrash gadol* (higher yeshiva) to train educators, expert rabbis. This *bet midrash*, if it is built and established, and if it succeeds, will serve to bridge the growing chasm between Torah and practical life, between those who uphold the Torah and the people of Israel. It will even be the creative workshop of a Torah state.[6]

## OBSERVING THE SABBATH IN THE STATE OF ISRAEL

Further criticism of the rabbis, like that of Elizur and yet vastly different, was expressed by Yeshayahu Leibowitz.

Yeshayahu Leibowitz (Riga, 1903–Jerusalem, 1994) was born in the Russian empire. In 1919, he immigrated with his family to Germany. He studied chemistry and philosophy at Berlin University and medicine at Basel University. In 1935, he immigrated to the Land of Israel. From 1936, he lectured at the Hebrew University in science and the philosophy of science. In the 1950s, he served as editor of the Hebrew Encyclopedia.[7]

In the 1940s, Leibowitz published several articles claiming that religious Jewry must be prepared to administer the sovereign state according to halakha. To this end a new halakhic constitution must be drawn up to face the challenge of sovereignty:

> The role of enacting new *halakhic* legislation, of establishing a religious law in a state-organized society in this day and age, is assigned to the religious public as a whole. For obvious historical-psychological reasons, the authoritative rabbinical institutions are incapable of doing so.

> The religious authority of the public to generate *halakha*—even contrary to an existing *halakha*—is unquestionable, provided that this public acts according to its best understanding of the Torah and is motivated by a sincere wish to fulfill it. Shape religion according to the needs of religion.[8]

He assigned the task of drawing up new halakhic legislation to the general public, not the rabbis, while making a distinction between his proposal and the halakhic reforms instituted by the liberal stream of Judaism. This distinction was contingent upon the underlying intention of the new legislation. Whereas the liberals concern themselves with needs that are external to religion, the proposed new legislation is concerned with the needs of religion itself. At the same time, he does not propose to employ well-known halakhic mechanisms of innovation such as rulings of the Sages, as others had suggested before him.

In the early 1950s, Leibowitz was a participant in the Religion and State Forum, whose goal was to discuss matters of current legislative authority according to halakha.

Among the dozens of participants were Rabbis Kalman Kahana and Raphael Kazenellenbogen, Judges Ben-Zion Sharshevsky and Benjamin Halevy, jurists Yitzhak Nebenzahl , Yaakov Breuer, and Zeev Falk, scientists Abraham Frankel and Yeshayahu Leibowitz, and Jewish studies scholars Ephraim Elimelech Urbach, Yechzkel Kutscher, Hayim Hillel Ben-Sasson, Yehuda Elitzur, Yaakov Levinger, and Nechama Leibowitz.

Along with Zeev Falk and Ephraim Elimelech Urbach, they drew up proposals on how halakha should deal with the challenge of sovereignty and submitted them to the forum. Urbach wrote the introduction, Leibowitz the chapter on Sabbath, and Falk the chapter on the role of women in society.

Their proposals were ultimately published in the form of a paper on the official position of the forum, but in 1951 Leibowitz published his personal viewpoint in *BeTerem*, under the title "Sabbath as a religious problem in the state." He viewed the Sabbath in the State of Israel as symptomatic of a serious problem that pitted Judaism against the reality of the new sovereignty.

Leibowitz argues that the most important question is not "What is the political significance of religion?" but rather "What is the religious significance of the state?" In a further article entitled "The Crisis of Religion in the State," he clarified the problem:

> The regime of the Torah as it has come down to us constituted a way of life for a community free of responsibility for internal and external security, for foreign relations, for national economy, for administration of the body politic, and even for a judicial system operating with state sanctions. Yet no community and no individual can manage without all these public functions, unless they are provided by some outside agent. Jewish community life as guided by *halakha* depended historically on

> gentiles, who provided the matrix of public law and order within which *halakha* functioned.[9]

To his understanding, the reality that secular Jews serve as the outside agent in the sovereign Jewish state has distorted Jewish religion, even leading to blasphemy, and is distancing the youth from Torah and mitzvah observance. He cites the Sabbath as a glaring example.

In the Jewish state, the attitude of the rabbinate and the religious political leadership toward the Sabbath in regular halakhic terms has, according to Leibowitz, resulted in a situation where the Sabbath is not a matter of the public domain but only the domain of the religious public. Halakha as it currently stands does not enable the modern state to function according to the Sabbath observance. Security services such as the army and police; essential services such as water, electricity, shipping, industry, and other branches of the economy; and cement and glassworks, all require work on the Sabbath. The sad result is that the religious public is like a parasite, resting on the Sabbath while enjoying the fruits of the labor of the secular public. As Leibowitz says:

> This sort of attitude can only discredit religion, even in the eyes of religious Jews, particularly the younger generation. It will, of necessity, be regarded as parasitic, in that a sectarian Judaism depends upon the secularity of the state and the non-observance of *halakha* by those who run the state. Let other Jews keep the electric current and water supply running on the Sabbath, they seem to say, so long as our group is exempted from that duty. Of course there must be police at work on the Sabbath; let its functions be performed by other Jews. There must be a navy; let nonreligious Jews be sailors.[10]

The religious public must offer a way of observing the Sabbath while maintaining the vital services of the state, one that will also obligate religious Jews. And religious Jews must be willing to implement it, using religious workers, when the state comes into being.

Leibowitz suggests that instead of relying on the assistance of the "shabbes goy,"[11] religious Jewry must work toward new halakhic legislation that would allow religious Jews and others to provide vital services on the Sabbath. He claims that "what was acceptable and possible in the Diaspora reality and in the absence of independent financial and economic responsibility, is liable to arouse resentment and aversion under conditions of sovereignty and national independence."[12]

Leibowitz, like Elizur, was opposed to flimsy dispensations and specific exemptions, but unlike him, he supported far-reaching comprehensive reform. He suggested that a definition be drawn up for every essential service that must function on the Sabbath, and these services should be designated as mitzvoth, to be carried out as they would on any other day, with no exemption for religious workers, nor should there be any change or mitigation in this work. According to Leibowitz, this general dispensation relied on the distinction between the fact that it is obligatory for every individual to observe the Torah, and the obligation for everyone—the state—to observe the Torah. The state and its citizens are permitted a great deal more than an individual. To bolster this point of view he gave the example of the institution of war, which overrides the injunction "thou shalt not kill," and the offering of sacrifices, which permitted those who were unclean to enter the temple and allowed many tasks to be carried out on the Sabbath:

> The general public—the nation, the state, society—is not the same as the individuals who comprise it. The general and its particulars should not be measured in the same way. Even the Torah was careful to distinguish between the one and the many. Therefore it is possible to conduct a serious *halakhic* inquiry as to whether Sabbath observance by the nation and the state and their institutions carries the same significance as for an individual and his actions. Perhaps the prohibition on Sabbath work bears the same weight as that for which there is none worse—"thou shalt not kill." This applies to each and every individual in his personal life and actions with no exemption, but it has no validity for the same individual when he is a soldier on a mission. Moreover, the state is even commanded by the Torah to spill blood in order to preserve that same society whose individuals comply with the injunction "thou shalt not kill."
>
> The same applies from a *halakhic* point of view between an unclean individual and public uncleanness, that is permitted or rejected in cases when it applies to the individual. Even on the Sabbath itself no prohibition on work applies to the temple and its work, which is the work of Israel and not the work of an Israelite for his own personal needs and enjoyment. In all earnestness we must deal with the question of whether we should impart the same *halakhic* importance to essential services and duties of the state in our day as to the offering of sacrifices when the Temple was in existence.[13]

Eight years earlier, Romanian born rabbi Eliezer Berkovitz (1908–1992), a graduate of the Orthodox rabbinical seminary in Berlin, objected to the concept of a "Sabbath goy" in the public domain in Israel, claiming that such unnatural arrangements are not compatible with the Torah. He was disappointed that "as of yet nobody has sufficiently researched and implemented a system to respond to the challenges historic Judaism poses in a modern world."[14]

However, he took a broad approach to the topic and it is not known whether he supported Leibowitz's specific proposal. Leibowitz's article aroused heated debate among religious Zionists.[15] Rabbi Moshe Zvi Neria (1913–1995) responded from the other side of the barricade. Rabbi Neria (1913–1995), who was born in Lodz, attended Lithuanian yeshivas before enrolling in the Mizrahi Teachers Seminary in Jerusalem. A student of Rabbi Abraham Isaac Kook, he went on to establish the Bnei

Akiva yeshiva in Kfar HaRoeh. Rabbi Neria negated both Leibowitz's presentation and his basic assumptions, which he viewed as foreign to halakhic discourse, while his deductions were not halakhically legitimate. According to him, Leibowitz's analogy between sacrificial work in the temple and essential services in the state was baseless. It raised questions from every angle that do not address the subject. He was sure the halakhic sages were competent to deal with the challenge using existing tools, without resorting to "religious amendments":

> It is not in Heaven, and it can all be learned from the Torah. In every generation our sages are capable of comparing *milta lemilta* (two sources) and extracting a clear *halakha* from the two Talmuds and their commentators. Moreover it has been said: Israel has no need of the Talmud of the Messiah, for it is said "the nations will seek it"—not Israel (Bereshit Raba, 98, 14).[16]

According to Rabbi Neria, existing halakhic definitions for *pikuach nefesh* (preservation of human life) are enough to sanction work on the Sabbath for all security and essential services. He legitimized the "Sabbath goy" solution formulated in the Diaspora as a halakhic expedient for observing the Sabbath under changing conditions, claiming it was permitted for certain branches of industry, on the grounds that the Torah does not forbid non-Jews to dwell in Eretz Israel, and the halakhic need for a gentile in certain cases, such as selling hametz, did not originate in the Diaspora. The patriotic sensibilities of teenagers who feel that this solution smacked too much of galut and therefore has no place in our sovereign land, should not influence the considerations of the halakhic authorities.[17]

To prove his point that the rabbis were indeed tackling the halakhic issue of the Sabbath in the sovereign state seriously, he brought in evidence Rabbi Eliezer Yehuda Waldenberg's treatise *Shevitat hayam* (Jerusalem 1950) dealing with Jewish shipping on the Sabbath, which had been published the previous year.[18] This comprehensive study of the halakhic problems involved in operating Jewish ships on the Sabbath also proposed practical solutions. The author had conducted extensive technical inquiries involving seamen and engineers, even including a preface with a technical description of a ship's structure and the manner in which it sails. Although his solutions did indeed depend upon a "Sabbath goy," he was aware of Leibowitz's criticism and responded that with regard to Israel's maritime activity, one-fifth of all sailors are not Jewish. In other words, the reality in this case is inevitable. While relying on the "Sabbath goy" in his proposed solution, he alluded to the solution offered by Rabbi Kook in his responsa *Da'at Cohen* (response no. 235), on the subject of milking on the Sabbath, which he only permitted to be carried out by a gentile "as our forefathers have always done":

> And in general it is impossible for a Jewish community not to include some gentiles for those things which are only permissible by gentiles on the Sabbath and holidays. The laws of the Holy Torah are certainly far stronger than all the nonsensical laws that people have invented. They are our lives and the length of our days in the Holy Land.[19]

According to Rabbi Neria, the real problem was that those who were responsible for essential services had no interest at all in Sabbath observance, so along with essential services they also operated non-essential services. This reality goes against halakha and creates a problem of conscience for the observant Jew who is careful not to commit halakhic transgressions. If those responsible for essential services were to operate according to halakhic guidelines there would be no problem for observant Jews to provide essential services on the Sabbath, just like secular Jews, who would also be fulfilling the commandment of preserving the state with this work. He believed that the halakha was suited to the reality of modern sovereignty just as it stands, but the condition for its adjustment was that society as a whole be committed to halakha:

> From here we see that the *halakhic* ruling by the writer, that "the form and the prohibitions (of Sabbath *halakhot*) do not permit a (religious) person to fulfill his duty as a soldier, a policeman, an official, or a citizen bearing state responsibility" is simply the opposite of the truth. It is devoid of any theoretical *halakhic* foundation, and is nothing more than a false accusation regarding the Sabbath laws. For it is not the Sabbath laws that prevent them from performing their duties. It is the laws of the state, which is largely secular, that is preventing them.[20]

Several years later, Rabbi Neria also objected to Rabbi Goren's innovation of basing permission for combat on the Sabbath on the dispensation of Shammai the Elder *ad rideta* (lit. until it has been reduced) even on the Sabbath,[21] claiming that from the time of Moses warfare has been permitted on the Sabbath on the general grounds of *pikuach nefesh* and there is no need for additional permissions. Nevertheless he, too, acknowledged that permission for combat on the Sabbath is broader than the permission granted for a normal case of pikuach nefesh.

> In the case of *pikuach nefesh* for an individual, a distinction can clearly be made between a dangerous condition and a normal condition, whereas in the case of *pikuach nefesh* for many, during a war emergency, it is impossible to make an accurate estimate, nor is it possible to predict developments in advance. Therefore the scope for contravening the Sabbath is broader, and there is no cessation of hostilities even in a situation where seemingly it is possible to do so.[22]

Eliezer Goldman (1918–2002) a New York born graduate of Yeshiva University who settled on Kibbutz Sde Eliahu and was affiliated with *Hakibbutz Hadati,* joined the dispute with his own proposal. On the one hand, he agreed with Leibowitz's definition of the problem and the pressing need for rabbis and the religious public to come up with halakhic solutions that would enable the state to function normally on the Sabbath. He rejected Rabbi Neria's claim that it was futile because the secular majority refused to compromise, maintaining that it is a fundamental obligation that does not depend on its results. On the other hand, he negated Leibowitz's concrete proposals, which he did not regard as halakhically legitimate. Instead, he called for a new religious constitution based on existing halakha. Goldman believed that the senior rabbis were disinclined to deal with this, fearing the reaction of the non-Zionist rabbis who ideologically repudiated the legitimacy of the state and had no interest in its succeeding.[23]

Leibowitz himself continued to voice his criticism in the ensuing years, but toward the end of the 1950s he ceased speaking of halakhic reform in view of the sovereign reality, calling instead for the separation of religion and state.[24] In an appeal published in 1959, he pointed out that his proposal was not made from a secular position but out of his deep concern for the future of the Jewish religion in the State of Israel, and his conviction that separation from the secular governmental apparatus was the only way to ensure its renaissance and its broad public influence.

> The separation of religion and state would involve neither withdrawal of religion to a secluded niche nor removal of religious Jewry from the political scene. On the contrary, it would signify the beginning of the great confrontation between Judaism and secularism within Jewry and the Jewish state and initiate a genuine struggle between them over the hearts and minds of the citizens. Religion as an independent force will be the principal opposition to the regime of the secular state, an opposition which can present a clear and unambiguous alternative in all areas of life in the state and society.[25]

## THE STATUS OF WOMEN

Another academician who joined the debate on halakha and the challenge of sovereignty was Professor Ze'ev Falk (1923–1998), who focused primarily on the status of women and proposed halakhic innovations in this sphere. Born in Breslau, Germany, to an Orthodox family, he came to Eretz Israel in 1939 to study at Hebron Yeshiva in Jerusalem. He attended law classes provided by the British Mandate government in 1945 and completed his degree at the Faculty of Law of the Hebrew University of Jerusalem. During the 1960s, he lectured on Jewish law at Tel Aviv University, and from 1970 he served as a professor at the Faculty of Law at the Hebrew University of Jerusalem.

In 1949, Falk submitted his proposal for a Torah constitution to Zerach Warhaftig, a lawyer and member of the First Knesset. He prefaced it with the following statements:

a. The State of Israel aspires to fulfill the Divine commandment: You shall be to Me a kingdom of priests and a holy nation.
b. The State of Israel regards Torah law as God's commandments to His people.
c. The State of Israel proclaims that the constitution of the state is Torah law as handed down from generation to generation.
d. The State of Israel recognizes God's rule over His people as it is said in the words of the prophet: God is our judge, He is our lawgiver, He is our king. The institutions of the state function in His Holy Name.
e. Every law, every action and every verdict issued in the State of Israel that goes against Torah law is null and void.[26]

Falk did not deal with the status of women in his constitution, other than proposing that the legislative body of seventy-seven seats include seven places for women, but rather in state institutions, the definition of citizenship, and the general rights of the individual. It was only within the framework of the Religion and State Forum of which he was a member that he first approached the question of women's status in religion.

Jewish tradition reduced women's economic rights compared to men (e.g., inheritance rights), as well as distancing women from any public position in community leadership and in the judicial system.

Actually, there had been deep social change with regard to the status of women, not only in Eretz Israel during the mandate period but throughout the Western world. Women had obtained many rights that had hitherto been denied them. In a report issued by Falk he described the gap between women's status in halakha and the reality in Israel:

> The social and economic changes that our nation has been subjected to in recent years have also left their imprint on the problem of women. In the social order that prevails today in the main sectors of the population, women take an equal part in duties and rights. It follows that large sections of the Jewish public feel there is an incompatibility between the actual situation of women and their *halakhic* status. The result is well-known; these groups are attempting to foist equality for women upon the rabbinical courts, or perhaps to expropriate exclusive judgment on family matters.[27]

Falk maintained that throughout the generations the Sages had enacted regulations aimed at adjusting the status and rights of women to the social reality of the time. Beginning with the ketubah, through various measures regarding inheritance, enforcing ketubah settlements, the prohibition of polygamy, forced divorce, and a woman's fitness to testify in cases of damages and quarrels. Now the chief rabbinate was charged with the task of enacting new regulations regarding the status of women and their rights, "giving legal expression to a state of affairs that already exists." In his opinion, failure on this issue would result in a situation where the legal authority of the rabbinical courts would no longer extend to the status of women.

Falk proposed four regulations: (1) That the ketubah would explicitly state that the woman can demand at any time that her property—the wages for her work, her profits, and inheritance from her parents—will be hers alone. (2) To include a condition stating that daughters will inherit equally with sons and the widow will receive a portion of the estate in addition to the ketubah. (3) To accept the testimony of women in monetary laws and all matters for which witnesses are required.[28] (4) To formulate laws as to when a woman can demand a get from her husband. It was his opinion that these regulations were essential in order to "achieve what the times require" without halakhic infractions.

Parallel to issuing his report, Falk published an article in *Hatzofeh*, suggesting that one should learn from the new regulations instituted by Moroccan rabbis with regard to uniform inheritance regulations in that country. The rabbis had adopted some of the Castilian Takanot (regulations) customary among exiled Spanish communities, ordaining among other things that the portion inherited by unwed daughters was equal to that of the sons, and the widow receive a portion of her husband's inheritance. Falk maintained that it was incumbent upon the Chief Rabbinate to institute new regulations aimed at improving the status of Jewish women.[29] He continued to address this subject throughout his academic career.

## EPHRAIM ELIMELECH URBACH AND THE MOVEMENT FOR TORAH JUDAISM

The third and most significant author of the Religion and State Forum memorandum that attempted to influence halakhic discourse in light of challenge of sovereignty was Ephraim Elimelech Urbach (1912–1991).

Urbach was born in 1912 in Białystok, Poland, to a Hasidic family. He received a traditional Jewish education. In the early 1930s, he studied at the Universities of Breslau and Rome and also attended the Jewish Theological seminary of Breslau, where he received rabbinic ordination. During this period he supported himself as a private Talmud teacher for German Jewish families. In his final years at the seminary Urbach, although only twenty-five years old, was a member of the teaching staff. He arrived in Eretz Israel in 1938. During World War II, he served as a chaplain in the British Army. He also took part in Israel's War of Independence and worked for several educational institutions before joining the faculty of the Hebrew University in 1953. Two years later he was awarded the Israel Prize for Jewish studies.[30]

It was in the early 1950s that Urbach wrote his introduction to the memorandum of the Religion and State Forum. He claimed that the new

Israeli sovereignty poses a challenge to religious leaders to reinterpret halakha according to political and moral reality, forcing them to be the "constructors" of the Torah rather than its "sons."[31] Furthermore, they should submit their new halakhic rulings to the Knesset (the Israeli Legislature), despite being aware that they would be rejected by the majority of its members, because "it is important that the words of the few be mentioned among the words of the majority, since the words of today's minority may become the majority words of tomorrow."[32]

Inherent in this proposal was the halakhic-democratic position that the Knesset is the arena for renewing halakha, since it is qualified by the general public to enact laws. This position is similar to that of Freiman, Urbach's friend, who also maintained that the Jewish parliament is qualified to enact laws by the power of the halakhic-traditional institution of state regulations.

The forum did not yield results and Urbach waited fifteen years before he publicly returned to this debate. In 1966, he, together with several other religious intellectuals, established the Movement for Torah Judaism, with the aim of transforming elements of religious life in Israel. The hegemony of religion in Israel belonged at the time to Orthodox Judaism and its political parties, particularly the circles of Lithuanian yeshivot. The new movement challenged the "gap between the people and the Torah and the gap between *halakha* and the political, economic and social reality," and called "to revive *halakha* through the clear assumption that the problems of the State are again included in the field of Torah." The six goals and principles of the movement were:

1. The Torah is the legacy of the whole people.
2. The commandments relating to interaction between man and man are an integral part of halakha.
3. The urgency of reviving halakha and the religious institutions.
4. Objection to religious coercion.
5. Religious tolerance for other religions.
6. Relevance for Diaspora Jewry.[33]

Urbach's movement espoused important ideas of the Breslau School, and was in fact an attempt to establish a Jewish "midstream movement" in Israel, like "positive-historical Judaism." The movement opposed the domination of Lithuanian Orthodoxy in religious life in Israel, as well as neo-Orthodoxy, which represented "technology sanctioned by the Torah." They were also opposed to Reform Judaism, which was dismantling Jewish unity. Although they opposed secularism, they were obliged to cooperate with the secular majority in all national-public enterprises. The three main items on their agenda were influenced by Zacharias Frankel's legacy: the method of ruling halakha; altering problematic prayers; and establishing a modern rabbinical seminary in Jerusalem.

The most important aspect of the new movement was its halakha committee. Urbach believed that he was living in a period of rabbinical conservatism and even retreat. Orthodox Jewry is intent on jealously guarding its inheritance rather than developing its heritage in the face of new challenges, particularly the challenge of the new Jewish state. The result has been halakhic stagnation and an almost total absence of creativity in a field that should be potentially vast: Jewish laws of the Jewish state.[34]

Urbach, like Frankel before him, believed in the total authority of halakha and its divine origin. He also believed that "*halakha* was not clear-cut and does not have to be clear-cut."[35] According to him, the codification of halakha is not final, and the Sages have permission and in fact an obligation to reinterpret halakha according to the changing reality. The authority of halakha lay in the acceptance of the people. He quoted Maimonides' introduction to Mishneh Torah: "But whatever is already mentioned in the Babylonian Talmud is binding on all Israel. And every city and country is bound to observe all the customs observed by the sages of the Gemara, to promulgate their decrees, and uphold their institutions, on the grounds that all these customs, decrees and institutions mentioned in the Talmud received the assent of all of Israel."[36] This should be our guiding principle when deciding whether to accept or reject a new interpretation. Like Frankel, he cited the principle in the Jerusalem Talmud (tractate Sabbath): "Every edict which the rabbinic court ordered the public and most of the public did not accept it, is void." He also pointed to precedents similar to the *Pruzbul* of Hillel the Elder, such as religious rulings of the *Gaonim* on issues of civil law, and Rabeinu Tam's ruling that when a non-Jew liaises in a business transaction the prohibition on usury does not hold. Urbach criticized Orthodoxy for adopting Moshe Sofer's slogan "*hadash assur min haTorah*" as a religious principle, while ignoring the internal mechanism of halakha.[37]

The agenda proposed by Urbach and his colleagues called for two main changes. First, to bring halakha in line with modern Jewish political reality. And second, to change irrelevant texts in the prayer book.

The specific halakha they wanted to implement was permission to perform an autopsy when there was even the remote possibility of saving a life, since the principle of *pikuach nefesh* takes precedence over the prohibition of desecrating the deceased. According to Jewish law the autopsy procedure amounts to desecration of a dead body. Therefore, it was frequently the subject of halakhic disputes, due to regulations and the systematic use of anatomy for medical research. As we have seen, Orthodox rabbis who followed Rabbi Yechezkel Landau and Rabbi Moshe Sofer did not find this acceptable. Only in specific cases where the anatomical examination of a dead body might possibly help a seriously ill patient, dissection was permitted, providing that the next of kin gave their consent.[38]

In 1966, the Minister of Health, formerly from the religious-Zionist Mafdal party, was replaced by a minister from socialist-Zionist Mapam party, who instituted a liberal policy regarding autopsies, ruling that they were to be carried out in every case, even when there were non-Jewish bodies from outside of Israel available for research. Public controversy flared and the Chief Rabbinate hastened to issue a halakhic response prohibiting autopsies except in life-threatening situations, and only with the consent of a rabbinical authority. This edict ignored the long-term importance of autopsies in saving the lives of others, preventing future diseases, and developing life-saving medicines.

Members of the movement saw the rabbis' objections to autopsies as tantamount to a declaration of war against modern medicine, limiting the halakha of *nivul hamet* to standard cases only. Their objections were fuelled by their deep respect for modern medicine.[39]

Ten years later Rabbi Shlomo Goren, who was appointed Chief Rabbi in 1973, ruled that autopsies be permitted for the purpose of furthering medical science, as well as for solving crimes and analyzing road accidents. It was also permitted to establish a skin bank for the future treatment of burns. He maintained that the halakhic rulings of Rabbi Yechezkel Landau and Rabbi Moshe Sofer only applied to individual queries posed by Jewish doctors and patients in the Diaspora, whereas in the State of Israel the Jewish government is responsible for the medical system. All planning must be for the long term. The state must ensure the availability of all medical means and aspire to a high standard of medicine and medical practitioners. This responsibility must take into account not only every patient currently in Israel but also future recipients of health care. In any case, one must relate to them as if they are at this moment requiring treatment. This is a matter of pikuach nefesh, which overrides nivul hamet.[40]

Another halakhic subject that required clarification was Judaism's attitude toward non-Jews. From its inception in April 1966, one of the movement's stated principles was its tolerance toward people of different religions: "The movement sees the need to base human relationships, in all religions, on the idea that 'God created man in His image *(tselem)*.' It is time to break free of opinions that are the result of historical circumstances. At the same time, the movement will fight missionary activities in our country by legal means."[41]

This issue was raised due to a false media report in 1966 that an Orthodox Jew had refused to save the life of a non-Jew on the Sabbath for halakhic reasons. The chief rabbi of Israel, Isser Yehuda Unterman, published his halakhic opinion that it is permitted to save the life of a non-Jew on the Sabbath, bringing the argument of *darchei shalom* (the avoidance of conflicts between Jews and non-Jews).[42] Secular Jews criticized this ruling, claiming that his argument perpetuates an unequal attitude toward non-Jews. Urbach and his colleagues sought to approach the issue in a positive halakhic manner. To this end they published several articles. At the founding conference of the movement, which was held that same week, Rabbi Eliezer Samson Rosenthal praised the ruling of Rabbi Unterman, although he pointed out that he was not in favor of political arguments, preferring ethical arguments.[43] In an unpublished article written at that time he offered a humanistic and egalitarian reason for the halakhic attitude toward non-Jews, based on the phrase "This is the book of the Chronicle of Adam (Gen. 5, 1)."[44]

Four years later, Ze'ev Falk, in his essay "A Gentile and a Ger Toshav in Hebrew Law" brought examples of positive and negative traditional attitudes toward non-Jews, with two explanations for the negative approach:

1. The attempt to preserve Jewish uniqueness in an alien society.
2. The archaic reaction of Jews in exile with no recourse who suffered at the hands of non-Jews.

He claimed that today we must preserve Jewish uniqueness through a positive attitude toward Judaism rather than a negative attitude toward non-Jews. Furthermore, in Israel we can defend ourselves, therefore there is no need for a negative halakhic approach.[45] On this issue he sought to bridge the gap between moral sensibilities and halakha.[46]

Urbach was also in favor of changing "problematic" prayers. After the Six-Day War and the reunification of Jerusalem, the movement published the Tisha B'Av letter, which called to amend the text of that day's prayers.[47] It claimed that the Jewish people can no longer refer to Jerusalem as a "destroyed city" and saying so implies ingratitude to the Almighty. The most problematic text was *Nachem,* an addition to the blessing *Boneh Yerushalayim* in the Amidah prayer. The original text depicts Jerusalem as a "city that is in sorrow, laid waste, scorned and desolate," which "sits with covered head like a barren woman," destroyed and conquered by foreign armies and idolaters. Urbach claimed that today we cannot identify with this text. The movement adopted his proposed changes, adapting the text to a plea for compassion (Rachem), instead of consolation (*Nachem*), for Jerusalem "which is being rebuilt upon its ruins, restored upon its devastation, and resettled upon its desolation."[48] The text includes a reference to those who perished in the Holocaust and in Israel's wars. Urbach relied in part on the Jerusalem Talmud's version (Berakhot, 4, 3), and in part on his own intuition. He ignored Orthodox rulings against changes in the original text, claiming they ignored the significance of the prayer. Unlike Orthodox rabbis, Urbach was not afraid to alter ancient texts when he thought them no longer relevant. Similarly, the movement's members proposed changes in a number of expressions in the liturgy that speak of Jerusalem as a destroyed city, for example at end of the third blessing of *Birkat Hamazon* (grace after meals). Instead of "May God rebuild Jerusalem, the holy city, speedily in our lifetime," its suggests "May God rebuild Jerusalem, the holy city, a complete building, speedily in our lifetime."[49]

In support of this, Urbach published an article by liturgical scholar Joseph Heineman in the movement's journal *Mahalakhim*.[50] Heineman maintained that since the Sages had not formulated the prayers, there was no monolithic version of the Amidah prayer. He claimed that the Sages simply ruled on the number of the blessings, their main import, and their order. His practical conclusion was that we must "find a path to express in our prayers the events of our time: the Holocaust, the rebirth of Israel, and the miracles which we have witnessed."[51] Otherwise, we decry the prayer or even deny its purpose.

Urbach also published the thesis of Moshe Samet on Jewish Orthodoxy in the movement's journal. According to Samet, Orthodoxy is not medieval but just as modern as the Reform and Conservative movements. Its theological slogan *Hadash Assur Min HaTorah* is a modern innovation and a reaction against liberal halakhic reforms.[52] Naturally, this thesis was in line with Urbach's agenda, which challenged the Orthodoxy's ultraconservative policy.

The movement's main endeavor was to establish a rabbinical seminary in Jerusalem. Urbach and his colleagues were dissatisfied with Israel's chief rabbinate and the cultural level of the rabbis. They believed the cultural gap between the intelligent public and the rabbis was the result of yeshiva world's opposition to science, progress, and enlightenment. They wanted to design a new model of rabbi. The proposed seminary was similar to the Breslau seminary, although they were attuned to the difference between the candidates and their audiences and did not want to imitate it per se.

Candidates were required to demonstrate a basic and appropriate knowledge of the Talmud and *Poskim*, in addition to worldly knowledge. The curriculum included historical and Talmudic research, study of Responsa literature, training in new and unprecedented halakhic questions, general education, and rhetoric, homiletics, philosophy, and modern Judaism.[53]

Urbach envisaged the first-year curriculum as follows:

The philological-historical method
Introduction to Tannaic literature, the Mishna, Tossefta, halakha, and Agadat Midrashim
The history of the siddur, its diverse styles, and wording
Medieval Jewish philosophy

In the second year:

Introduction to Amoraic literature
Introduction to mystic literature
Modern Jewish history

Homiletics

In the third year:

The history of rabbinical literature
Introduction to law, sociology, and psychology
Modern Jewish philosophy[54]

Urbach emphasized that a philological-historical method should be applied for teaching halakha. The students were required to employ the discipline of Jewish studies even though they would not be pursuing research. There were already enough researchers in Israeli universities; they were being groomed as adjudicators. Urbach wanted the rabbinical seminary to be established specifically by scholars of Jewish studies because of their exceptional contribution to Judaism. Like Frankel, Urbach regarded Jewish studies in a positive light, but he believed the students had to be convinced of the sanctity of the sources. Like Frankel, Urbach excluded Bible criticism from the curriculum, maintaining that a positive affinity is preferable to critical interest.[55]

The movement for Torah Judaism never succeeded in attracting more than a few hundred members. The secularists had no desire to become involved and the ultra-Orthodox were deterred by its Zionist character. The religious-Zionists, unlike American Jewry in the early twentieth century, were not a small minority and therefore did not feel the need to challenge tradition for the sake of Israelization. The movement also failed to establish the rabbinical seminary, the heart and soul of their movement, with its promise of vitality and continuity. Ten years later the movement ceased to exist. It had fulfilled the needs of religious academicians, especially scholars of Jewish studies, and although it no longer exists, its legacy remains among the many religious intellectual academics in Israel.

The reality that was beginning to take shape in the young State of Israel ignored halakhic tradition, the lack of agreement among rabbis regarding the amendment of the Sages' regulations that had become necessary in the light of historical developments, such as inheritance by daughters, and rabbinical opposition to the implementation of halakhic means. Consequently, a group of religious scholars of Jewish studies were impelled to join the discussion as a practical alternative to the rabbinic world, adding their professional and ideological concepts to the argument. They sought to apply methods from the academic world to the field of halakhic ruling, taking into account the achievements of science and the values of enlightenment, and to introduce a democratic dimension to halachic ruling as a criterion for its renewal, as did Rabbi Zacharias Frankel in his time. But beyond expanding and reviving the discourse on the subject, they were unable to obtain the support of the religious public for their initiatives and arrive at a position of religious leadership. The alternative intellectual leadership, which accorded them public prestige, had no effect on their ability to significantly influence halakhic rulings.

## NOTES

1. Yehuda Elizur, "Medinat Heterim o Medinat HaTorah," *Yavneh* 3 (1948): 65.
2. Ibid., 66.
3. Ibid.
4. Ibid., 67.
5. Isaac Unna, "The High Court of Justice in the Past and in the Future," in Leo Jung (ed.), *Israel of Tomorrow*, ed. Leo Jung (New York: Herald Square Press, 1946), 353.
6. Elizur, "Medinat Heterim," 70.
7. On the early thought of Leibowitz, see: Moshe Hellinger, "A Clearly Democratic Religious-Zionist Philosophy: The Early Thought of Yeshayahu Leibowitz," *The Journal of Jewish Thought and Philosophy*, 16, 2 (2008): 253–82.
8. Yeshayahu Leibowitz, *Torah u-Mitzvot ba-Zeman ha-Zeh* (Tel-Aviv: Massadah, 1954), 73. Quoted in Hellinger, "Religious-Zionist Philosophy," 268.
9. Yeshayahu Leibowitz, *Judaism, Human Values and the Jewish State*, trans. by Eliezer Goldman and others (Cambridge, MA: Harvard University Press, 1992), 162.
10. Leibowitz, *Judaism*, 170.
11. On the history of this term, see: Katz, *The "Shabbes Goy."*
12. Leibowitz, *Judaism*, 167.
13. Leibowitz, *Torah u-Mitzvot*, 98–99.
14. Eliezer Berkovitz, *Towards Historic Judaism* (Oxford: East and West Library, 1943), 39–40.
15. On this debate, see also: Cohen, *The Talit*, 137–54.
16. Moshe Zvi Neriah, *Kuntres ha-Vikku'ah* (Jerusalem: 1952), 4.
17. It should be borne in mind that a notable precedent for the "Sabbath goy"—permission to purchase the land of a gentile on the Sabbath by instructing a non-Jew to write the deed of sale—was introduced specifically in the context of settling Eretz Israel, and not in the context of Jewish life in the Diaspora. *bGitt.* 8b.
18. On Waldenberg's legal pluralism, see: Kaye, "The Legal Philosophies," 84–91.
19. A. Y. Kook, *Daat Cohen* (Jerusalem: Mossad Harav Kook, 1942), 427.
20. Neriah, *Kuntres ha-Vikku'ah*, 7.
21. On this, see chapter 5.
22. Moshe Zvi Neriah, *Al Heter Milchamah Be-Sabbath* (Tel Aviv 1962), 5.
23. Cohen, *The Talit*, 150–52.
24. A similar but not identical stand was taken by Eliezer Goldman at the same time.
25. Leibowitz, *Judaism*, 183–84.
26. Proposed Constitution for the State of Israel, March 1949, NLI Archives, Falk Collection, Arc 4° 1789.
27. "On New Social Problems in the *Halakha*," Chapter III, Iyar 1951, NLI Archives, Urbach Collection, Arc 4° 1873.
28. Witnesses whose purpose is not to determine what really happened (as with regular witnesses) but without whom religious law does not apply.
29. Ze'ev Falk, "LeTakanat Benot Israel," *Hatzofeh*, May 18, 1951, 3.
30. Jacob Zussman, "The Scientific Project of Ephraim Elimelech Urbach," *Jewish Studies*, addendum/ special volume 1 (1993): 7–116.
31. According to the Talmudic Midrash: "Rabbi Elazar said on behalf of Rabbi Chanina: Torah scholars increase peace in the world, as it is said 'And all your sons will be students of G-od, and your sons will have peace'—do not read [בניך] your sons but [בוניך] your constructors." *bBer.* 64a.

32. "On New Social Problems in *Halakha*," Chapter I, Iyar 1951, NLI Archives, Urbach Collection, Arc 4° 1873.
33. "The Movement's Program," *Ha-Chadash Yitkadesh*, 1 (1966): 24–27.
34. Urbach, "Life with the Torah," *The Jerusalem Post*, June 5, 1973, 3–4.
35. Urbach, "Samchut haHalakhah Beyameinu," *Mahalakhim* V (1971): 4.
36. Ibid., 3.
37. Ibid., 7.
38. Breuer, *Modernity*, 57.
39. "The Movement for Torah's Judaism's Manifesto on Autopsy," *Ha-Chadash Yitkadesh* 1 (1966): 38–39.
40. Shlomo Goren, *Torat HaRefu'ah* (Tel Aviv: HaIdrah Rabah, 2001), 150–62, 209–41.
41. "The Movement's Programs," *Ha-Chadash Yitkadesh* 1 (1966): 26–27.
42. Isser Yehuda Unterman, *Haaretz*, April 4,1966.
43. Eliezer Samson Rosenthal, "Closing Remarks at the Founding Conference," *Ha-Chadash Yitkadesh* 1 (1966): 19.
44. Benjamin Lau, "Rabbinate and Academy in the writings of Rabbi Eliezer Samson Rosenthal on Saving the life of a non-Jew on Sabbath," *Akdamot* 13 (2003): 21. On similar opinion of Rabbi Hayyim David Halevi, see: Hellinger, "Religion and State," 242.
45. Zeev Falk, "A Gentile and a Ger Toshav in Hebrew Law," *Mahalakhim* II (1970): 14.
46. Ibid., 15.
47. "The Tisha B'Av letter," *Ha-Chadash Yitkadesh* 2 (1968): 58–60.
48. Ibid., 59.
49. Ibid., 61–63.
50. Yosef Heineman, "Changes in the wording and order of worship in the synagogue," *Mahalakhim* I (1969): 23–27.
51. Ibid., 24.
52. Moses Samet, "Hayahadut Hcharedit Bazman Hachadash," *Mahalakhim* I (1969): 29–40; ibid., III (1970): 15–27.
53. "The Program to Establish a Rabbinical Seminary," *Mahalakhim* IV (1970): 5–7.
54. Ibid., 9–10.
55. Ibid., 13.

# Epilogue

As the new Yishuv and national aspirations began to escalate in Eretz Israel, Zionist political ideology took center stage. This when the question of halakha and the challenge of sovereignty emerged. The Yishuv grew and struck roots, the political Zionist concept met with success in the diplomatic arena, and as more and more scholars joined the debate, it became more diverse and detailed. Not only were rabbis and adjudicators involved, but also religious scholars and secular jurists.

It was clear that in order to respond to the challenge, it would be necessary to transition from protective and defensive halakha to innovative, and even groundbreaking halakha. Various suggestions were put forward as to how halakha should respond to the challenge. The two basic premises were that in the Jewish state, law and society must be guided by halakha, while at the same time, international realities and democratic Western values must be taken into consideration in halakhic decisions.

In actual fact, up until the establishment of the state most of the proposals for contending with the challenge of sovereignty were fairly general. Some were evolutionary, others revolutionary, some supported legal pluralism, others were in favor of legal centralism: moderate reform, a renewed Sanhedrin, a renewal of the monarchical legal system, using rulings of the Sages and public regulations. Very few of them were specific, such as the institution of the *Heter Mechira* in a *Shmita* year. Consequently, the allegation took root that the rabbis and the religious public were not paying attention to halakhic questions that were likely to arise when sovereignty became a reality, and they were not prepared accordingly. This complaint was unjustified, as this study shows. The main reason why specific proposals were not put forward was because halakha's responsive casuistic nature, formed during exile, responds mainly to real-time issues but does not take initiatives or preplanning. The genre of Responsa literature that originated during the time of the Gaonim best expresses this trend.

Specific halakhic discourse on a reality that had yet to occur was unacceptable. It was perceived as building castles in the air. The halakhic enterprise of future-thinking Rabbi Chaim Hirschensohn was not acknowledged by his rabbinical colleagues. On the other hand, the paramount example of early methodical engagement with Messianic law—Maimonides' *Hilchot Melachim*—did not relate to the political reality of the modern national state and international law, and therefore could not provide solutions to major problems that arose in real time.

It must be borne in mind that the secular majority in Eretz Israel during the mandate period did not regard halakha as a binding set of rules in the same way that the religious public regarded them. An attempt to present halakha as a national asset, like the national territory of Eretz Israel, the Hebrew language, and *Aggadic* literature, was unsuccessful, both its full religious formulation and the pared-down version of Jewish law. As a result, halakha never fully withstood the test of modern sovereign reality, because in many spheres the state authorities were never required to apply it.

Furthermore, the Haredi (ultra-Orthodox) sector, who were opposed to Zionism, feared a Jewish state ruled by a secular majority, and thus rejected any change in traditional halakhic rulings. They regarded the endeavors of Zionist rabbis to solve the halakhic issues as ongoing cooperation with the secular majority in the Zionist movement. Due to this attitude, and the fact that leading haredi rabbis were opposed to the Chief Rabbinate and to newly instituted halakhic regulations such as the Heter Mechira and bringing the inheritance of daughters in line with the inheritance of sons, the religious public did not present a united front when it came to the laws and institutions of the state. This had a detrimental effect on their insistence that halakha be taken into consideration in the formation of the state.

It also altered the purpose of dealing with the question of halakha and the challenge of sovereignty during the mandate period. At the beginning of this period Zionist rabbis sought to shape the laws and institutions of the embryonic state according to halakha, but by its end, when the machinery of government and society had been formed by the mostly secular Jews in Eretz Israel, and it was clear that this reality would not change in the near future, the Zionist rabbis hoped that the laws and institutions of the state would at least not go against halakha, as actually occurred in the IDF under the leadership of the first military chief rabbi—Shlomo Goren.

Nevertheless, halakhic writings made great strides to narrow the gaps between halakhic precedents arising from the realities of ancient times and the Middle Ages, and modern sovereign reality. They took into account the principle of democratic representation, more equality for women and minorities, maximal functioning of the defense forces on the Sabbath, removing impediments on medical and agricultural advances, and adapting to international law. The gaps that nonetheless remained between the halakhic positions reviewed in this book and the liberal-democratic values of Western nations (some of which are still disputed between conservatives and liberals in these countries) go far deeper than the contradictions that exist in any democratic regime. For example, how do we weigh the security of the state against the freedom of the individual and his right to privacy? Do we accord preference to the dominant national culture or do we give equal weight to the culture of the minority?[1] And do we choose the traditional character over the freedom of the individual and freedom of occupation, in the public domain?[2]

After the Six Day War (1967) and the occupation of areas of Judea, Samaria, the Golan Heights, the Gaza Strip, and the Sinai desert, the political debate on the future of these territories was joined by a halakhic dispute regarding the validity of the prohibition against handing over parts of Eretz Israel to non-Jewish dominion.[3] This debate, which still continues today, overshadowed all other halakhic debates on the question of religion and state and became the nucleus of religious Zionist policy. It even spilled over to the concrete question facing every IDF soldier: Is it permitted to obey an order to evacuate settlements in these regions and hand them over to non-Jewish control?[4] A further argument that arose in the wake of the Six Day War and the unification of Jerusalem, one that has become more weighted in recent years, centers on the halakhic prohibition against going up to the Temple Mount and the proper government policy for this site.[5]

From time to time other halakhic issues relating to government policy emerge, but they are generally solved by political compromises, rather than by decisions that either take the halakhic position into consideration or else reject it outright. For example, sometimes the need arises for essential infrastructural work to be carried out on the Sabbath on roads, railroad tracks, or power stations, in order to cause a little as possible disruption to everyday life and the general economy during the other six days. These activities draw fire from religious political elements and are limited or halted under instructions from the political echelon, and so it goes.

Other controversial issues that arise from time to time, some even creating political crises, are the recruitment of yeshiva students to the IDF, state sanctioned Jewish conversions, non-Orthodox prayer services at the Western Wall, and organ transplants.

The study of halakha in light of the challenge of sovereignty is being constantly upheld by rabbis and scholars of every religious stripe, from the liberal group represented by the Shalom Hartman Institute to the national ultra-Orthodox represented by the *Chotam* forum. Part of their involvement stems from a revolutionary outlook that regards halakha as a source of inspiration for the sovereign state along with modern sources of inspiration. The Shalom Hartman Institute has undertaken a four volume literary enterprise entitled *The Jewish Political Tradition*, tracing the political thought of the Jewish people from biblical times to the present. Each volume contains a selection of primary sources—from the Bible, the Talmud, Midrashic literature, the Responsa, halakha, and philosophy of the Middle Ages and the Modern Age—that illuminate the richness and diversity of the Jewish political tradition. The first two volumes have already been published: *Authority* (2000) and *Membership* (2003). Another liberal body dealing with the same sphere is the Israel Democracy Institute which, since its establishment in 1991, has published dozens of studies and position papers on religion and state in Israel, each dealing to some degree with the question of halakha and the challenge of sovereignty. Nearly all of them were written by religious scholars in the field of philosophy and law.

A great part of the current involvement with this topic maintains the perception that halakha is the primary source that is supposed to guide the state and its institutions. The Zomet Institute, which is identified with mainstream Zionist Orthodoxy, has since 1977 published *Tchumin*, a yearbook that is in fact a continuation of the *HaTorah veHamedina* yearbook. This is a rabbinical literary podium for debates on the encounter between halakha and the state, its institutions, technological developments, and modernism. The guideline of the institute is that "*halakha* is designed to direct the course of the world of action, to accompany its progress, and in order to do so we must delve more deeply into the sea of *halakha*, find *halakhic* innovations, and glean guidance for an ever-renewing world."[6]

Rabbis who are not affiliated with an institute designated to deal with this field nevertheless do not refrain from writing on these topics. For example, in 2007, Rabbi Naftali Bar Ilan, the grandson of Rabbi Meir Berlin, published a four-volume anthology entitled *Regime and State in Israel According to the Torah* (Hebrew), a collection of hundreds of halakhic sources throughout the ages relating to sovereign reality, from a practical point of view. Rabbi Eliezer Melamed, author of *Pninei Halakha* (Pearls of *Halakha*), a popular series that has been published in several languages, also addresses the challenge of sovereignty. After publishing an entire volume on the subject of the Nation and the Land, he went on to discuss it in subsequent volumes. In the volume devoted to the laws of *shvi'it* and *yovel* (2005), he added a chapter entitled "Hazon haShvi'it" (Vision of the Seventh Year) in which he expounds on his theory of the correct way to observe these laws in our time.

The Chotam Forum is comprised of several Torah research institutes that deal with questions of halakha, state, and modernism. It came into being because:

> Along with the development of the State of Israel on social, economic, scientific lines and so on, suitable spiritual development is also required. Topics that have emerged on the public agenda, in the Knesset, in professional forums, and the media demand a response from a professional *halakhic* perspective, one that investigates them in depth and is capable of providing a consolidated Torah-based position suited to the needs of the generation and the time.[7]

An integral part of the activities of the forum consists of writing position papers for the political echelon and mounting media campaigns on topical matters.

Nevertheless, the last three decades have witnessed an accelerated process of secularization among the Israeli public, one that has distanced the State of Israel even further from the religious Zionist aspiration of a state in the spirit of the Torah or at least not opposed to it. This secularization finds expression in four spheres: significantly increased commerce on the Sabbath, with large shopping centers opening on the outskirts of the cities; the import and sale of non-kosher meat; de facto recognition of civil marriages; and secular burials in private cemeteries.[8] The religious public has come to terms with these changes in Israel's public sector, and for the time being it has abandoned its efforts to restore the situation to what it was before through religious legislation. Thus, the focus of those who support this aspiration remains academic and educational, their appeals to the legislative channel are rare, and they mainly take the form of a rearguard action against further erosion of the status quo as regards religion and state.

## NOTES

1. Charles Taylor, *The Malaise of Modernity* (Toronto: House of Anansi Press, 1991), Ch. 5; idem, *Philosophy and the Human Sciences: Philosophical Papers*, vol. II (Cambridge, UK: Cambridge University Press, 1985), 248–88.
2. Alan Roucher, "Sunday Business and the Decline of Sunday Closing Laws: A Historical Review," *Journal of Church and State*, 36 (1994): 13–36.
3. On this, see: S. Fischer, "Self-Expression and Democracy in Radical Religious Zionist Ideology" (PhD dissertation, The Hebrew University, Jerusalem 2007); M Inbari, *Messianic Religious Zionism Confronts Israeli Territorial Compromises* (New York: Cambridge University Press, 2012).
4. On this, see: Geiger, *Leaving the Shtetl*, 230–66.
5. On this, see: M Inbari, *Jewish Fundamentalism and the Temple Mount: Who will Build the Third Temple?* (Albany: State University of New York Press, 2009).
6. "Odot Machon Zomet," April 1, 2019, https://www.zomet.org.il/?CategoryID=204.
7. http://www.chotam.org.il/%D7%90%D7%95%D7%93%D7%95%D7%AA/.
8. Guy Ben-Porat, *Between State and Synagogue: the Secularization of Contemporary Israel* (New York: Cambridge University Press, 2013).

# Bibliography

Abramov, Shlomo Zalman, *The Perpetual Dilemma: Jewish Religion in the Jewish State*, New York: Associated University Presses, 1979.
Ahituv, Yosef, "From Bible to Sword: The Torah Image of the Israel Defense Forces during Israel's Early Years," in *On both Sides of the Bridge* (in Hebrew), edited by Mordechai Bar-On and Zvi Zameret, 414-434. Jerusalem: Yad Ben-Zvi Press, 2002.
———. "Halakhic Vacillations of Chief Rabbi Isaac Halevi Herzog during the Early Years of the State of Israel," in *The Challenge of Independence: Ideological and Cultural Aspects of Israel's First Decade* (in Hebrew), edited by Mordechai Bar-On, 199–213. Jerusalem: Yad Ben-Zvi Press, 1999.
Adler, J., "Religion and Herzl: Fact and Fabel," *Herzl Year Book* 4 (1961–2): 271–303.
Ahad, Ha'am, *The Collected Writings of Ahad Ha'am* (in Hebrew), Tel Aviv: Dvir, 1961.
Albeck, Shalom, *The Law of Property and Contract in the Talmud* (in Hebrew), Tel Aviv: Dvir, 1976.
Altmann, Alexander, "Moses Mendelssohn's Political Philosophy," *The Solomon Goldman Lectures* 3 (1982), 31–38.
Angel, Marc, *Loving Truth and Peace: The Grand Religious Worldview of Rabbi Benzion Uziel*, Northvale, N.J.: Jason Aronson, 1999.
Appel, Judah Leib, *Be-Tokh Reshit ha-Tehiyya: Zikhronot ve-Ketavim Mi-Yemei "Hovevei Ziyyon" be-Russia* (In the Beginning of the Rebirth: Memoirs and Documents from the Period of Hovevei Zion in Russia; in Hebrew), Tel Aviv: Gutenberg, 1936.
Ascher, Mauritius, *Kein Widerspruch zwischen Judentum, Wissenschaft und Leben!*, Neuchâtel: H. Itzkowski, 1908.
Assaf, Simcha, *Bate ha-Din ve-Sidrehem Ahare Hatimat ha-Talmud* (Courts and Procedure in the post-Talmudic Era; in Hebrew), Jerusalem: HaSifria HaMishpatit, 1923/4.
———. *Ha-Onshin Ahare Hatimat ha- Talmud* (Penal Law in the Post-Talmudic Period; in Hebrew), Jerusalem: HaSifria HaMishpatit, 1921/2.
Avineri, Shlomo, "Herzls utopische Vision," *Internationales Theodor Herzl Symposion* 5 (2004): 25–35.
Backford, J. A., "Politics and Religion in England and Wales," *Deadalus* 120 (1991): 179–201.
Bakon, Gershon, "The Rabbinical Conference in Krakow (1903) and the Beginnings of Organized Orthodox Jewry," in *Let the Old Make Way for the New* (in Hebrew), edited by David Assaf and Ada Rapoport-Albet, Vol. II, 201*-202*. Jerusalem: Shazar Centre, 2009.
Barak-Erez, Daphne, *Outlawed Pigs: Law, Religion and Culture in Israel*, Madison: University of Wisconsin Press, 2007.
Baram, Eshel E., "A Rootless Hebrew Writer Interprets the Second Commandment: An Inquiry into Reuven Breinan's Novella *Notes of a Hebrew Artist*," *Moed* 19 (2010): 160–170.
Bar-On, Mordechai and Zameret, Zvi, eds., *On both Sides of the Bridge: Religion and State in the Early Years of Israel* (in Hebrew), Jerusalem: Yad Ben-Zvi Press, 2002.
Belke, I., ed., *Moritz Lazarus und Heymann Steinthal—die Begründer der Völkerpsychologie in ihren Briefen*, Tübingen: Mohr Siebeck, 1971.
Bartelson, J., *A Genealogy of Sovereignty*, Cambridge: Cambridge University Press, 1995.
Benadmon, Mikhael, *Religion and Creativity in Religious Zionist Thought: Moshe Unna and the Religious Kibbutz Revolution* (in Hebrew), Ramat Gan: Bar-Ilan University Press, 2013.

Ben-Artzi, Hagi, *The New Shall be Sacred: Rav Kook as an Innovative Posek* (in Hebrew), Tel Aviv: Miskal, 2010.

Benayahu, Meir, "The Revival of Ordination in Safed," In *Yitzhak F. Baer Jubilee Volume* (in Hebrew), edited by S. W. Baron and others, 248–69. Jerusalem: The Historical Society of Israel, 1960.

Ben-Porat, Guy, *Between State and Synagogue: the Secularization of Contemporary Israel*, New York: Cambridge University Press, 2013.

Berlin (Bar-Ilan), Meir, *Bishvilei HaTechia* (in Hebrew), Tel Aviv: Hapoel Hamizrachi, 1940.

———. "Hok u-mishpat bi-Medinateinu [Status and Law in our State]," *Yavneh* 3 (1948): 29–32, 151.

Berlin, Naftali Zvi Yehudah (Neziv of Volozhin), *Responsa Meishiv Davar* (in Hebrew), repr. Jerusalem, 1968.

Berliner, Abraham, *Randbemerkungen zum tagelichen Gebetbuch*, Berlin: M. Poppelauer, 1909.

———. *Ueber den Einfluss des ersten hebraeischen Buch-drucks auf den Cultus und die Cultur der Juden*, Berlin:

Berkovitz, Eliezer, *Towards Historic Judaism*, Oxford: East and West Library, 1943.

Berkovitz, Jay R., *Rites and Passages: The Beginnings of Modern Jewish Culture in France 1650-1860*, Philadelphia: University of Pennsylvania Press, 2004.

Bialik, Haim Nachman, *Halachah and Aggadah*. Translated by Leon Simon, London: Education Department of the Zionist Federation of Great Britain and Ireland, 1944.

———. *Divrei Safrut* (in Hebrew), Tel Aviv: Dvir, 1965.

Biemann, Asher D., "Isaac Breuer: Zionist against his will?" *Modern Judaism* 20 (2000): 129–46.

Bleich, David J., "Survey of Recent Halachik Periodical Literature: A 19th Century 'Agunah' Problem and a 20th Century Application," *Tradition*, 38, 2 (2004): 15–48.

Bleich, Judith, "Rabbinic Responses to Nonobservance in the Modern Era," in *Jewish Tradition and the Non-Traditional Jew*, edited by Jacob J. Schacter, 37–115. Northvale, N.J.: Jason Aronson, 1992.

Blidstein, Gerald J., "On Lay Legislation in Halakhah: The King as Instance," in *Rabbinic and Lay Communal Authority*, edited by Suzanne Last Stone, 1–18. New York: KTAV Publishing House, 2006.

Braemer, Andreas, *Rabbiner Zacharias Frankel*, Hildesheim: G. Olms, 2000.

———. "The Dilemmas of Moderate Reform: Some Reflections on the Development of Conservative Judaism in Germany, 1840-1880," *Jewish Studies Quarterly*, 10 (2003): 73–87.

Breuer, Isaac, *Mein Weg*, Jerusalem: Mossad Yitzhaq Breuer, 1988.

———. *Messiasspuren*, Frankfurt am Main: R. L. Hammon, 1918.

———. *Concepts of Judaism: Isaac Breuer*, edited by Jacob S. Levinger, Jerusalem: Israel Universities Press, 1974.

———. "Tokhnit la-Hukkah ba-Medinah ha-Yehudit [A Constitutional Program for the Jewish State]," *Yavneh* 3 (Nissan 1949): 33–40.

———. *Weltwende*, Jerusalem: Mossad Yitzhaq Breuer, 1979.

———. "Jewish State and Torah-Front," in *Fundamentals of Judaism*, edited by Jacob Breuer, 264–69. New York: Kessinger Publishing, LLC, 1969.

———. *Nahaliel* (in Hebrew), Jerusalem: Mossad Yitzhaq Breuer, 1951.

Breuer, Mordechai, *Modernity within Tradition—the Social History of Orthodox Jewry in Imperial Germany*, New York: Columbia University Press, 1992.

Brown, Benjamin, "Breuer, Hirsch and Jewish Nationalism: Change and Continuity—Principle versus Supra-Principle," *Journal of Jewish Studies*, 64 (2013): 383–402.

———. *The Hazon Ish: Halakhist, Believer and Leader of the Haredi Revolution* (in Hebrew), Jerusalem: Magnes Press, 2011.

———. "'Let Us Not Be Presumptuous': The Hazon Ish's Opposition to Commemoration of the Holocaust," in *When Disaster Comes from Afar: Leading Personalities in the*

*Land of Israel Confront Nazism and the Holocaust, 1933-1948* (in Hebrew), edited by Dina Porat, 210–34. Jerusalem: Yad Ben-Zvi Press, 2009.

Broyde, Michael J., *Marriage, Divorce and the Abandoned Wife in the Jewish Law*, New York: KTAV Publishing House, 2000.

Burgansky, Chaim, "Community and Kingdom: The Halakhic Approach of R. Isaac Halevi Herzog and R. Shaul Yisraeli towards the State of Israel," in *Religion and State in Twentieth-Century Jewish Thought* (in Hebrew), edited by Aviezer Ravitzky, 267–94. Jerusalem: Israel Democracy Institute, 2005.

Burton, Antoinette, *Empires and the Reach of the Global 1870-1945*, Cambridge, MA: Harvard University Press, 2014.

Caplan, Kimmy, "Reaction of Five Orthodox Rabbis of the Hebrew University of Jerusalem," *Contemporary Jewry*, 10 (1996): 139–63.

Cassuto, David, ed., *Art and Judaism* (in Hebrew), Ramat Gan: Bar-Ilan University Press, 1989.

Churgin, Pinkhos, "*Lishe'elat Haregah* [The Question of the Moment]," *HaIvri*, 8 (1918), vol. 2, 3–4.

———. "Binyan Olam [An Everlasting edifice]," *HaIvri*, 8 (1918), vols. 29–31, 2–4, 3–4, 2–4.

———. "*Knesiah, Dat, Umemshala* [Church, Religion and Government]", *HaToren* (1919), vols. 35, 42–44, 3–6, 3–5, 5–8.

Cohen, Asher, *The Talit and the Flag—Religion Zionism and the Concept of a Torah State, 1947-1953* (in Hebrew), Jerusalem: Yad Ben-Zvi Press, 1998.

———. & A. Kampinsky, "Religious Leadership in Israel's Religious Zionism: The Case of The Board of Rabbis," *Jewish Political Studies Review*, 18, 3–4 (2006): 119–39.

Cohen, Stuart A., "The Concept of the Three Ketarim: Their Place in Jewish Political Thought and Implications for Studying Jewish Constitutional Theory," in *Kinship & Consent: The Jewish Political Tradition and its Contemporary Uses*, edited by Daniel Judah Elazar, 47–76. New Brunswick, N.J.: Transaction Publishers, 1997.

David, Joseph, "The 'Jewish Law' Vision: Background, Trends and Aspirations," in *Religion and State in Twentieth-Century Jewish Thought* (in Hebrew), edited by Aviezer Ravitzky, 77–113. Jerusalem: Israel Democracy Institute, 2005.

Daykan (Dickstein), Paltiel, *Toldot Mishpat ha-Shalom ha-'Ivri: Megamotav, Pe'ulotav ve-Hesegav* (A History of the Hebrew Courts of Arbitration, in Hebrew), Tel Aviv: Yavneh, 1964.

———. "Review: Kitve M. Z. Rapaport al ha-Mishpat ha-'Ivri [The Works of M. Z. Rapaport on Hebrew Law]," *He-Avar* 1 (1918): 198–200.

———. "She'elat ha-'Ona'ah be-Mishpat ha-Shalom ha-'Ivri [The Question of Fraud in the Hebrew Courts of Arbitration]," *Ha-Mishpat ha-'Ivri* 1 (1925/6): 149–52.

Don-Yehiya, Eliezer, "Religion, National Identity, and Politics: The Crisis over 'Who is a Jew' 1958," in *On both Sides of the Bridge* (in Hebrew), edited by Mordechai Bar-On and Zvi Zameret, 88–143. Jerusalem: Yad Ben-Zvi Press, 2002.

Drachman, Bernard, *The Unfailing Light: Memoirs of an American Rabbi*, New York: Rabbinical Council of America, 1948.

———. *HaGalut Betoch HaGeulah* (The exile inside the redemption, in Hebrew), Jerusalem: Defus Shi'sh, 1920.

Druyanow, Alter (ed.), *Ketavim LeToldot Hibbat-Zion VeYishuv Eretz Israel* (Documents on the History of Hibbat-Zion and Settlement of Eretz Israel (in Hebrew), Odessa: HaVa'ad Leishuv Eretz-Israel, 1919.

Dubnov, Arie M., "Jewish Nationalism in the wake of World War I: A 'State-in-the-Making' or The Empire Strikes Back,?" *Israel* 24 (2016): 5–36.

———. "Notes on the Zionist passage to India, or: The analogical imagination and its boundaries," *Journal of Israeli History* 35 (2016): 177–214.

Edrei, Arye, "Identity, politics, and Halakhah in modern Israel," *Journal of Modern Jewish Studies* 14, 1 (2015): 109–25.

———. "From Orthodoxy to Religious Zionism: Rabbi Kook and Sabbatical Year Polemic," *Dine Israel* 26–27 (2009–2010): 45–145.

———. "The Foundations of Religious-Zionist Halakhah: Rabbi Kook and the Polemic over the Sabbatical Year," in *Religion and Politics in Jewish Thought: Essays in Honor of Aviezer Ravitzky*, vol. II (in Hebrew), edited by B. Brown, M. Lorberbaum, A. Rosenak, Y. Z. Stern, 833–96. Jerusalem: Shazar Centre, 2012.

———. "Divine spirit and physical power: Rabbi Shlomo Goren and the military ethic of the Israel Defense Forces," *Theoretical Inquiries in Law*, 7,1 (2006): 255–97.

———. "Law, Interpretation, and Ideology: the Renewal of the Jewish Laws of War in the State of Israel," *Cardozo Law Review* 28,1 (2006): 187–227.

Eliash, Shulamit, Warhaftig Itamar and Desberg Uri, eds., *Masu'ah LeYitzhak* (in Hebrew), Jerusalem: Yad Harav Herzog, 2008.

Elizur, Yehuda, "Medinat Heterim o Medinat HaTorah [Permissions' State or the Torah State]," *Yavneh* 3 (1948): 64–71.

Elon, Menachem, *Jewish Law: History, Source, Principles: Ha-Mishpat ha-'Ivri*. Translated by Bernard Auerbach & Melvin J. Sykes, Philadelphia: Jewish Publications Society, 1994.

———. "On Power and Authority: The Halakhic Stance of the Traditional Community and Its Contemporary Implications," in *Kinship & Consent: The Jewish Political Tradition and its Contemporary Uses*, edited by Daniel Judah Elazar, 293–326. New Brunswick, N.J.: Transaction Publishers, 1997.

Falk, Zeev, "LeTakanat Benot Israel [A Regulation for the Daughters of Israel]," *Hatzofeh*, May 18, 1951, 3, 6.

———. "A Gentile and a Ger Toshav in Hebrew Law," *Mahalachim* II (1970): 9–17.

Federbush, Simon, *Mishpat ha-Melukhah be-Yisrael* (The Kingdom Laws in Israel, in Hebrew), Jerusalem: Mossad Harav Kook, 1952.

Feiner, Shmuel, *Haskalah and History: The Emergence of a Modern Jewish Historical Consciousness*, Oxford: The Littman Library of Jewish Civilization, 2002.

———. *The Jewish Enlightenment*, Philadelphia: University of Pennsylvania Press, 2004.

———. "'Humani nil a me alienum puto': Theodor Herzl's Vision of the Secular Jewish Society and Culture," in *Memoria—Wege jüdischen Erinners*, edited by Brigit E. Klein and Christiane E. Mueller, 709–31. Berlin: Metropol, 2005.

———. "Critique of Modernity: Samuel David Luzzatto and the Counter-Enlightenment," in *Samuel David Luzzatto: Two Hundred Years since His Birth* (in Hebrew), edited by R. Bonfil, Y. Gottleib and H. Kasher, 146–65. Jerusalem: Magnes Press, 2004.

Ferziger, Adam, *Exclusion and Hierarchy: Orthodoxy, Nonobservance, and the Emergence of Modern Jewish Identity*, Philadelphia: University of Pennsylvania Press, 2005.

Finkelstein, Louis, *Jewish Self Government in the Middle Ages*, New York: The Jewish Theological Seminary of America, 1964.

Friedman, Menachem, "The structural foundation for religio-political accommodation in Israel : fallacy and reality," in *Israel—the First Decade of Independence*, edited by S. Ilan Troen and Noah Lucas, 51-81. Albany: State University of New York Press, 1995.

———. "On the Social Significance of the Polemic on *Shemita*," *Shalem: Studies in the History of the Jews in Eretz-Israel* 1 (1974): 455–79.

Friedman, Shuki and Radzyner, Amichai, *The Religious Community and the Constitution: What Can History Teach Us?* (in Hebrew) Jerusalem: Israel Democracy Institute, 2006.

Freimann, A. C., "Die Ascheriden [The Descendants of Asheri]," *Jahrbuch der Juedisch-Literarischen Gesellschaft*, 13 (1920): 142–254.

———. *Seder Kiddushin ve-Nissu'in Aharei Hatimat ha-Talmud: Mehkar Histori-Dogmati be-Dinei Yisra'el* (Law of Betrothal and Marriage after the Completion of the Talmud: A Historical-Dogmatic Study in Jewish Law, in Hebrew), Jerusalem: Mossad Harav Kook, 1945.

———. "Mezonot Shel Yeled she-Nolad she-lo be-Nissu'in al pi Dinei Yisra'el (Maintenance of a Child Born out of Wedlock, According to Jewish Law)," *Ha-Praklit* 2 (1945): 163–73.

———. "Ha-Takanot Ha-Hadashot Shel Ha-Rabbanut ha-Rashit le-Erez Yisra'el be-Dinei Ishut (The New Enactments of the Chief Rabbinate of Israel on Family Law)," *Sinai* 14 (1944): 254.

———. "Dinei Yisra'el be-Erez Yisra'el (Jewish Law in the Land of Israel)," *Lu'ah ha-Arez* (1946): 110–25.

———. "Darkhei ha-Hakikah be-Yisra'el (The Methodology of Jewish Legislation)," *Yavneh* 1 (1946): 41–44.

———. "Rov u-Mi'ut ba-Zibbur (Majority and Minority in the Community)," *Yavneh* 2 (Tishri 1948): 1–6.

———. "Die Behandlung der Volksfremden bei den Juden," *Mitteilungsblatt des Juedischen Volksrats* 8 (1919): 102–03.

———. "Batei ha-Din ha-Rabbani'im ba-Medina ha-Yehudit (The Rabbinical Courts in the Jewish State)," *Yavneh* 3 (Nissan 1949): 124–25.

Frumkin, G., "Disabilities of Women under Jewish Law—Can they be Remedied?" *Journal of Comparative Legislation and International Law* 3rd Ser. Vol. 12 (November 1930).

Fuchs, Ilan and Hollander, Aviad Yeiel, "National Movements and international Law: Rabbi Shlomo Goren's Understanding of International Law," *Journal of Law and Religion* 29, 2 (2014): 1–16.

Fund, Yossef, *Separation or Participation: Agudat Israel Confronting Zionism and the State of Israel* (in Hebrew), Jerusalem: Magnes Press, 1999.

Geiger, Itzchak, *Leaving the Shtetl: Religious Zionists Rabbis and the Challenge of Jewish Sovereignty* (in Hebrew), Alon Shvut: Herzog College Press, 2016.

Ginsburg, Yaakov M., "Ha'ashamah Atzmit lefi Mishpat HaTorah [Self-Blame, according to Torah Law]," *HaTorah veHamedinah*, 9-10 (1958-9): 82–90.

Goldman, Eliezer, *Religious Issues in Israel's Political Life*, Jerusalem: World Zionist Organization, 1964.

Goldstein, Yossef, *Ahad Ha'am and Herzl: The Struggle for Political and Cultural Nature of Zionism in the Shade of Altneuland Affair* (in Hebrew), Jerusalem: Dinur Centre & Shazar Centre, 2011.

Gordon, J. L., "Hashmatah," *HaSchachar*, 2 (1871): 154–56.

Goren, Shlomo, *Meshiv Milhama: She'elot U-teshuvot Be-inyene Tsava Milhamah U-vitahon* (Response to War: Responsa on Matters of the Military, War, and Security), vol. 1 (in Hebrew), Jerusalem 1983.

———. *Mishnat HaGoren* (in Hebrew), Tel Aviv: Miskal, 2016.

———. *Torat HaRefu'ah* (in Hebrew), Jerusalem: Haldrah Rabah, 2001.

———. "Lechimah beSabbath leOr haMekorot (Fighting on Sabbat in light of the Sources]," In *Sinai: Jubilee Volume* (in Hebrew), edited by Yehuda Leib Maimon, 149-189. Jerusalem: Mossad Harav Kook, 1958.

Graetz, Heinrich, *Geschichte der Juden*, I-IX, Leipzig: Oskar Leiner, 1908.

Gries, Zeev, "Nationalism and Religion in the Writings of 'Rav Tzair' (Rabbi Chaim Tchernowitz)," In *Jewish Thought and Jewish Belief* (in Hebrew), edited by D. J. Lasker, 191–247. Beer Sheva: Ben-Guryon University Press, 2012.

Gulak, Asher, "Le-Sidur Hayenu ha-Mishpatiyim ba-Arets, (On Organizing our Legal Life in Palestine)," *Ha-Toren*, 33–34 (1930/1). Reprinted in *Ha-Mishpat ha-'Ivri u-Medinat Yisra'el: Leket Ma'amarim* (Jewish Law and the State of Israel: Collection of Articles, in Hebrew), edited by Jacob Bazak, 28–35. Jerusalem: Mossad Harav Kook, 1969.

———. *Yesodei ha-Mishpat ha-Ivri* (The Foundations of Jewish Law, in Hebrew), Warsaw: Defus Universal, 1923.

Gutel, Neria, *Both New and Old* (in Hebrew), Jerusalem: Magnes Press, 2005.

HaCohen, Aviad, *The Tears of the Oppressed: An Examination of the Agunah problem: Background and Halachic Sources*, New York: KTAV Publishing House, 2004.

———. "'The State of Israel—This is a Holy Place!': Forming a 'Jewish Public Domain' in the State of Israel," in *On both Sides of the Bridge* (in Hebrew), edited by Mordechai Bar-On and Zvi Zameret, 144–72. Jerusalem: Yad Ben-Zvi Press, 2002.

HaCohen, Mordechai ben Hillel, "Mishpat HaShalom [Magistrate Court]," *HaOlam*, 9 (1920), vol. 17–19.

Haddayah, Ovadyah, "Dose *dina de-malkhuta dina* Apply to the State of Israel?" *HaTorah VehaMedinah*, 9-10 (1958-9): 36–44.

Halbertal, Moshe, "'Ones Possessed of Religion': Religious Tolerance in the Teachings of the Me'iri," *Edah*, 1, 1 (2000): 1–24.

Ha-Levi, Yehudah, *The Kuzari: in Defence of the Despised Faith*, translated by D. Korobkin, Northvale, N.J.: Jason Aronson, 2010.

Harris Ron, Ron Harris, *The Israeli Law—The Formative Years; 1948-1977* (in Hebrew), Tel Aviv: Hakibbutz Hameuchad-Sifriat Poalim Publishing Group, 2014.

———. "Absent-minded Misses and Historical Opportunities: Jewish Law, Israeli Law and the Establishment of the State of Israel," in *On Both Sides of the Bridge: Religion and State in the Early Years of Israel* (in Hebrew), edited by Mordechai Bar-On and Zvi Zameret, 21–55. Jerusalem: Yad Ben-Zvi Press, 2002.

Harvey, Warren Zev, "Liberal Democratic Themes In Nissim of Girona," *Studies in Medieval Jewish History and Literature*, III, edited by In Isadore Twerski and Jay M. Harris, 197–211. Cambridge, MA.: Harvard University Press, 2000.

Havlin, Shlomo Zalman, "The Ralbah," *Jeschurun* 11 (2002): 884–900; 14 (2004): 997–1011.

Heilman, Samuel C., "The Many Faces of Orthodoxy," *Modern Judaism* 2 (1982): 23–51.

Heineman, Yosef, "Changes in the wording and order of worship in the Synagogue," *Mahalachim* I (1969): 23–27.

Hellinger, Moshe, "Religion and State in Sephardi Religion-Zionist Thought: R. Meir Hai Uziel and R. Hayyim David Halevi," in *Religion and State in Twentieth Century Jewish Thought* (in Hebrew), edited by Aviezer Ravitzky, 219–65. Jerusalem: Israel Democracy Institute, 2005.

———. "A Clearly Democratic Religious-Zionist Philosophy: The Early Thought of Yeshayahu Leibowitz," *The Journal of Jewish Thought and Philosophy* 16, 2 (2008): 253–82.

Herzl, Theodor, *The Jewish State*, translated by H. Zohn, New York: Herzl Press, 1970.

———. *Old-New Land*, translated by Paula Arnold, Haifa: Haifa Publishing Company, 1960.

———. *Old New Land*, translated by L. Levensohn, New York: Wiener, 1987.

Herzog, I. E., *Tehuqah leYisrael Al-Pi haTorah* (Constitution and Law in a Jewish State According to the Halakha, in Hebrew), vols. 1–3, Jerusalem: Yad Harav Herzog, 1989.

———. "Ha-Tehiqah ve-ha-Mishpat ba-Medinah ha-Yehudit (Legislation and Law in the Jewish State)", *Yavneh* 3 (1948): 9–10.

———. "The Law in the Jewish State," *HaTorah VehaMedinah*, 7-8 (1955-6): 13–20.

———. "Al Darchei Shmirat HaBitachon HaPnimi BaMedinah BeSabbat veYom Tov (The Ways to Maintain the Internal Security in the Country on Sabbat and Holidays)," *HaTorah VehaMedinah*, 5-6 (1953-4): 25–33.

Hirsch, S. R., *The Collected Writings*, vols. 1–10, New York and Jerusalem: Feldheim Publishers, 1992.

———. *The Hirsch Siddur: The Order of Prayers for the whole Year*, New York and Jerusalem: Feldheim Publishers, 1978.

———. *The Pentateuch—with Translation and Commentary*, New York: Judaica Press, 1962.

Hirschensohn, Chaim, *Malki BaKodesh* (in Hebrew), vols. 1–6, St. Louis: Moinester Printing Co., 1919–28.

———. *Eileh Divrei HaBrit* (This is the Covenant, in Hebrew), vol. 1, Jerusalem: HaIvri, 1926.

———. *Torat HaHinnukh HaYisraeli* (Theory of Jewish Education, in Hebrew), Seini: Defus Jacob Wieder, 1927.

Hoffmann, David Zvi, *Der Schulchan-Aruch und die Rabbinen über das verhältnis der juden zu Adersgläubigen*, Berlin 1885.

Holtzman, Avner, *Art Work: The Revival of the Nation—Hebrew Literature in the Light of Plastic Art* (in Hebrew), Haifa: Kinneret Zmora-Bitan Dvir, 1999.

Inbari, Motti, *Messianic Religious Zionism Confronts Israeli Territorial Compromises*, New York: Cambridge University Press, 2012.

———. *Jewish Fundamentalism and the Temple Mount: Who will Build the Third Temple?* Albany: State University of New York Press, 2009.

Israel-Vleeschhouwer, Amos, "A Jewish Ultra-Orthodox Critique of Nationalism Individualism and Rights-Based Regimes: The Alternative Model and Thought of Yitzhak Breuer," *HaMishpat: Law Review* 15, 2 (2010):607–46.

Jabotinsky, Vladimir, *From the Pen of Jabotinsky*, edited by I. Benari, Cape Town: Unie-Volkspers BPK, 1941.

Jackson, Bernard S., ed., *Jewish Law Association Studies* V - *The Halakhic thought of R. Isaac Herzog*, Atlanta: Scholars Press, 1991.

Jackson, Robert, Sovereignty: The Evolution of an Idea , Cambridge: Polity Press 2007.

Jawitz, Zeev, *Toledot Yisrael* (in Hebrew), vols. 1–14, Tel Aviv: Achi'ever, 1954–62.

———. "In Days to Come," *Ha-Mizrach* 1 (1904): 324–33.

———. "Unity," *Ha-Mizrach* 1 (1903): 10–17.

———. "Swords into Ploughshares," in *The Grape Basket: Stories From the Land of Israel at the Time of the First Aliyah* (in Hebrew), edited by G. Yardeni, 56–105. Jerusalem: Bialik Institute, 1967.

———. "Transitory Worlds and an Enduring World," *Sefer ha-Shana* 1 (1900): 43–54.

Jo-Kim, B., "Schatz's Bezalel: Zionist Icon and Hebrew Art," *Historia veTeoria* 5, 2007.

Junovits, Y., "Al ha-Sifriyah ha-Mishpatit (On the Legal Library)," in Simcha Assaf, *Ha-Onshin Ahare Hatimat ha-Talmud* (Penal Law in the Post-Talmudic Period, in Hebrew), Jerusalem: HaSifria HaMishpatit, 1921/2), 4–8.

Kahana, Maoz, *From the Noda BeYehuda to the Chatam Sofer: Halakha and Thought in their Historical Moment* (in Hebrew), Jerusalem: Shazar Centre, 2015.

Kampinsky, Aharon, *The Development of the Military Rabbinate in Israel* (in Hebrew), Jerusalem: Carmel Press, 2015.

———. "The Rise and Fall of the 'War *Get*' in the Early Days of the IDF," *Jewish Law Association Studies* 18 (2008): 103–22.

Kanarfogel, Ephraim, "Unanimity, majority, and communal government in Ashkenaz during the high Middle Ages: a reassessment," *Proceedings—American Academy for Jewish Research* 58 (1992): 79–106.

Kaniel, Yehoshua, *In Transition: The Jews of Eretz Israel in the Nineteenth Century Between Old and New and Between Settlement of the Holy Land and Zionism* (in Hebrew), Jerusalem: Yad Ben-Zvi Press, 2000.

Kaplan, Y. S., "The Public Welfare," *Dine Israel* 17 (1993-4): 27–91.

———. "The Status and Authority of Communal Leaders in the Middle Ages," *Dine Israel* 18 (1995-6): 255–319.

———. "Majority and Minority in the Decisions of the Jewish Community in the Middle Ages," *Annual of the Institute for Research in Jewish Law* 20 (1996-7): 213–80.

Karelitz, Abraham Yeshayahu, *Kovetz Iggrot* (in Hebrew), Jerusalem: HaMassorah, 1955.

Katz, Jacob, *Divine Law in Human Hands: Case Studies in Halakhic Flexibility* (in Hebrew), Jerusalem: Magnes Press, 1998.

———. *A House Divided: Orthodoxy and Schism in Nineteenth-Century Central European Jewry*, Hanover, NH: Brandeis University Press, 1998.

———. *The "Shabbes Goy": A Study in Halakhic Flexibility*, Philadelphia: Jewish Publication Society, 1989.

———. *Exclusiveness and Tolerance: Studies in Jewish-Gentile Relations in Medieval and Modern* Times, Oxford: Oxford University Press, 1961.

———. "The Controversy on the Semikha (Ordination) between Rabbi Jacob Bei-Rav and the Ralbah," *Zion*, 16, 3-4 (1951): 28–45

Katz, Yossi, "Religion and Zionism in the Yishuv Era: The Sabbath Observance Clause in Lease Contracts between the Jewish National Fund and the Agricultural Settlements," *Zion*, 68 (2013): 207–36.

Kaye, Alexander, "The Legal Philosophies of Religious Zionism 1937-1967." PhD diss., Columbia University, New York 2013.

Klier, J. D., "The Kahal in the Russian Empire: Life, Death and Afterlife of a Jewish Institution, 1772-1882," *Jahrbuch des Simon-Dubnow-Instituts* 5 (2006): 33–50.

Kolatt, Israel, "The Idea of the Hebrew University in the Jewish National Movement," in *The History of the Hebrew University of Jerusalem: Origins and Beginnings* (in Hebrew), edited by S. Katz and M. Hed, 3–74. Jerusalem: Magnes Press, 1997.

———. "Religion, society, and state during the period of the National Home," in *Zionism and Religion*, edited by Shmuel Almog, Jehuda Reinharz, and Anita Shapira (eds.), 273–301. Hanover, NH: University Press of New England, 1998.

Kook, A.Y., *Iggrot haReaya* (Collected Letters of Rav Kook, in Hebrew), vols. 1–2, Jerusalem: Mossad Harav Kook, 1943–1961.

———. *Sabbath Ha-Aretz* (in Hebrew), Jerusalem: Defus Levy & co., 1909.

———. *Orot* (in Hebrew), Jerusalem: Mossad Harav Kook, 1950.

———. "Streams in the South," *Ha-Peles* 4 (1904): 138–44.

———. *Eder Hayakar* (in Hebrew), Jerusalem, 1906.

———. *Mishpat Kohen* (The Priest's Due, in Hebrew), Jerusalem: Mossad Harav Kook, 1966.

———. *Daat Cohen* (in Hebrew), Jerusalem: Mossad Harav Kook, 1942.

———. *Ma'amarei Hare'ayah* (in Hebrew), Jerusalem 1984.

Lahav, P., "The Formative Years of Israel's Supreme Court: 1948-1955," *Tel Aviv University Law Review*, 14 (1989): 479–501.

Laskow, Shulamit, "The 'Altneuland' Controversy," *Ha-Tzionut* 15 (1991): 35–54.

Lau, Bnjamin, "Rabinate and Academy in the writings of Rabbi Eliezer Samson Rosenthal on Saving the life of a non-Jew on Sabbath," *Akdamot* 13 (2003): 7–32.

Leibowitz, Yeshayahu, *Torah u-Mitzvot ba-Zeman ha-Zeh* (Torah and Mitzvoth in our Days, in Hebrew), Tel-Aviv: Massadah, 1954.

———. *Judaism, Human Values and the Jewish State*, translated by Eliezer Goldman and others, Cambridge, MA: Harvard University Press, 1992.

Levin, Isaac, ed., *Material for the Preparation of a Constitution for the Jewish State on a Religious Basis* (in Hebrew), New York: Research Institute for Post-War Problems of Religious Jewry, 1948.

Liberles, Robert, *Religious Conflict in Social Context: The Resurgence of Orthodox Judaism in Frankfurt am Main, 1833-1877*, Westport, Conn: Greenwood Press, 1985.

Likhovski, Assaf, "The invention of 'Hebrew law' in Mandatory Palestine," *American Journal of Comparative Law* 46,2 (1998): 339–73

Lilienblum, M. L., *Complete Writings of Moshe Leib Lilenblum* (Kol kitvei Moshe Leib Lilenblum in Hebrew), Krakow: Yossef Zeitlin, 1910.

Lipkin, B., "Shittot ha-Rishonim be-Takkanot ha-Kahal (The Approach of the *Rishonim* to Communal Enactments)," *Ha-Torah ve-ha-Medinah* 2 (1950): 41–54.

Liebman, Charles and Don-Yehiya, Eliezer, *Religion and Politics in Israel*, Bloomington: Indiana University Press, 1984.

Luz, Ehud, *Parallels Meet: Religion and Nationalism in the Early Zionist Movement, 1882-1904*, Philadelphia: Jewish Publication Society, 1988.

Luzzatto, S. D., "Judaism Versus Atticism: S.D. Luzzatto's Song for his Generation," *Zion*, vol. 1 (Frankfurt am Main, 1841): 81–93.

Manekin, Rachel, *The Jews of Galicia and the Austrian Constitution; The Beginning of Modern Jewish Politics* (in Hebrew), Jerusalem: Shazar Centre, 2015.

Manela, Erez, *The Wilsonian Moment: Self-determination and the International Origins of Anticolonial Nationalism*, Oxford:

Margolies, Reuben, *Kavei Or* (Lines of Light, in Hebrew), Lvov: Praca, 1921.

Mashiach, Amir, "Offensive Ethos of Orthodox Jewish Rulers: Primarily Thoughts," *Daat: A Journal of Jewish Philosophy & Kabbalah* 76 (2014): 231–58.

Mautner, Menachem, "Herzl veHa-Mishpat Ha-Yisraeli (Herzl and Jewish La)," in *The Jewish State* in the Jewish State (in Hebrew), edited by A. Sagi and Y. Stern, 227–50. Jerusalem: The Shalom Hartman Institute, 2008.

Medhurst, K. and Moyser, G., *Church and Politics in a Secular Age,* Oxford: Clarendon Press, 1988.

Mendelssohn, Moses, *Jerusalem and other Jewish Writings,* translated by A. Jospe, New York: Schocken Books, 1969.

Meyer, Michael, *Response to Modernity: A History of the Reform Movement in Judaism,* New York: Oxford University Press, 1988.

Michael, Reuven, *The Writing of Jewish History* (in Hebrew), Jerusalem: Bialik Institute, 1993.

Mirsky, Samuel Kalman, "Mishpat HaMedinah HaIvrit (The Law of the Hebrew State)," *Talpioth* 3 (1948): 338–79,

———. "Ha-Yesod Ha-Democrati be-Dat Yisrael (The Democratic Element in Judaism)," *Ha-Doar,* 25 Nisan, 5699, 391–92

———. "Megilat Hayyay (hereinafter Memoir)," in *Samuel K. Mirsky Memorial Volume: Studies in Jewish Law, Philosophy and Literature,* edited by Gersion Appel, Morris Epstein and Hayim Leaf, Hebrew section, 279--91. New York & Jerusalem: Yeshiva University & Sura Research Institute, 1970.

Mirsky, Yehudah, *Rav Kook: Mystic in a Time of Revolution,* New Haven and London: Yale University Press, 2014.

Mittleman, Alan L., *Between Kant and Kabbalah: An Introduction to Isaac Breuer's Philosophy of Judaism,* Albany:

Monsma, S. V. and Soper, J. C., *The Challenge of Pluralism: Church and State in Five Democracies,* Lanham MD: Rowman & Littlefield, 1996.

Morgenstern, A., *Ha-Rabbanut ha-Rashit le-Erez Yisra'el: Yissuda ve-Irgunah* (The Chief Rabbinate of Israel: Foundations and Organization, in Hebrew), Jerusalem 1973.

Morgenstern, Matthias, *From Frankfurt to Jerusalem: Isaac Breuer and the History of the Secession Dispute in Modern Jewish Orthodoxy,* Leiden: Brill, 2002.

Myers, David N., *Resisting History: Historicism and Its Discontents in German-Jewish Thought,* Princeton, N. J.: Princeton University Press, 2003.

Myers, Jody E., *Seeking Zion—Modernity and Messianic Activism in the Writings of Tsevi Hirsch Kalischer,* Oxford: The Littman Library of Jewish Civilization, 2003.

Nahmanides, *Commentary on the Torah,* Volume 1: *Genesis,* (in Hebrew) Jerusalem: Mossad Harav Kook, 1976.

Neriah, Moshe Zvi, *Kuntres ha-Vikku'ah* (The Pamphlet of the Debate, in Hebrew), Jerusalem 1952.

———. *Al Heter Milchamah Be-Sabbath* (On the Permission to Fight on Sabbath, in Hebrew), Tel Aviv 1962.

Nehar, Andre, *David Gans and his Times* (in Hebrew) Jerusalem: Rubin Mass Ltd., 1982.

Neuberger, Benjamin, "The Relation between Religion and State in Europe," in *The Conflict—Religion and State in Israel* (in Hebrew), edited by N. Langental and S. Friedman, 336–53. Tel Aviv: Miskal, 2002.

Neuman, Kalman and others, *When Judaism Meets the State* (in Hebrew), Tel Aviv: Miskal, 2015.

Nordau, Max, *Zionist Writings,* Volume 2: *Speeches and Articles* (in Hebrew) Jerusalem: HaSifria HaZionit, 1960.

Novak, David, *The Image of the Non-Jew in Judaism,* Portland: The Littman Library of Jewish Civilization, 2011.

Olin, M., "The Search for a Jewish Art in Palestine: Bezalel 1906–1948," *Das Jüdische Echo* 48 (1999): 375–89.

Penslar, Derek, "Herzl, Zionism and the Origins of Jewish Social Policy," in *Theodor Herzl, Visionary of the Jewish State,* edited by G. Shimoni and R. Wistrich, 215–26. Jerusalem: Magnes Press, 1999.

Pines, Y.M., *Children of my Spirit*, vol. 2 (in Hebrew), Mainz: Defus Yechiel Brill, 1872.
Pinsker, Y. L., *Herald of the National Rebirth: Auto-Emancipation and its Critics: Open Letters, Speeches and Correspondence*, translated by M. Yoeli (in Hebrew), Jerusalem 1960.
Porat, Benjamin, ed., *Reflections on Jewish Democracy* (in Hebrew), Jerusalem: Israel Democracy Institute, 2009.
Presner, T.S., *Muscular Judaism: The Jewish Body and the Politics of Regeneration*, London: Routledge, 2007.
Rabinovich, Itamar and Reinharz, Jehuda, eds., *Israel in the Middle East: Documents and Readings on Society, Politics, and Foreign Relations, Pre 1948 to the Present*, Waltham, MA: Brandeis University Press, 2008.
Radzyner, Amihai, "Rabbi Uziel, the Tel-Aviv-Jaffa Rabbinate and the Rabbinical Court of Appeal: A Play in Four Acts," *Bar-Ilan Law Studies* 21 (2004): 129–243.
———. "'Hefqer Bet-Din Hefqer' (the Court has the Power to Expropriate) in Talmudic Sources," *Sidra: A Journal for the Study of Rabbinic Literature* 16 (2000): 11–133.
———. "'Jewish Law' between 'National' and 'Religious': The Dilemma of the Religious-National Movement," *Bar-Ilan Law Studies*, 26 (2010): 91–178.
———. "The Origins of Procedural Regulations for Rabbinical Courts: 'Takkanot Ha-Diyun' 1943," *Dine Israel*, 25 (2008): 185–260.
———. "A Constitution for Israel: The Design of the Leo Kohn Proposal, 1948," *Israel Studies* 15, 1 (2010): 1–24.
———. "Forgotten Basic Elements in 'The Law and Administration Ordinance' and the Covert Struggle over Religion and State in Israel," *Cathedra* 136 (2010): 121–50.
Rafael, Yitshak (ed.), *The Encyclopaedia of Religious Zionism*, vol. 2 (in Hebrew), Jerusalem: Mossad Harav Kook, 1960.
Ravitzky, Aviezer, ed., *Religion and State in Twentieth Century Jewish Thought* (in Hebrew), Jerusalem: Israel Democracy Institute, 2005.
———. *Messianism, Zionism And Jewish Religious Radicalism*, Chicago and London: The University of Chicago Press, 1996.
———. "Is a Halakhic State Possible? The Paradox of Jewish Theocracy," *Israel Affairs* 11, 1 (2005): 137–64.
Renton, James, *Masquerade: the Birth of the Anglo-Zionist Alliance 1914-1918*, New York: Palgrave Macmillan, 2007, 149–55.
Roness, A. Y., "Interpretation, Political Ideology and the Re-Establishment of Jewish Laws of State: R. Shaul Yisraeli on Securing the Release of Prisoners of War," *Jewish Law Association Studies* 24 (2013): 206–20.
Rosenberg, Shalom, *Torah and Science in Modern Jewish Thought* (in Hebrew) Jerusalem: Ministry of Education, 1988.
———. "Heart and Uniqueness: The Idea of Chosenness in the Thought of R. Yehudah Ha-Levi and in Modern Jewish Philosophy," in *The Philosophical Thought of R. Yehudah Ha-Levi* (in Hebrew), edited by Haya Schwartz, 109–18. Jerusalem: Ministry of Education, 1978.
Rosenthal, Eliezer Samson, "Closing Remarks at the End of the Founding Conference," *Ha-Chadash Yitkadesh* 1 (1966): 17–23.
Rozenak, Avinoam, *The Prophetic Halakhah* (in Hebrew) Jerusalem: Magnes Press, 2007.
Ruderman, David, *Jewish Thought and Scientific Discovery in Early Modern Europe*, New Haven: Yale University Press, 1995.
Salmon, Yosef, Ravitzky Aviezer and Ferziger Adam, eds., *Orthodox Judaism—New Perspectives* (in Hebrew), Jerusalem: Magnes Press, 2006.
———. *Do not provoke Providence: Orthodoxy in the Grip of Nationalism*, Boston: Academic Press, 2014.
———. *Religion and Zionism: First Encounters*, Jerusalem: Magnes Press, 2002.
———. "Tradition and Nationalism," in *Essential papers on Zionism*, edited by J. Reinharz and A. Shapira, 94–116. New York: New York University Press, 1996.

———. "Enlightenment Rabbis as Reformers in Russian Jewish Society," in *New Perspectives on the Haskalah*, edited by Shmuel Feiner and David Sorkin, 166–83. London: The Littman library of Jewish civilization, 2001.
———. "Christians and Christianity in the Responsa Literature from late 18th century to the second half of the 19th century," in *By the Well* (in Hebrew), edited by Uri Ehrlich and others, 635–51. Be'er Sheva: Ben-Guryon University Press, 2008,
Samet, Moshe, *Chapters in the History of Orthodoxy* (in Hebrew), Jerusalem: Dinur Centre, 2005.
———. "Hayahadut Hacharedit Bazman Hachadash (The Orthodoxy in the modern Period)," *Mahalachim* I (1969): 29–40; III (1970): 15–27.
Saposnik, Arieh Bruce, *Becoming Hebrew: The Creation of a Jewish National Cukture in Ottoman Palestine*, Oxford: Oxford University Press, 2008.
Schatz, Uffenheimer Rivka, *The Messianic Idea from the Expulsion from Spain* (in Hebrew), Jerusalem: Magnes Press, 2005.
Schorsch, Ismar, *From Text to Context: The Turn to History in Modern Judaism*, Hanover, NH: Brandeis University Press, 1994.
Schmitt, Carl, *Political Theology: Four Chapters on the Concept of Sovereignty*, Chicago: University of Chicago Press, 2005.
Schwartz, Dov, *Religious-Zionism: History and Ideology*, Boston: Academic Press, 2009 .
Schweid, Eliezer, *A History of the Philosophy of the Jewish Religion in Modern Times* (in Hebrew), vols.1–3, Tel Aviv: Am Oved Publishers , 2003.
———. *Democracy and Halakhah*, Lanham, MD: University Press of America, 1994.
Segal, Esther, "The Historical Thought of Ze'ev Jawitz," (in Hebrew) M.A. thesis, Bar-Ilan University, 1992.
Seidler, Meir, "Isaac Breuer's Concept of law," *Jewish Law Association Studies* 8 (2000): 167–71.
Shamir, Ronen, *The Colonies of Law—Colonialism, Zionism and Law in Early Mandate Palestine*, Cambridge: Cambridge University Press, 2000.
Shapira, Amnon, *Primitive Democracy in the Bible: Ancient Foundations of Democratic Values* (in Hebrew), Tel Aviv: Hakibbutz Hameuchad-Sifriat Poalim Publishing Group , 2009.
Shapira, Herman, *Zionist Writings* (in Hebrew), Jerusalem: Defus Zion, 1925.
Shavit, Y. and Reinharz, J., *Darwin and His Kind* (in Hebrew), Bnei Brak: Hakibbutz Hameuchad-Sifriat Poalim Publishing Group , 2009.
Shilo, Margalit, *Girls of Liberty: The Struggle for Suffrage in Mandatory Palestine*, Brandeis University Press, Waltham 2016.
Shilo Shmuel, Dina De-Malkhuta Dina (The Law of the State is Law, in Hebrew), Jerusalem: The Institute for Research in Jewish Law at the Hebrew University of Jerusalem, 1974.
Shimoni, Gideon, *The Zionist Ideology*, Hanover, NH: University Press of New England, 1995.
Shochetman, Eliav, "The Halakha's Recognition of the Laws of the State of Israel," *Jewish Law Annual* 16–17 (1990–1991): 417–500.
Sigad, Ran, "Moses Mendelssohn, Judaism, Theocratic Politics and the State of Israel," *Da'at* 7 (1981): 93–103.
Silver, Michael, "Orthodoxy," in *The Yivo Encyclopedia of Jews in Eastern Europe*, vol. 2, edited by Gershon David Hundert, New Haven: Yale University Press 2008, 1292–97.
———. "The emergence of Ultra-Orthodoxy—the invention of a tradition," in *The Uses of Tradition*, edited by J. Wertheimer, 23–84. Jerusalem and New York: Jewish Theological Seminary of America, 1992.
Smolar, Leivy and Aberbach, Moses, *Studies in Targum Konathan to the Prophets*, Baltimore/ Hoboken: Baltimore Hebrew College/ Ktav, 1983.
Stern, Yedidia, *State, Law and Halakhah* (in Hebrew), vols. 1–4, Jerusalem: The Israel Democracy Institute, 2001–2006.

Stone, Suzanne Last, "Religion and State: Models of Separation from within Jewish Law," *International Journal of Constitutional Law* 6, no. 3 and 4 (2008): 631–61.
———. "Law Without Nation? The Ongoing Jewish Discussion," in *Law Without Nations*, edited by Austin Sarat, Lawrence Douglas, and Martha Merrill Umphrey, 101–37. Stanford, Calif.: Stanford University Press, 2011.
Taylor, Charles, *The Malaise of Modernity*, Toronto: House of Anansi Press, 1991.
———. *Philosophy and the Human Sciences: Philosophical Papers*, vol. II, Cambridge, UK: Cambridge University Press, 1985.
Tchernowitz, Chaim, *BeSha'arei Zion* (in Hebrew), New York: Schulsinger Brothers, 1936.
———. *Chevley Geulah* (in Hebrew), New York: Shoulson Press, 1949.
———. "Merkaz Dati (Religious Center)," *HaIvri* 10 (1920), no. 20: 2–4, no. 21: 2–5, no. 22: 2–3, no. 23: 2–4, no. 25: 3–4.
———. "LiShe'elat HaDat VeHaMedinah BeIsrael (Questions of Religion and State in Israel)," *Betzaron* 9 (1948), 293–304.
Tchorsh, Katriel Fishel, "Ma'arechet HaMissim LeOr HaTorah (The Tax System in light of the Torah)," *HaTorah VehaMedinah*, 5-6 (1953–1954): 233–82.
Tikochinski, Yechiel M., *Sefer Ha-Shemittah* (in Hebrew), Jerusalem: Mossad Harav Kook, 1952.
Trunk, Yahushua, *Yeshu'ot Malko*, repr. New York 1958.
Tobi, Yosef, "The Organization of the Jewish Communities in the East in the 19-20 th Centuries, " in *Kehal Yisrael: Jewish Self-Rule Through the Ages* (in Hebrew), Vol. 3, edited by Israel Bartal, 191–209. Jerusalem: Shazar Center, 2004.
Unna, Isaac, "The High Court of Justice in the Past and in the Future," in *Israel of Tomorrow*, edited by Leo Jung, 347–53. New York: Herald Square Press, 1946.
Urbach, Ephraim Elimelech, "Life with the Tora," *The Jerusalem Post*, June 5, 1973.
———. "Samchut Hahalakha Beyameinu (The authority of Halakha Today)," *Mahalachim* V (1971): 3–10.
Uziel, B. C., *Mikhmannei Uziel* (in Hebrew), Tel Aviv: Hapoel Hamizrachi, 1939 .
———. *Mishpatei Uziel* (in Hebrew), vols. 1–4, Jerusalem: Mossad Harav Kook. 1947.
———. "HaTorah ve-HaMedinah (The Torah and the State)," *Sinai*, 22 (1948): 117–25.
———. "Mishpat Yerushat HaBat (Law of Inheritance of Daughters)," *Talpioth*, 5–6 (1952–1953): 451-474, 51-64.
Vital, David, *The Origins of Zionism*, Oxford: Oxford University Press, 1975.
Walzer, Michael et al., eds., *The Jewish Political Tradition*, vols. 1–2, New Haven and London: Yale University Press, 2000–2003.
Warhaftig, Itamar, "Rabbi Herzog's approach to modernity," in *Engaging Modernity: Rabbinical Leaders and the Challenge of the Twentieth Century*, edited by Moshe Z. Sokol, 275–319. Northvale, N.J.:
Warhaftig, Zerach, *Constitution for Israel—Religion and State* (in Hebrew), Jerusalem: Messilot, 1988.
Wissotzky, K.Z., *Collected Letters* (in Hebrew) Jerusalem: Yad Beb-Zvi Press, 1981.
Yardeni, Galia, *The Hebrew Press in Eretz-Israel 1863–1904* (in Hebrew) Tel Aviv: Hakibbutz Hameuchad Publishing House,1969.
Yedidya, Asaf, *Criticized Criticism: Orthodox Alternatives to Wissenschaft des Judentums 1873–1956* (in Hebrew) Jerusalem: Bialik Institute, 2013.
———. "Benjamin Menashe Levin and Orthodox *Wissenschaft des Judentums*," *Cathedra*, 130 (2008): 103–28.
———. "Orthodox Reactions to *Wissenschaft des Judentums*," *Modern Judaism* 30 (2010): 69–94.
———. "The Nazi Attacks on the Talmud and the Apologetic Responses of the Jews in Germany and Austria in the 1930s," *Search and Research*, 25 (2016): 7–66.
Yehoshafat, Y. Y., "Hit'hadshut ha-Mishpat (Legal renewal)," *Ha-Mishpat ha-'Ivri* 2 (1927): 1–7.
Yisraeli, Shaul, "Im HaKovetz," *HaTorah veHamedinah* 1 (1949): 11–13.
———. "Im HaKovetz," *HaTorah veHamedinah* 5–6 (1954): 5–7.

———. "Samchut HaNassi UMossdot Mimshal Nivcharim BeYisrael (The Authority of the President and Elected Government Institutions in Israel)," *HaTorah veHamedinah* 1 (1949): 67–78.

———. "Tokef Mishpatey HaMeluchah BeYameynu (The Validity of Kingdom Laws in our Day)," *HaTorah VehaMedinah* 2 (1950): 76–88.

———. "HaBitachon HaPnimi BaMedinah BeSabbat (The Internal Security in the Country on Sabbat)," *HaTorah VehaMedinah* 5–6 (1953–1954): 335–47.

———. "Hilchot Koalitzia [Coalition]," *HaTorah VehaMedinah* 11-13 ( 1960-2): 75–102.

———. "Takrit Kibiyeh le-Or ha-Halakha (The Kibiyah Incident in Light of Jewish Law)," *HaTorah VehaMedinah* 5–6 (1954): 71–113.

Yust, Ariav, "Aspects of the Halakhik Approach of R. Shaul Yisraeli to Matters of Public Concern: The Deployment of Police on Sabbath as a Test Case," *Dine Israel* 28 (2011): 145–84.

Zipperstein, Steven J., *Elusive Prophet: Ahad Ha'am and the Origins of Zionism*, Berkeley: University of California Press, 1993.

Ziwan, Gili, "The Seperation of Religion and State and the Religious Meaning of the State of Israel: Yeshayahu Leibowitz, Eliezer Goldman and David Hartman," in *Religion and State in Twentieth Century Jewish Thought* (in Hebrew), edited by Aviezer Ravitzky, 431–48. Jerusalem: Israel Democracy Institute, 2005.

Zohar, David, *Jewish Commitment World: R. Hayyim Hirschensohn and His Attitude Towards the Moderna* (in Hebrew) Tel Aviv: Hakibbutz Hameuchad-Sifriat Poalim Publishing Group, 2003.

Zohar, Zvi, *The Luminous Face of the East: Studies in the Legal and Religious Thought of Sephardic Rabbis of the Middle East* (in Hebrew), Tel Aviv: Hakibbutz Hameuchad-Sifriat Poalim Publishing Group, 2001.

———. "Ahrayut Hakneset Leitzuv Hahalacha-Iyun Bema'amaro shel Harav Uziel Behagdarat Pesuley Edut," in *Rav Tarbutiyut Bemedinah Demokratit Veyehudit: Sefer Hazikaron LeAriel Rozen-Tzvi Z'L* (in Hebrew), edited by Menachem Mautiner et al., 301–39. Tel Aviv: Ramot, 1998.

Zussman, Jacob, "The Scientific Project of Ephraim Elimelech Urbach," *Jewish Studies*, addendum/ special volume 1 (1993): 7–116.

# Index

# About the Author

Dr. Asaf Yedidya is the head of the Department of History at Efrata College (Jerusalem) and a senior lecturer at Ariel University. His research discipline is intellectual history and his primary research interests include Jewish nationalism and Jewish orthodoxy in the modern period.

He was Matthew Family Fellow at the Center for Advanced Holocaust Studies at the USHMM in Washington, DC (2011), Kennedy Leigh Fellow at the Oxford Center for Hebrew and Jewish Studies, Oxford University, UK (2012), and fellow at the Helen Gartner Hammer Scholars-in-Residence Program, at HBI, Brandeis University (2016).

He is the author of *Criticized Criticism: Orthodox Alternatives to Wissenschaft des Judentums 1873-1956* (in Hebrew) and *'To Cultivate a Hebrew Culture': The Life and Thought of Zeev Jawitz* (in Hebrew). He is also the editor of *Ashkenazi Batei Midrash: Memoirs of Graduates of German and Austrian Rabbinical Seminaries* (in Hebrew) and *Rabbi Zvi Hirsch Kalischer and the Awakening to Zion* (in Hebrew).

www.ingramcontent.com/pod-product-compliance
Ingram Content Group UK Ltd.
Pitfield, Milton Keynes, MK11 3LW, UK
UKHW041630031026
15587UKWH00001B/178

9 781498 534970